Elementary Thinking
for
Modern Management

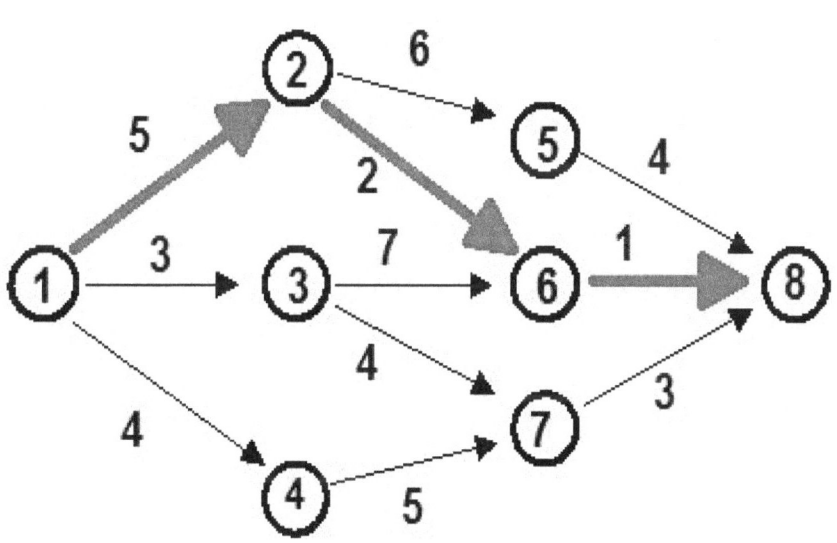

G. A. MOHR, PHD
WORLD HONS MULT

ELEMENTARY THINKING FOR MODERN MANAGEMENT

G. A. Mohr, PhD

© G. A. Mohr, 2018

All rights reserved. No part of this publication may be reproduced, stored in a retrieval system, or transmitted in any form or by any means, electronic, mechanical, photocopying, recording, or otherwise, without the prior written permission of both the author and publisher.

G. A. Mohr
Elementary Thinking for Modern Management

TRI

Transworld Research & Innovation
9 Hampstead Drive
Hoppers Crossing VIC 3029
AUSTRALIA

Contents

Chapter		Page
	Preface	1
1	Introduction	3
2	Learning	17
3	Memory	31
4	Thinking	53
5	Critical Thinking	65
6	Group Thinking	75
7	Corporate Thinking	83
8	Surveys of Public Opinion	95
9	Mathematical Logic	107
10	Computer Programming	117
11	Planning and Scheduling	127
12	Linear Programming	139
13	Finite Element Networks	149
14	Optimization Techniques	161
15	Optimal Networks	173
16	Economic Modelling	195
17	Conclusions	209
	Appendix A: Introduction to Basic	221
	Appendix B: Two-Dimensional Finite Elements	231
	Appendix C: Mohr Ideas	251
	References	281

PREFACE

As far as we can discern, the sole purpose of human existence is to kindle a light in the darkness of mere being.
C.G. Jung, Erinnerungen, Traüme, Gedunken (1962).

The present book is about thinking processes, many of which break a problem into parts or *elements* to examine it.

First, however, learning and memory are discussed briefly as these, of course, play an important part in our ability to think. A simple *precedence model* for memory structure is proposed and this could be modelled using a program for DC networks given later in the book.

Then creative thinking, critical thinking and various decision processes are discussed.

Group thinking, corporate thinking and surveys of public opinion are discussed as, of course, getting ideas from other people can be an important part of thinking and planning processes.

The remaining chapters deal with thinking in terms of elements which may, for example, be propositions, sections of a computer program, parts of a plan, parts of a physical object, or parts of a distribution or traffic system.

In this important part of the book mathematical logic is first discussed. Here propositional calculus in particular is sometimes both appealing and useful.

Then computer programming, various planning and scheduling techniques and linear programming are discussed.

Next comes the important step of introducing the *Finite Element Method* (FEM) into the discussion via the simple example of a DC network. Then FEM is used to model distribution and traffic flow networks.

Preface

Next techniques for optimization of nonlinear problems are introduced and then used to optimize FEM network models.

The penultimate chapter discusses modelling of economic problems, of particular note being my inverse law of supply and demand for mass produced products, as well as my modification and use of Jack Vernon's equations for the liquid money supply (LMS) and interest sensitive expenditure (ISE) curves to show that increasing interest rates increases inflation.

An appendix on BASIC programming is given, along with an appendix which introduces two-dimensional finite elements for flow problems.

Readers should note that QBASIC, which is the version of BASIC used in nearly all the coding given in this book, can easily be downloaded free from the internet, as can QuickBASIC, a later version which includes a compiler.

The book concludes with an Appendix of 'Mohr Ideas', that is, just some of the most interesting and useful ideas I came up with in a lifetime of research in a wide variety of fields. Having finished my memoirs after over twenty years of work on them, but not published them, I thought this short appendix a better alternative.

I hope some of the methods in this book, some of which are new, prove helpful as everyday techniques for thinking, getting ideas, and solving problems in personal life and in business.

I am grateful to my sons Richard and 'Ned', and also 4 ladies in the sales department of OUP Oxford, for discussing with me aspects of this and other works.

Finally, once again I am grateful to the publishers for yet again doing an excellent job of promptly publishing this book.

Geoff Mohr
Melbourne, 2018

Chapter 1

INTRODUCTION

*The longest part of the journey is said
to be the passing of the gate.*
Marcus Terentius Varro, *On Agriculture* (circa 37 B.C.)

THE EVOLUTION OF HOMO SAPIENS SAPIENS

We modern humans regard ourselves as different from other species, and do not regard ourselves as animals, though it is increasingly clear that we have animal origins.

Charles Darwin's 1859 book *On the Origin of Species by Means of Natural Selection* established the theory of evolution firmly, whilst the botanical studies of Alfred Russell Wallace helped broaden and strengthen that theory. The sciences of genetics and molecular biology have since confirmed it.

Evidence of the evolution of modern humans from chimpanzees, with whom we share circa 98% of our DNA, continues to accumulate. A key step in this evolution was the appearance of hominids with bipedal locomotion between 5 and 6 million years ago in Africa, remains of the first Ramapithecus species of Hominidae having been found in Kenya dating back to the middle of the Miocene epoch, that is, about 19 million years ago (Weiss & Mann, 1978).

According to fossil records, about 5 million years ago the first of seven species of Australopithecines appeared in Africa, there being two types, the Robust and the Gracile Australopithecines. These species were from 1.2 to 1.4 metres tall and weighed from 30 to 45 kg. The Robusts, as their name suggests, were more solidly built but became extinct about a million years ago.

1. INTRODUCTION

The more fleet-footed Gracile's survived, however, evolving from the Australopithecus afarensis form to the species Australopithecus africanas by about 2.5 million years ago (Smith & Davies, 2008).

The earliest evidence of stone tools comes from sites in Africa dated to about 2.5 million years ago. These tools have not been found in association with a particular hominine species.

About 2 million years ago Australopithecus africanas evolved into the first Homo species, Homo habilis, the forerunner of modern man. Homo habilis evolved into Homo ergaster about 1.5 million years ago in Africa and spread into Asia, where it evolved into Homo erectus, a species which survived until about 250 thousand years ago (Encarta, 1999).

Later H. erectus skulls possess brain sizes in the range of 1100 to 1300 cc (67.1 to 79.3 cu in), within the size variation of *Homo sapiens*.

A number of archaeological sites dating from the time of Homo erectus reveal a greater sophistication in tool making than was found at earlier sites. Evidence found at the cave site of "Peking Man" in northern China, suggests that H. erectus used fire.

The remains of the foundations of an oval structure built by a Homo erectus group were found at the Terra-Amata site in France, and within this structure there was a fireplace (Weiss & Mann, 1978).

Homo ergaster then spread from Africa into Europe, evolving into Homo Heidelbergensis, so named because the first remains of this species were discovered in Heidelberg, Germany, in 1903. This species appeared between 0.6 and 1.3 million years ago and survived until 200 to 250 thousand years ago.

The Homo species spread widely and by 350,000 years ago planned hunting, fire making, wearing of clothes, and probably burial rituals, were well established.

1. Introduction

It seems likely that Homo Heidelbergensis then evolved into Homo sapiens Neanderthalis between 200,000 and 300,000 years ago. The Neanderthals had similar DNA to modern man and lived only in family groups, the men being hunter-gatherers to feed the family.

The Neanderthals left cave paintings which were an important evolutionary advance. These often depicted a simple activity, perhaps a precursor to the highly pictorial hieroglyphic script of the ancient Egyptians (Egerton Eastwick, 1896).

Meanwhile, in Africa, Homo ergaster evolved into Homo sapiens sapiens at around the same time, spreading to Europe and interbreeding with the Neanderthals so that circa 4% of the DNA of non-African modern humans comes from them.

The Neanderthals had slightly larger brain size than Homo sapiens sapiens, but disappeared about 30,000 years ago, in part as a result of interbreeding.

Fragments of another subspecies of Homo sapiens, the Denisovans, dating back 40,000 years were recently discovered in Siberia, along with Neanderthal remains. Study of the nuclear genome of this species suggested that it came from the same origins as the Neanderthals. The Denisovans ranged from Siberia to Southeast Asia and up to 6% of their DNA is found in Melanesians, Australian Aborigines and the Mananwa, a Negrito people of the Philippines.

Comparison of the Denisovan and Neanderthal genomes showed that there was considerable interbreeding between the two species, the Denisovan DNA being 17% Neanderthal.

Some scientists believe in the 'replacement model', which holds that Neanderthals were replaced by migrating Homo sapiens sapiens. As noted above, however, the evidence now supports the 'assimilation model' in which there was a significant amount of interbreeding.

1. Introduction

The 'assimilation' or 'multiregional evolution model' proposes that modern humans evolved more or less simultaneously in the major regions of the world, for example modern Chinese are thought to be evolved from archaic Chinese humans.

The present author believes this is true in this instance at least, and that modern Chinese people evolved from the Homo erectus species that evolved from the spread of the Homo ergaster species from Africa to Asia.

Like chimpanzees, homo sapiens sapiens formed tribes and there is evidence of religion, recorded events and art dating from 30,000 to 40,000 years ago implying the advanced language and ethics required for the ordering of social groups.

An example of relatively recent evolution, the body shapes of people in central Africa contrast greatly with those of Eskimos, the latter being shorter and carrying much more body fat to cope with cold climate (Weiss & Mann, 1978).

Thinking and learning in animals

Man is a thinking animal but not the only one. Our closest relatives, chimpanzees, use tools effectively and most species are capable or learning and thence thought.

Pavlov's classical conditioning experiments with dogs are well known (Pavlov, 1960).

Conditioning has also been successfully applied to flatworms whose brains have only about 400 cells (Packard, 1978). In these experiments the worms were conditioned to "scrunch up" when seeing a light go on when this was followed by electrical shocks. It was found that when the worms were cut in half, or even several pieces, the pieces regenerated brains that remembered the conditioning.

Similar results were then obtained with various species of vertebrates.

1. INTRODUCTION

Even more startling was the 'memory transferability' achieved by making soup of the brains of rats conditioned to shun darkness and feeding it to hamsters. The injected hamsters soon began to shun darkness!

This led before too long to the suggestion that students should eat their professors!

Later Georges Ungar and coworkers detected a peptide[1] compound in the brain of a conditioned rat that caused it to avoid darkness.

They pooled the brains of 4000 rats to obtain a sample of this compound large enough for analysis and synthesis of the compound (Ungar et al., 1972).

Subsequently Ungar's group reported discovering several other brain peptides that seemed to transfer learning from one animal to another (Jonas, 1974).

Classical conditioning involves a passive reflex response being associated with a stimulus. *Operant conditioning* involves an animal learning some operation and in Skinner's classical experiments rats learnt to operate a lever to deliver food (Skinner, 1972).

Behaviour shaping, that is, progressive use of operant conditioning, can be used to train bears to ride bicycles (Lindzey et al., 1978).

Some species of primates, of course, are capable of quite advanced learning and chimpanzees have been taught to recognize number symbols and count out the corresponding number of tokens to obtain a reward. Indeed, after years of study of chimpanzees in the Gombe National Park Jane Goodall became quite disillusioned with their all too human-like behaviours, for example those of regular tribal confrontations (Goodall, 1971).

---

[1] Peptides link chains of up to thousands of amino acid molecules to form *polypeptides*. Proteins are naturally occurring polypeptides.

1. Introduction

A BRIEF HISTORY OF HUMAN THOUGHT

We have little evidence of what Neanderthal man thought save for his cave paintings, nevertheless a great evolutionary advance.

It is not a great step in human history to the thinking of the Greek and Roman philosophers upon which much of Western society is based. Aristotle's comment on democracy:

A democracy exists whenever those who are free and are not well-off, being in the majority, are in sovereign control of government, an oligarchy when control lies with the rich and better-born, these being few.

still begs for notice today.

Much of that legacy is worthy, much of it not, for example our continuing predilection for war.

The invention of God has had a profound effect, not all of it for the better, as continuing religious conflict around the world attests (Mohr & Fear, 2015).

Jacob Bronowski in his celebrated TV series *The Ascent of Man* implored us that we must not forget Newton. No less, therefore, should we forget da Vinci and many of the other great thinkers in human history.

Einstein, despite the fact that his celebrated Theory of Relativity is misconceived and highly erroneous (Mohr, Sinclair & Fear, 2014; Mohr GA, Mohr RS, Mohr PE, 2018), we place on the highest mental pedestal to vainly try and convince ourselves we are not self-destructive animals doomed by famine, plagues and wars of our own making (Cowie et al., 1994).

I say only Einstein here because we tend to have little space for hero models in the intellectual area and give them but token attention. We have far more time, however, for our sporting heroes and pop music and movie stars. These biff it out or perform like wild animals, which seems to appeal to our baser animal thoughts.

1. Introduction

In Western society we also have little time for God now and churches of most denominations are almost empty and one has to be an insomniac to hear much of God in the early hours of Sunday morning on TV where the same old hackneyed bible bashing is repeated.

Nevertheless, our leaders still have time to invoke the old 'God excuse' for wars and, if anything, religious conflict is more prevalent that at any time in history (Mohr, 2014; Mohr & Fear, 2015).

Modern thought

At best the modern world is an impending disaster, at worst a catastrophe of biblical proportions.

In Africa famine, AIDS and war are reaping an increasing toll whilst throughout the world Muslim extremists continue terrorist activities (Mohr, 2014; Mohr & Fear, 2015; Mohr et al. 208d).

In more affluent countries we are being reduced to brainwashed zombies by mass advertising of often dubious, if not downright rotten products (Packard, 1963; Mohr, 2013b).

There are no better examples than the tobacco and mobile phone industries. The degree to which humans were able to be persuaded to become addicted to the highly ridiculous and dangerous practice of smoking dried leaves was remarkable enough.

The degree to they have now been persuaded en masse to wear jeans and carry a drink bottle in one hand and a mobile phone in the other beggars belief.

Some 20 years ago it was reported that the average American IQ was decreasing at the rate of one or two points per generation and a similar result was reported in the UK three decades earlier (Vernon, 1960).

In part this is the result of decreasing standards of education (Sykes, 1995), in part the result of advertising and media which teach children poor behaviours and addict them to, at best, pointless and wasteful products.

1. Introduction

The result is a generation of boys that enjoy a primitive form of cave painting throughout our cities and a generation of girls that dress increasingly like those in primitive tribes.

Reminiscent of declining Rome we place great value on contests such as rugby in which teams fight over leather balls, a process that was designed to take the animal out of pubescent youths, not as a spectator sport to be viewed in modern coliseums.

This can only be called *reverse evolution,* a subject I discuss at some length in my book *The Pretentious Persuaders.*

Now children experiment with drugs and sex at younger ages than ever before and half of their parents divorce sooner, rather than later.

Transnational companies employ what can only be called slave labour in poorer populations, and escalating house prices in growing megacities force both parents to work and very young children to be incarcerated in long day care centres that would have disturbed Hitler (Mohr, 2013b).

This can only be seen as an increasingly amoral society in a process of decay of biblical proportions.

What have we done wrong?

Several authors have prognosticated on what we are doing wrong, for example Ralph Nader, JK Galbraith and Vance Packard. In his renowned book *The Peter Principle, Why Things Always Go Wrong,* Laurence Peter provides the root cause with his Peter Principle (Peter & Hull, 1969):

> *In a hierarchy every employee tends to rise to his own level of incompetence.*

He cites such notable examples as Hitler who was an extremely effective politician and an incompetent commander-in-chief. He then goes on to point out that, ambitious and often ruthless people having risen to positions of authority and incompetence, they stay there. As one might expect, recent research finds that a high proportion of 'bosses' are psychopaths, their symptoms including lying, bullying etc.

1. Introduction

Then these incompetents live up to Parkinson's Law of triviality:

Committees will pass major decisions without demur but prognosticate interminably over trivia.

This is a special case of the original Parkinson's Law:

Work expands so as to fill the time available for its completion.

Summing it all up is Parkinson's Law of the Vacuum, a generalization of his original law (Parkinson, 1980):

Action expands to fill the void created by human failure.

The result, of course, is that bad decisions create problems which are usually followed by more bad decisions and so the human race careers at an accelerating rate towards disaster.

The present author sums it all up with *Mohr's Laws,* ten laws proposed for the new religion Mohronism (Mohr & Fear, 2015; Mohr GA, Mohr PE & Mohr RS, 2018).

Of relevance to the present discussion, the second (Mohr's mentation) is that education is largely brainwashing in the colloquial sense of the term (Mohr, 2013b).

The sixth (Mohr's Mechanism) is that proposed by Zorba the Greek in the movie of that name: *"A man must have a little madness"* to achieve much and, indeed, that the term 'mad scientist' is much used illustrates our belief in this proposal.

The ninth is that Murphy is the Prophet, and all history seems to prove it as, indeed, almost everything does go wrong and at the worst possible time etc. (Hughes-Wilson, 1999). Consistent with this law, one of the mankind's greatest discoveries, that of penicillin, was an accident!

The tenth, Mohr's Metrology, is that everything should be rated with a score from 1 to 9, this because, for example, zero aggressiveness would be petrifaction whilst ten would be meltdown. In other words, everything is not black and white and one should not simply think of a person as mad but give them a rating from 1 to 9.

1. Introduction

These laws are made tongue-in-cheek, but have more than a little truth.

The real truth, however, is rather grimmer, namely that greed for money and possession and hunger for power have played a very great part in human history (Mohr, 2013b).

We all know the maxim *power corrupts* and we are all well aware of the corruption that occurs in most organizations, ranging from paedophilia in the church to gigantic salaries and bonuses given to executives who often cheat consumers.

Now we have an education system that exploits our children and often ruins their lives. It does so by insisting on twelve years at school (after too many years in day care) when clearly ten better organized years would achieve better results (Mohr, 2004a, 2013b). Careers are then chosen by a lottery system unless you are sufficiently affluent to buy your chosen tertiary qualifications.

Francis Bacon *left* Cambridge at 14 and Michelangelo and da Vinci were apprenticed at the same age. This makes a mockery of an education system that has many people studying ludicrous postgraduate courses in Sexology and Puppetry until they are middle-aged.

This too is part of our reverse evolution, signs of which include decreasing IQ in decadent Western Societies, and many signs of physical deterioration of the species including epidemics of obesity, male baldness, and reduction in fertility.

What can we do about it?

There are several ways in which we can improve our bad record of thinking, including:

[1] Better understanding of the interactive processes of learning, memory and thinking.

[2] Better decision processes for management that, for example, might involve more than just a single motive such as profit.

[3] The use of logical thinking, whether this is in terms of language or mathematical symbols.

1. Introduction

[4] Designing better products and systems through the use of mathematical models, for example using the increasingly widely applicable Finite Element Method (FEM).

[5] Using optimization techniques to improve these products and systems.

[6] Using techniques such as Critical Path Planning (CPM) to plan our activities optimally.

[7] Viewing human history objectively so that we understand, for example, that:

(a) We are animals, albeit the only ones capable of what we might choose to call 'higher thinking.' Minor racial differences between us, therefore, were never a good enough excuse for conflict.

(b) That God is an invention of the human mind and that thousands of years of conflict over different interpretations of the 'God myth' have been unjustified lunacy.

[8] Give ourselves a little "Reality Therapy" (Glasser, 1975) in order to understand the problems we face, for example a population that cannot be sustained in the manner to which it aspires, continuing war all over the globe and the increasing possibility of nuclear and biochemical (NBC) warfare (Alibek, 2000; Bethe, 1991; Miller et al., 2001; Mohr, 2012a & 2014).

[9] Think hard about how best to deal with these problems, for example by unilaterally banning NBC weapons.

[10] Think hard and realistically about our goals. Some, such as freedom, we should all readily agree upon. Others, such as interminable prognostication about the origin of the Universe, border on lunacy bearing in mind that, for example, one cannot have a 'big bang of nothing' (Mohr et al, 2014).

The question of our goals is, perhaps, the most important, and amongst those goals should be to achieve a global understanding that God is, indeed, an invention, and it is only we, indeed, who can play God to any extent.

Then, surely, the interminable religious wars might cease (Mohr, 2014; Mohr & Fear, 2014; Mohr et al., 2018d).

1. Introduction

Differing religions are not the only cause of war, of course, far from it. Just as Joan Goodall was ultimately disillusioned by the repeated conflicts between neighbouring tribes of chimps, so mankind should be disillusioned by conflicts about political, racial, territorial, financial or any other issues.

Our endless history of such conflict is illustrated well by our very primitive and tribal practice of competitive sport, particularly team sports. Rugby is a good example of this, myself having always thought of it having been devised as a way of conditioning young men to unthinkingly 'charge' at the enemy when told to, whether the issue be that of winning a moronic game or winning a war.

As Newton so eloquently put it:

Nature is pleased with simplicity and hath no wont of the pomp and glory of superfluous causes.

And the superfluous causes that modern man espouses are many, ranging from religion to politics and the consumer society in which we have become *consumer zombies* creeping around with a mobile phone in one hand and a cigarette or drink bottle in the other wearing uncomfortable clothes such as jeans to keep up with 'fashion' (Mohr, 2013b).

It should be clear then that our primary purpose on this lonely planet should be to live life well, each and every one of us, and to pass on the future generations a better world in which they may *hope* to live a little better, a little more humanely, and, indeed, *hope* and positive thinking are important in helping us cope with and achieve much in life, as discussed in the recent book *The Psychology of Hope* (Mohr et al., 2018).

At present our prospects of achieving this continue to diminish as our population grows far beyond that sustainable, and we continue to deplete the planet's finite resources and pollute and degrade it (Mohr, 2012a).

1. Introduction

Mohr's Laws of Decisions

Essentially, the major problem of the human race is the habit of making bad decisions.

Some of us, at least, are very good at creative thinking to produce new ideas and products, and others are good at making the things we most need such as food, clothing and shelter.

As a result of the devastatingly accurate Peter Principle all too many of our leaders and managers are, more often than not, guilty of bad decisions, if not corruption. If a leader commits us to an unjustified war then, just as architects do, he praises his mistake. If a worker makes a small error or two he is dismissed.

Self-evident as they may be, Mohr's Laws of Decision are some help:

1) Don't rush.
2) Don't take the first offer or run with the first idea.
3) Look for alternative ideas and build an ideas/options list.
4) List the requirements or inputs for each option.
5) List the results or outputs for each option.
6) Calculate the ratio of the outputs to inputs for each option.
7) Double check the accuracy of 4 - 6.
8) Select the option with the highest output/input ratio.
9) Ask at least a second opinion.
10) Sleep on it.

The analysis of steps 4 - 6 corresponds to *cost-benefit* analysis, a simple technique widely used in economic studies of infrastructure and other plans to decide on the best program of work.

Many a housewife probably uses a somewhat similar decision making approach but the morons who run countries find such stuff hard going and have to employ thousands of economists and statisticians to perform these rudimentary analyses.

1. Introduction

Needless to say they usually get it wrong, often when somebody's palm is greased, for example by a construction company seeking the contract for a major government project.

This short book attempts to briefly consider organized processes of thinking that should lead to better results.

To this end, early chapters briefly discuss the interactive processes of human learning, memory and thinking.

Following chapters discuss group and corporate thinking using such tools as agendas for meetings, decision tables, benefit-cost analysis, and surveys of public opinion.

Further chapters then discuss symbolic logic, computer programming, planning and scheduling, finite element models of network systems and optimization of these.

It is hoped that this introduction to thinking in an organized fashion, usually breaking a problem or task into several 'elements', will prove far more useful than such popular but trivial concepts as lateral thinking and the silly word 'po' that it uses as an alternative to the word 'no' (de Bono, 1982).

Finally, note that the QBASIC programs in this book can be copied, however, and saved in Plain Text format with the file extension .BAS so that QBASIC can then run them.

Chapter 2

LEARNING

LEARNING IN INFANTS

Habituation is the basic learning process of adjustment to one's environment. The young child plucked from the womb has every reason to feel disturbed and it takes time for it to adjust to the new environment of a cot. There, *accommodation* is the process by which it comes to terms with the new objects and activities which then confront it.

Imprinting is an important part of the early learning process in higher animals that plays a key role in brain development.

Konrad Lorentz, an Austrian ethologist, demonstrated this by being the first moving object seen by ducklings after hatching. He waddled in a squatting position and quacked and before long the ducklings assumed him to be their mother and followed him about and flew to him when he quacked.

In the first months of life there is considerable growth in the network of brain cells and connecting fibres, especially in the speech area of the infant brain (Foss & Hakes, 1978).

Much of our language learning is stored as *semantic memory*, one of five basic memory types discussed in the next chapter. Semantic memory is very stable so that the meanings of words or the rules for their use are not forgotten.

Some experiments have shown that semantic memory stores information in logical hierarchies that go from general categories to specific ones, so that clusters of words with related meanings are stored in the same location in the brain.

2. Learning

According to some experts the critical period in a child's intellectual, social and emotional development is between eight and eighteen months.

During this period in particular much of a child's learning is by *modelling* or *imitative learning*, also referred to as *learning by observation*. For example, infants learn to smile by imitating the smiles of doting mothers, nurses and relatives.

They also try to imitate speech and at six months lallation begins and the baby utters repeated sounds such as ma-ma or da-da. At 10 months the baby begins to try to copy sounds made by the parents and by the end of the first year it may have learnt one or two real words.

At age two a child will have learnt about 250 words. From here the number of words learnt increases at an approximately linear rate up to about 2500 words at age 6 when the rate slows down and there are new subjects to be learnt at school.

In the early childhood years parents instinctively use *conditioning*, that is, repetitive presentation of items associated with simple skills to be learnt, often followed by praise when satisfactory progress is made.

Cognitive learning

In the early primary school years children should be guided through the processes of 'learning to learn.'

They will already have learnt many *activities* by modelling and conditioning before starting school. By the time they have learnt to read a little, however, they are able to learn things by *cognitive* learning which *processes* and stores *abstract* information.

Latent learning occurs when subjects are exposed to a body of information, rather than in small parts, and they then apply that information later on, perhaps in a test.

A laboratory example of this is that an experimental group of rats allowed to roam a maze will then do better in learning to get through it for a reward than a control group with no prior experience of the maze.

2. LEARNING

Insight learning occurs when, given a problem, we make little or no progress until suddenly we find the solution using both prior knowledge and information specific to the problem. Such learning occurs by processes of reorganizing the information pertinent to the problem until a solution is devised.

Imitative learning or *modelling* is the primary learning process in infancy and is important in human learning of language, attitude formation and personality development.

It occurs later in life too, however, for example the speed with such things as new dance styles or other crazes propagate is often remarkable and a boon to the advertising industry.

CLASSICAL CONDITIONING

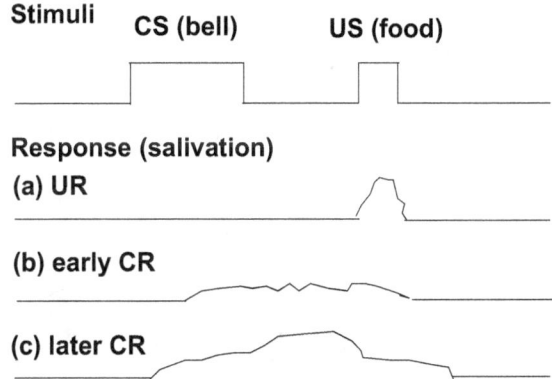

Figure 2.1. Pavlov's classical conditioning experiment:
(a) Bell precedes food presentation.
(b) Only stimulus is the bell.
(c) US resumed temporarily - then only CS giving result shown.

Classical conditioning, or learning by association, was first demonstrated by Ivan Pavlov's celebrated experiments with dogs in the 1890s.

In these he noted that a caged dog's mouth salivated when it saw food on a pan swung within its reach. Here the food is the *uncontrolled stimulus* (US) and salivation is the dog's *uncontrolled reaction* (UR)

2. Learning

Next, a bell was rung shortly before presentation of the food and the dog's saliva collected in a cup to measure the amount. Here the bell is the *controlled stimulus* (CS).

It was found that, after a few repetitions of the paired stimuli of bell and food, the dog would begin to salivate with the ringing of the bell alone, this being the *controlled reaction* (CR).

Similar results can be obtained with almost any stimulus that consistently evokes a reflex response such as electrical shock. A dog or a human given a mild shock to a leg will quickly withdraw the leg.

If the electrode giving the shocks is attached to the leg, on the other hand, flexion of the leg will occur in response to shock, the US. Then when a prior conditioned or 'neutral' stimulus is given as warning conditioned response is developed and remains after the US is removed.

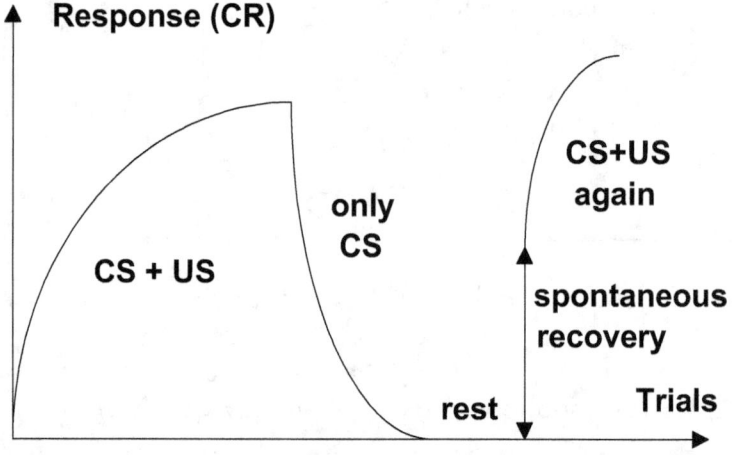

Figure 2.2. Conditioning, extinction and recovery.

After many trials the results can be graphed as a *learning curve*. Typically this takes the form shown in Figure 2.2 where the curve gradually flattens as the number of trials increases.

Here the US and CS remain paired. If the US is removed, however, *extinction* occurs and the response (the CR) decreases. Then, if the US is again added after the CS the response recovers, the initial amount of response being called the *spontaneous recovery*.

Advertising often uses classical conditioning by repeatedly associating a product with positive ideas and images, thereby encouraging people to have positive feelings towards the product itself.

Operant conditioning

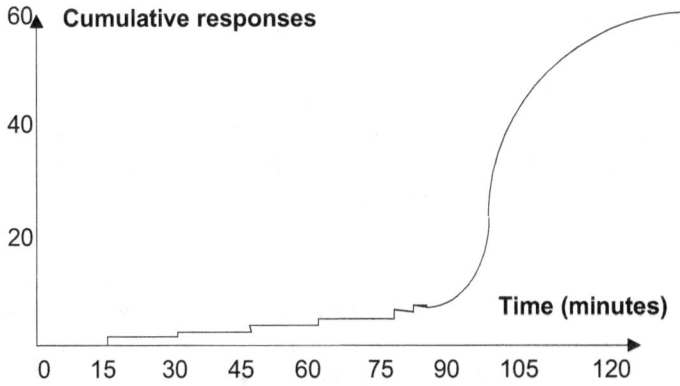

Figure 2.3. Operant conditioning responses by rat in a Skinner Box. First response at 15 minutes, second at 30, third at 45, but after 75 minutes the rate of response becomes high.

Operant conditioning, or learning by consequences, is characterized by the use of *reinforcement* which encourages a response in which the subject *operates* in some way, rather than just exhibiting a passive reflex response as in classical conditioning.

The classical experiments in operant conditioning were conducted in the 1940s by Skinner, a Harvard psychologist. In these he placed a rat in a box in which there was a lever that delivered food to it when pressed.

2. Learning

Initially the lever was operated from outside and soon the rat learnt the association between seeing the lever move and the appearance of food.

After a while it operated the lever itself to obtain food and continued to do so with increasing frequency as it becomes more familiar with the routine, as shown in Figure 2.3.

In the result of Figure 2.3 the rat in the 'Skinner Box', as it came to be called, took 15 minutes to successfully operate the feed lever. Four more intervals of about 15 minutes occurred before following operations when, the rat having fully learnt the procedure, the rate of operation accelerated markedly.

We instinctively use operant conditioning in bringing up children, the reinforcement to encourage desired actions being smiles and vocal approval.

Note that the timing of reinforcement is important. In a Skinner box, for example, the greater the time delay between the rat pressing the lever and the delivery of the food the longer it will take the rat to associate the two events and thus learn the feeding operation.

As with classical conditioning, *extinction* occurs when reinforcement ceases. This 'unlearning' process may be stronger still when *negative reinforcement*, typically some form of punishment in the educational context, is used.

Conditioned physical responses may be accompanied by emotional feelings or responses and many of our feelings are developed by conditioning.

In the case of classical conditioning *conditioned emotional responses* (CERs) may develop. Indeed, our feelings about many people and other things in our lives develop in this kind of way.

Advertising is also a case in point where an ad reminds us of a familiar product, evoking feelings of recognition and approval whilst the implications for education are all too obvious.

2. Learning

ATTITUDES

Attitude can be defined as 'psychological *tendency* expressed by *evaluating* a particular entity with some degree of favour or disfavour.'

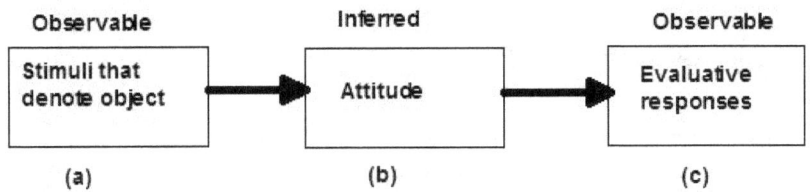

Figure 2.4. Psychological responses

Figure 2.4 illustrates the three types of response involved in attitudinal psychology. These are:
1. *Cognitive response*. This response is that of recognition of, for example, a name, a picture or other stimulus.
2. *Affective response*. This is a hypothetical construct and a latent variable. Here the sympathetic nervous system responds to (1) with feelings or emotions.
3. *Behavioural response*. This is the outward expression of (2) and may be a positive, neutral or negative response of some degree or intensity involving some observable action.

In this context, for example, conservatism, environmentalism or racism are objects. Then when we label a person a conservative, environmentalist or racist we infer an attitudinal position. Such attitudes are evidenced and also developed by the *'CAB'* mechanism illustrated in Figure 2.4.

Schemas

Schemas are cognitive structures that represent a person's past experience in a stimulus domain by a higher order or abstract cognitive structure. Then attitude is a subset of such a schema.

2. Learning

Schemas have a selective effect on the retention, retrieval and remembering of information so that people have a better remembrance of stimuli that 'fit' their schemas and also for those that 'oppose.' This same selectivity applies to the 'input' of information as well as its output.

Functions of attitudes

Attitudes are necessary as part of our information processing system and have the following functions:

1. Knowledge function. Attitudes play an important role in summarizing past experience.
2. Adjustment or 'utilitarian' function. This proposed function has its roots in learning theory and enables people to maximize rewards in their environment and minimize punishment or losses.
3. Ego-defensive function. This has its roots in the idea of a defence mechanism and involves trying to avoid unpleasant realities.
4. Value-expressive function. This is related to the concept of the ego and social psychology and involves the expression of personal values and self-concept through attitude formation.

It follows from this theory that people like, and hence are motivated, to organize and simplify stimuli and collate related cognitions. Thus attitudes themselves energize and direct behaviour, that is, they motivate action as well as determine the form of reactions.

ATTITUDE FORMATION

Of particular importance is McGuire's reception-yielding model of attitude formation shown in Figure 2.5 (Eagly & Chaiken, 1993). Here 'reception' refers to comprehending a 'message', for example an advertisement. This model postulates that the probability of attitude change is given by:

$$P(C) = P(R) \times P(Y)$$

so that a maximum change is obtained where the reception and yielding curves intersect, as shown in Figure 2.5.

2. LEARNING

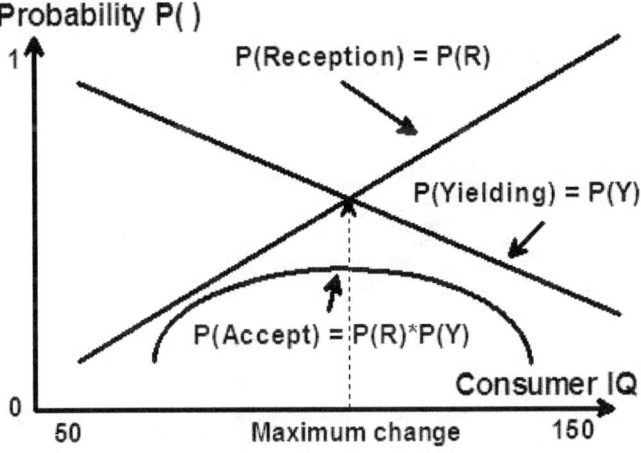

Figure 2.5. Probability of reception, yielding & attitude change.

One application of this idea is to 'get them young' so that advertising companies target the young and naive before they have the maturity or 'consumer intelligence' to develop resistance. Thus, once an idea like 'beer is for the men' is buried in a boy's brain he may become a beer drinker for life, the habit occasionally reinforced by ads that make the habit look completely appropriate.

An excellent example of this was given by Sir Edgar Saunders addressing the Brewer's Society in Birmingham in 1930 (Sargent, 1979):

The chief customers of the public house today are the elderly and middle-aged men. Unless you can attract the younger generation to take the place of the older men, there is no doubt that we shall have to face a steadily falling consumption . . . if we begin advertising in the press we shall see the continuance of our advertising is contingent upon the fact that we get educational support as well in the same papers.

In that way it is wonderful how you can educate public opinion, generally, without making it too obvious that there is a public campaign behind it all.

2. LEARNING

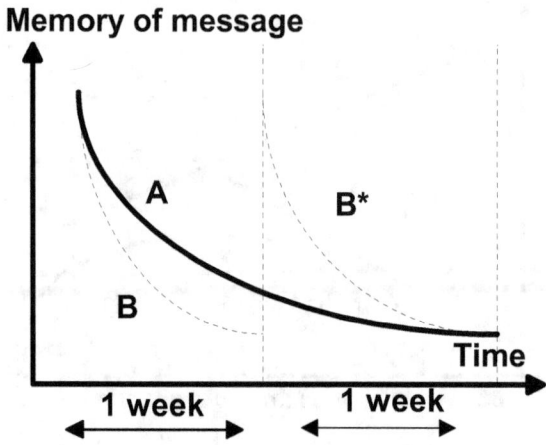

Figure 2.6. Forgetting curves.

The forgetting curves of Figure 2.6 have important application in developing long term marketing plans. Here curves A and B are for two messages and curve B* is the result after the second message is repeated.

Then, after time has elapsed after an advertisement, its 'residual' effect depends upon both the *primacy,* or strength of the ad compared to others, and its *recency.* In Figure 2.6, after two weeks ad B* has greater recency than ad A, but less primacy so that they have nearly equal effect.

In such studies, however, correlation between retention and persuasion is by no means guaranteed.

MOTIVATION

Aristotle was first to assert that our goal was to become more nearly what we were intended to be. Psychologists refer to this is as *self-actualization* and Maslow viewed this as striving to reach our potential (Lindzey at al., 1978). He defined two kinds of needs:

(a) *Basic needs* such as hunger, thirst, sex and security.

(b) *Metaneeds* such as achievement, beauty, goodness, justice, order and unity.

2. Learning

Maslow defined achievement as a basic need but the present author prefers to classify it as a 'higher' or more human metaneed.

First, we must meet our basic or 'animal' needs. That done, we can turn our attention to the higher 'human' metaneeds, and thence self-actualization as a human being.

These needs provide *primary goals* that may motivate us towards *secondary goals* such as money in order to achieve them.

Most of our basic needs are *intrinsic motivations*. Of these, *competence motivation* is perhaps the most basic and is learnt by infants challenged by goals such as standing up in their cot or walking.

Most of our metaneeds are *learned goals*. Achievement motivation, for example, can be inculcated by parents or teachers. *Social motivations* such as justice are also acquired in this way.

What has this got to do with thinking? One's motivations will, of course, greatly influence how one thinks and acts.

Some studies have found, however, little correlation between motivation and efficiency of learning, suggesting that genetics and practice are more important factors.

Practice

In a classical experiment Hermann Ebbinghaus found that after reading through a list of 16 syllables for 0, 8, 16, 24, 32, 42, 53, or 64 repetitions, and then 24 hours later assessing how many further repetitions were needed to re-learn the list, the result was the almost linear relationship shown in Figure 2.7.

This result shows that more practice (on day 1 here) gives greater learning. More important, it shows that each learning trial on day 1, which takes about 7 seconds, saves about 12 seconds on day 2. Thus it is better to spread learning trials out over time and this phenomenon is known as *distribution of practice* (Baddeley, 1990).

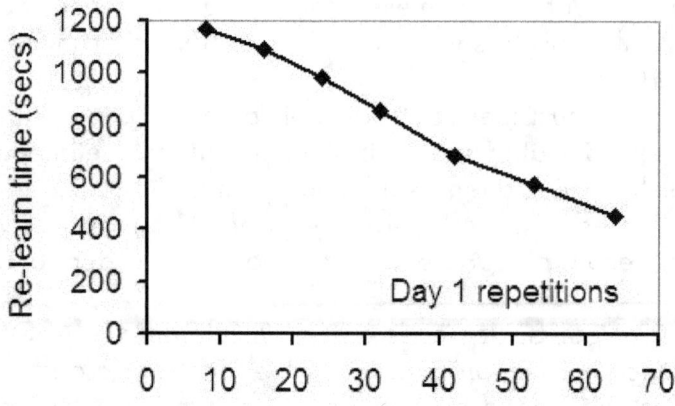

Figure 2.7. Influence of number learning repetitions on retention 24 hours later.

One trial of distributed learning had four groups learning to type with (Baddeley, 1990):
1. One session of one hour/day.
2. Two sessions of one hour/day.
3. One two-hour session/day.
4. Two two-hour sessions/day.

It was found that the first group learnt the keyboard more efficiently than the other groups. That is, the rate of learning per hour of practice was greater for the group with greater distribution of learning.

CONCLUSION

Learning often involves a good deal of thinking, and what we have learnt will then greatly influence how we think thereafter, if not for the rest of our lives.

So too will the attitudes we have developed. All too many of us have tunnel vision for our own ideas and goals, and a negative attitude to the ideas and aspirations of others. In other words many of us are not aware of the power of positive thinking.

2. Learning

Many of our attitudes may have been formed by conditioning, for example by parents and teachers, or by the ubiquitous, incessant and increasingly 'heavy' advertising of today.

Be that as it may, if we have some understanding of learning and attitude formation, our thinking may be the better for it.

If our goal is to influence the thinking of others, on the other hand, then an understanding of conditioning is absolutely essential.

As for advertising, we should be aware, regardless which side of the advertising fence we are on, of the extent to which advertising plays upon our basic feelings and needs and literally conditions us to accept, if not desire, products.

A good example is the ads for beer which promote the idea that some beer brands are manly and appropriate after a hard days work. Higher priced and imported beers, on the other hand, will be promoted as 'cool' beside a luxurious swimming pool, for example, but the drinker will always be a man.

Several authors such as Ralph Nader, Vance Packard and JK Galbraith have lamented that all too many American products are somewhat second rate because they concentrate on 'image' rather than quality (Packard, 1961; Galbraith, 1963). Nevertheless, such companies are often remarkably good at selling these products thanks to advertising which effectively uses such principles as the reception-yielding model of Figure 2.5 to influence our thinking.

2. Learning

Chapter 3

Memory

Human learning and memory

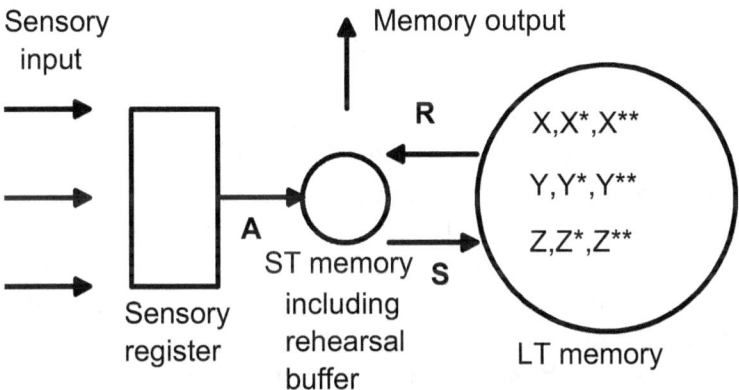

A = Attention, S = storage, R = retrieval

Figure 3.1. Information processing model of memory.

Learning is an important prerequisite to thinking and memory is an important part of both the learning and thinking processes. Figure 3.1 shows a simple information processing model of memory (Atkinson & Shiffrin, 1968). In this, the *sensory register*, located in a part of the brain called the thalamus, processes information from sensory channels associated with vision, hearing and other senses.

The visual sensory register can hold 10 - 20 bits of information for only about 1 second, whereas the auditory sensory register can hold information for up to 4 or 5 seconds.

3. Memory

Of the up to 20 bits of information that our visual registers can accommodate with a brief glance, for example an array of letters of the alphabet, we can only remember four or five of them, this number being called the *span of apprehension*.

As a consequence most information in the sensory registers is lost but that to which sufficient attention is paid is transferred to the *short-term-memory* (STM), located in a part of the brain called the hippocampus. Here it is held for about 20 - 30 seconds and some of it is processed by being rehearsed in the *rehearsal buffer*, the rest being lost.

This model fits everyday life fairly well. For example, when somebody tells you a phone number and you are interrupted while dialing it you are likely to forget it because it will be lost from STM. This is because the STM holds only about 5 - 9 items and, under certain conditions, as few as two or three.

Sternberg (1966) conducted an experiment that illustrates how memory, in this case STM, works. He showed a group of people sets of from 1 to 6 digits and seconds later asked them if the set contained a particular digit. Response times were closely proportional to the number of digits shown, demonstrating that the coding of the set in STM was searched serially or one digit at a time.

In the rehearsal buffer such processes as repetition of the information link it to information already stored in memory and then pass it to *long-term-memory* (LTM) where it remains for periods of days up to a lifetime. In LTM information is *consolidated*, a process that may take from half an hour up to months. If consolidation is somehow interrupted some memory loss occurs.

Most LTM information is stored in the cerebral cortex, the 'thinking' part of the brain which is much more developed in humans than in other species.

3. Memory

Simple passive repetition of information, or *maintenance rehearsal,* is not sufficient to ensure that items are passed to LTM. The active process of *elaborative rehearsal,* involving reorganization of the material and attaching meaning to it is more likely to pass information to LTM.

There are four types of LTM:

[1] *Procedural memory* or implicit memory is 'knowing how' to perform some skill, often learnt by procedural or implicit learning. Procedural learning is discussed later in this chapter.

[2] *Declarative memory* is 'knowing that' or memory of data or facts and events.

[3] *Episodic memory* of prior life experiences is a type of declarative memory.

[4] *Semantic memory* such as words and language rules is another type of declarative memory which involves more 'preprocessing' in STM than episodic memory.

In such processing even inherently organized material is *subjectively organized* by the learner into categories. Up to a point, it is found that the more categories used the better the material can be recalled.

Semantic memory uses *constructive processes* to store information in an organized manner, often into a hierarchical structure of categories and sub-categories.

Recall of the information then occurs by *reconstructive processes.* With these speed of recall depends upon the hierarchical level at which information is recalled, more general 'heading' information being recalled more rapidly than specific information.

Thus, when we have difficulty remembering a person's name, for example, we often can only remember one or more names similar in some respect such as their first letter, and then finally remember the required name anything from seconds to days later.

3. Memory

Memory processing also makes much use of images and *concrete* images are easily formed for words like 'cat' whilst *abstract* images for words like 'mercy' are more difficult to form.

Australian aborigine elders, for example, remember centuries of tribal history by associating important events with environmental features and recall and pass on this history by 'walking through' these places.

Information stored in LTM is easier to recall if it is stored with *retrieval cues* which are associated with 'blocks' of information. Individual items within these blocks are then stored with 'tags'.

How easily information is recalled later depends much upon how well it has been associated with images, categorized, and provided with cues.

An example of how images affect information recall from LTM occurs if witnesses who saw a speeding car crash are asked:

"How fast do you think the car was going when it _ _ _ _?"

with the final verb having such variations as *contacted, hit,* and *crashed.*

Speed estimates will increase in the order of these three verbs by as much as 25% because the new information in the wording of the question may conflict or *interfere* with the memory and associated images of the event in LTM.

Information that has been stored in a well-organized fashion can sometimes be recalled by *redintegration*, the process by which some event such as a 'leading question' unlocks a rapid sequence of memories that may be connected by a chain of associations.

This is the ideal situation when we read an exam question. One or more words in the question quickly trigger recall of a stream of relevant information. If the exam is the usual written answer one we tend to forget part of the answer before we can write it down.

3. MEMORY

LEARNING CURVES

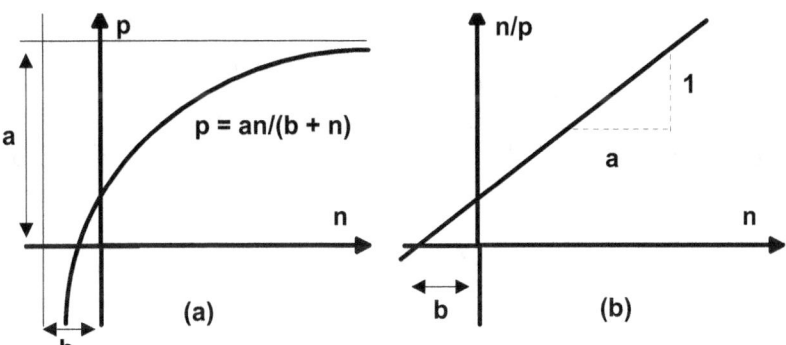

Figure 3.2. Mohr Plot for learning.

Suppose the degree to which a person or group has learnt something or been conditioned is given by the probability $p = 0$ to 1, and this probability depends on n, the number of repetitions of the learning process.

If we assume that the learning process is hyperbolic so that the degree of learning gradually increases towards 100% or the asymptote $p = a$ with $a = 1$, then this is represented by the hyperbola of Figure 3.2(a), the equation for which is

$$p = an/(b + n)$$

This equation is easily rearranged to give $n/p = (b + n)/a$ so that if we plot n/p against n the straight line of Figure 3.2(b) is obtained and the magnitude of the intercept with the n axis = $-b$ whilst, of more interest, the inverse slope of the line equals the horizontal asymptote a of the hyperbola.

In experimental situations this plot is useful in testing whether results are indeed hyperbolic and, if so, estimating the 'ceiling' value towards which some dependent variable is converging.

Applied to the memory of a single person, for example, a typical result might be $b = 3$, $n = 3$, giving $p/a = 50\%$, or 50% memory retention after three repetitions.

3. Memory

Here p is either:

(a) How well an item is learnt and people's names might be a good example of this. Myself, I often think I need about three repetitions of such things to remember them.

(b) How much of a 'block' of information is learnt. An example might be a list of names where, because of *interference,* words at the beginning (the *primacy effect*) and end (the *recency effect*) are remembered best.

For a slower learner, on the other hand, b might double to 6 so we need $n = 6$ to get $p = 50\%$ learning.

Applied to conditioning of the populace by advertising, p is the proportion of the population affected, and larger values of the asymptote b which flatten the curve might occur when there are two or more competing advertisers in the market. In politics this highlights the advantage of dictatorship.

In education it perhaps highlights the importance of avoiding conflicting messages so that it is often best to learn one subject at a time.

Skill learning

Learning some skills requires a large number of repetitions n, for example 'touch' typing where when fully proficient we do not have to consciously think of which key to associate with each letter of the alphabet to be typed. Such memory is called *procedural memory* or implicit memory.

Skill learning has three stages:

[1] The cognitive stage in which the requirements and components of the skill are learnt.

[2] The association stage in which the components are performed together and the skill is perfected.

[3] The automation stage at which the skill is completely remembered.

In learning skills *feedback* is important in stage [1] to help perfect each component of the skill and again important in stages [2] and [3] to help assess which components require further learning.

3. Memory

If the requirements of a new skill overlap those of one previously learnt *positive transfer* makes the new skill easier to learn. Conversely, if some parts of the new skill contradict those of an 'old' skill then *negative transfer* may make learning the new skill more difficult.

An example might be riding a bike where turning the handlebars to the right steers to the right. Used to this, in yachting one might have some difficulty becoming accustomed to pushing the tiller to the right to steer left.

Effective study

As prelude to thinking study may be needed and effective study techniques are desirable. In studying a chapter of a book, for example:

Motivate yourself and make time for the learning task. Relax for a while before starting to clear your mind, then summon your concentration and start, making sure there are no distractions.

Then apply the **HEART** routine suggested by Mohr (2004a):

H. Skim through to see the different topics/sections in the chapter, trying to spot the highlight or key point in each.

E. Exposition. Carefully read through, not word for word, but focusing on the key points and searching for their meaning, if not already clear, in the surrounding text.

A. Again. Go through the material again, writing brief notes on the topics you identified in **H** with key words as headings, followed by brief elaboration of the key points.

R. Review the material to see how well you remember it, especially the key points.

T. Test how well you remember the material.

In studying *positive transfer* occurs when subjects overlap and well designed curricula take advantage of this wherever possible. When studying try to make a habit of letting previous learning help by noticing where subjects overlap in some way.

When we have negative attitudes towards a subject, however, *negative transfer* may occur. Hence the importance of motivating yourself for study, for example by thinking about the usefulness of the material under study.

FORGETTING

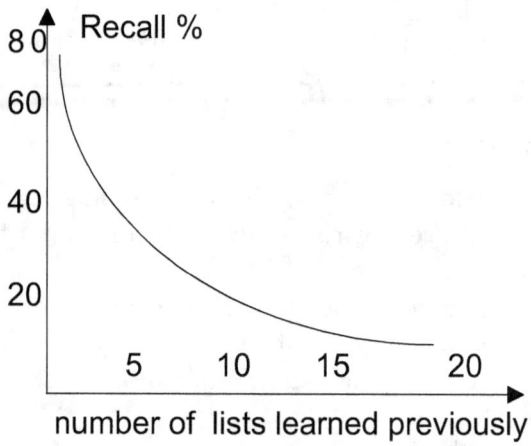

Figure 3.3. Decrease in recall of a list with increasing number of lists learnt previously.

Figure 3.3 shows an example of *proactive interference* in which the accuracy with which lists are remembered declines as the number of lists learnt previously increases (Morgan et al., 1979).

Here the increasing number of previously learnt lists interferes with the learning of the last list. At the same time *retroactive interference* will occur so that learning of further lists reduces recall of the earlier lists.

A similar effect, called the *serial position effect,* applies to the items of a single list so that items early in the list are remembered better than those in the middle (the *primacy effect)* whilst items late in the list are remembered much better than those in the middle (the *recency effect).*

3. Memory

Interference is one of the major causes of forgetting and forgetting curves generally take roughly the same form as that of Figure 3.3 where the curve is hyperbolic like that of Figure 3.2 but 'upside down.'

Interference is *trace-dependent* forgetting because of physical changes in memory traces when something new is learned.

Memory traces can also be changed by *decay* or by *motivated forgetting*, for example when we deliberately *repress* a memory.

Retrieval failure is when we lack or fail to use the right cues to retrieve stored memories. This is called *cue-dependent* forgetting.

Pseudoforgetting is when we fail to recall something, not realizing that it was not stored in LTM in the first place.

Generally, memory can decline with age, for example with the onset of senile dementia of the Alzheimer type (SDAT), Alzheimer's disease, or brain damage caused by injury, alcohol or other drugs.

IMPROVING MEMORY

Sometimes *mnemonic* techniques are used to improve memory.

The *method of loci*, as in the example of the use of association by Australian aborigine elders given earlier, associates items to be remembered with physical objects in one's environment.

The *word peg method* typically uses a list of ten number-word pairs, for example one-sun, two-shoe and so on. Then to remember a list of food items the first two of which are bread and butter one might visualize:

[1] White bread as being bright like the sun,

[2] Our shoes slipping on butter on the floor.

3. Memory

The method may only be useful for one or two very important lists and can fix many items of a short list for many years.

An example of the *link method* is *narrative chaining* in which a list of words is remembered by inventing a story involving each item in the list.

The *method of word associations* uses a phrase with the first letter of each word corresponding to each item of a list, for example:

My very energetic mother just sits up near pop is used to remember the names of the planets in order from the sun, that is Mercury, Venus, Earth, Mars, Jupiter, Saturn, Uranus, Neptune, Pluto.

This method is often used by medical students to remember anatomical names.

Acronyms are another useful mnemonic in which words are formed from the first letters of a group of words, for example WHO for World Health Organization. Abbreviations of the names of companies (e.g., IBM) and mathematical and other methods (e.g., MIS = Management Information Systems) are also formed in this way.

The way in which text is remembered provides an insight into why key words are important in the memory process. It is believed that text is not stored in memory literally, but as a number of *propositions*, each of which has a *relational term* for which there are *arguments* (using the latter word in the same way it is used in connection with mathematical functions, especially when they are used in computer programs).

The sentence "Tom hit Jack", for example, is remembered as: (HIT, TOM, JACK)

If later "Tom apologized for hitting Jack" this is stored as

((APOLOGIZE, TOM), (HIT, TOM, JACK))

with the simple proposition of the original memory embedded in a complex one. Here the 'strong' word HIT acts as a key word and it is linked directly to the word TOM in long-term memory.

3. Memory

UNDERSTANDING THE WORKINGS OF THE BRAIN

The role of chemicals

The experiments with flat worms and then rats which led Ungar's group to isolation and then synthesis of several peptide compounds that were able to transfer memory of conditioned learning to other animals were mentioned in the second section of Chapter 1.

The 'strength' of memories

Memory storage is sometimes so effective and indelible that sometimes we can't forget things we would like to such as bad habits.

Sometimes *motivated forgetting* suppresses memories of traumatic experiences but this generally occurs subconsciously and we are not able to control the repression process at will.

One clue is that when we do consciously forget certain things we quickly dismiss them from our thoughts as soon as they enter them. When happier thoughts cross our minds, on the other hand, they may linger a little longer and almost involve a euphoria comparable to that which might be induced by small doses of tranquilizers like alcohol.

In other words we use processes like elaborative rehearsal to 'tag' memories with appropriate emphasis as important, good, bad and so on.

It is also clear that we have different 'layers' of memory so that past memories are in 'background memory' and take from seconds to days to recall.

Presumably items in foreground memory are chemically tagged and, over time, the pathways and neurons that store them become depleted in these markers.

Supporting this view, research by Hyden's group in Sweden found changes in RNA in rat's brains compared to those of a control group after they had been given a learning task.

Such work clearly demonstrates that, just as DNA stores genetic coding, macromolecules of RNA play an important role in memory processes.

3. Memory

Effect of experience

The importance of *enrichment* of the learning environment was tellingly demonstrated by the work of social psychologist David Krech and his group at UC Berkeley (Packard, 1978).

In this they provided a group of rats with an "enriched environment" of large cages with various things rats enjoy such as slides, wheels and the like. Then a maze with a sugar reward at the end was added. This had a dark and a lighted alley and the rats soon learnt which led to the sugar.

Then the maze lighting was reversed regularly so that the rats had to relearn the 'sugar route.'

A second control group of rats lived normally and a third group was kept in a deprived dark and noiseless area.

After 90 days it was found that the 'enriched' rats had developed thicker cerebral cortexes!

This was perhaps the first evidence that the brain is modified by experience. The enrichment conditions caused the following changes (Atrens & Curthoys, 1982):

[1] The size of the cerebral cortex was increased.

[2] The size of the cortical neurons increased.

[3] The size and number of synaptic contacts increased.

[4] The quantity of acetylcholinesterase, the compound responsible for breakdown of the neurotransmitter acetylcholine, increased.

Therefore, the rats which had experienced early environmental enrichment were apparently anatomically and biochemically superior to those which had endured a deprived environment.

This result provided laboratory evidence that environmental enrichment might be able to reverse the deficiencies in brain development resulting from an environmentally deprived childhood.

3. MEMORY

Nutrition also plays a part as proteins are needed for growth of all cells in the body, including neurons. Poor nutrition, therefore, might be expected to inhibit brain development.

It should be noted, however, that apparently greater brain development such as that experienced by Krech's rats does not necessarily lead to corresponding improvements in behaviour or performance of such processes as learning.

BIOCHEMICAL LEARNING AND EVOLUTION

Three important research results indicative of the biochemical nature of learning processes were:

[1] Increases in the quantity of acetylcholinesterase, the compound responsible for breakdown of the neurotransmitter acetylcholine, in the brains of Krech's environmentally enriched rats (Packard, 1978).

[2] The work by Ungar's group in which peptides in rats conditioned to shun darkness were isolated. These peptides seemed able to transfer the conditioning to other rats (Ungar et al., 1972; Ungar, 1974).

[3] Changes in RNA in rats given a learning task found by Hyden's group in Sweden (Hyden, 1967; Traill, 1999).

Hyden's group also found an increase in a brain-specific protein S-100 in rats trained to use their non-preferred paw. They then found that an antiserum to S-100 stopped this learning.

Subsequently much further work has been done to investigate the effects of inhibition of protein and RNA synthesis by antibiotics upon memory. One finding was that drugs that interfere with the uptake of amino acids by cells can selectively interfere with memory retrieval or formation.

Peptides are small organic molecules that link hundreds or even thousands of amino acid molecules together to form polypeptides.

Proteins are naturally occurring polypeptides.

3. Memory

Genes are nucleoproteins formed by combination of polypeptide and DNA (deoxyribonucleic acid) chains.

The process of cell reproduction or *mitosis* occurs when the two strands of the DNA double helix separate and manufacture protein and a new 'opposite' strand to form a new cell.

This process is assisted by RNA (ribonucleic acid).

If learning changes RNA then perhaps a process like the cell mutation that causes cancer (Mohr, 20013a) might also be responsible for human evolution, both physically (Selmes, 1974) and mentally (Darwin, 1999).

Cell mutation is the result of a DNA copying error. This may just be a statistical fluke, having a probability of one in a million or less.

A ground breaking case study of the mutation process was the *ras* oncogene[2] found in a smoker with bladder cancer (Weinberg, 1999).

After 30 years of smoking some of the many highly toxic carcinogens he had inhaled had not been detoxified in his liver and had passed into his urine.

The ras oncogene is 5000 DNA bases long but one base was incorrect where a sequence that should have been GCC GGC GGT but instead was GCC GTC GGT with just one base incorrect, a T appearing instead of a G.

The incorrect gene then governed the growth of this cell and its descendants, resulting in a cancer tumour years later.

In like fashion, it might be possible that, over time, environmentally induced and other learning processes produce lasting changes in human RNA and thence DNA that result in physical and mental evolution.

That we have a comparatively large brain size, therefore, might indeed be the evolutionary result of sometimes vicarious thinking over millennia, as often assumed.

---

[2] The ras proto-oncogene is so named because it was first isolated in the rat sarcoma virus.

3. Memory

Another example of human evolution is the vitamin D theory of why some races have dark skin. Doubtless such changes are the result of DNA changes caused by environmentally induced biochemical processes.

Baldness is perhaps part of an evolutionary process that has generally reduced the distribution of human hair compared to that of our chimpanzee cousins.

In the last century alone some populations have become taller as a result of improved diet. During the same period there appears to have been a reduction in the fertility of some populations.

In the period 1920 – 1950 average IQ in the UK decreased by 1.5% (Vernon, 1960), and IQ in the USA has been reportedly decreasing by 1 point per generation. This alone may be clear evidence of evolutionary changes in DNA so that, as with Krech's rats, there has presumably been a corresponding change (now a decrease) in the average cerebral cortex size.

Furthermore, it may be that learnt human behaviours such as facial expressions can be inherited and thus be the result of DNA changes (Darwin, 1999).

MEMORY STRUCTURE

Figure 3.4 shows a proposed structure in which the brain stores information about animals, that is, as categories and sub-categories with properties attached to each 'node' in the structure (Collins & Quillian, 1969; Baddeley, 1990).

Some experimental results do not fit this model, for example Ripps et al. (1973) found that people were quicker to agree to the truth of the statement: *A cat is an animal* than they were to the truth of the statement: *A cat is a mammal.* They argued that MAMMAL should be closer to CAT than ANIMAL in the hierarchy.

More important, however, is that the word ANIMAL is much more frequently used than the word MAMMAL and frequency of reference to a memory certainly does enhance the speed of recall.

3. Memory

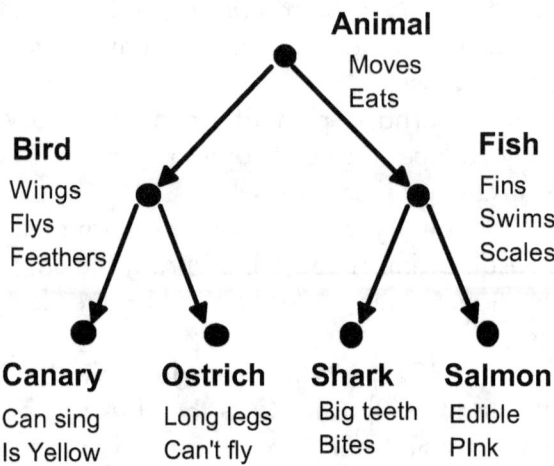

Figure 3.4. Hierarchical organization of the mental lexicon.

The present author would also argue that the brain almost certainly must store memories in a *precedence network* based on the order in which learning occurs.

In such a network a memory search that succeeds in finding a 'connection' or *common* property shared by a 'new' item in short term memory, and an item in long-term memory, might then store the data for the new item in the same physical area.

Then, for example, the first live animals that most children encounter might well be cats or dogs so that they will begin forming the memory structure shown in Figure 3.5.

Here four memories have the *common property* 'animal' and cat is the first animal encountered by an infant and thence the first memory stored (at node 1, perhaps one or more brain cells). The second memory is dog, the third lion, and so on. Then cat and dog are associated by the property *domestic* (in the child's language perhaps 'house' or 'nearby') whilst lion and elephant are associated by the common property *jungle*.

3. MEMORY

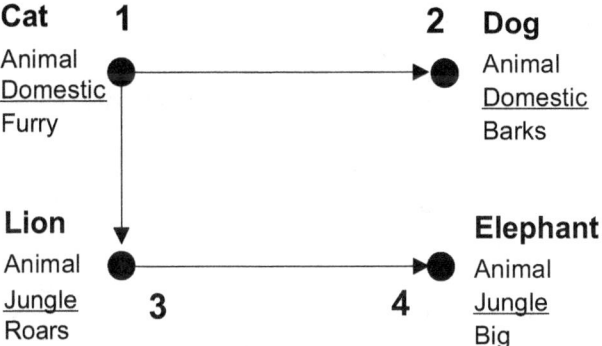

Figure 3.5. Precedence memory network.

Such memories have a considerable visual 'content' and the ease of recall of a memory will depend upon its 'strength', which will depend on such factors as the degree of elaboration with which it was committed to long-term memory, and the frequency and recency with which the memory has been revisited, the latter factor being comparable to that of *long term potentiation* (Vander et al., 1960).

NETWORK MODELS OF THE BRAIN

That electrical stimuli play an important part in brain function was demonstrated graphically by Jose Delgado by rigging a bull for radio-triggered mild electrical stimulation of a part of its brain (Delgado, 1971). He then stood in front of the animal. When it charged the tiny electrode in its brain was triggered and the bull stopped. After triggering the stimulation several times the bull was so pacified that it allowed witnesses of the experiment into the ring without charging them.

In humans, electrodes implanted in the brain have been found to cause recall of long forgotten memories.

3. Memory

It has been found that the speed of conduction of impulses or *action potentials* in nerves is approximately proportional to the square root of the fibre diameter, a result familiar in cable theory (Schmidt-Nielsen, 1979). In myelin coated axons, however, the conduction speed is approximately proportional to the fibre diameter.

The brain consists of a network of long axons extending from neurons, and their terminals connect to the short dendrites of other neurons in the brain.

Such networks can be modelled using the *Finite Element Method* (FEM). The simple example of a direct current (DC) electrical network modelled using FEM is given in Chapter 13 and this might be likened to the network of Figure 3.5.

As a crude analogy the resistance of each element in such a model might be compared to the *frequency* of use of a path in the network of the brain and the voltage at each node might be compared to the *strength* of a memory 'image' or information 'bundle' stored in a neuron.

In practice a signal between two neurons is an electrical impulse passed along the axon of the first to the dendrites of the second via a synaptic junction. At this junction neurotransmitter chemicals pass the signal across a 'synaptic gap.'

Evidently these chemicals react with RNA or peptide macromolecules in the neurons that play a role in memory *coding*.

In the case of classical conditioning, therefore, with frequent 'dosing' in this way the storage of a memory is made more permanent.

Therefore, a more realistic FEM model of a neural network might include a capacitance property for nodes so that the charge stored at these could model the strength and/or recency of a memory.

FEM network models lend themselves to 'structural' models of memory such as those of Figures 3.4 and 3.5.

3. Memory

That the resulting numerical model is a matrix suggests that some form of database model might also be used to model memory storage in the brain, not a particularly startling idea!

Another possibility is to combine the two model types so that each node in Figure 3.5 is a database of some category like those in the upper levels of Figure 3.4, and the links between the nodes are the *joins* between common *fields* in these databases.

As there are about 10^{12} neurons in the human brain, however, we can only hope to model its memory processes on a small scale.

Memory search

Dunne (1934) claimed that dreams might allow us to predict the future. This may seem a little farfetched but if we consider the *memory search* process that occurs in the brain while we are asleep his idea might not be completely ridiculous.

In Dunne's time REM sleep had not been discovered. It is during these periods that occur about every 90 minutes that dreaming occurs.

When awake and relaxed we have alpha wave brain activity (8 - 13 cycles per second) and when thinking analytically we have beta activity (15 - 30 cycles per second). These frequencies vary slightly with age and vascular and psychiatric condition (Mayeux & Rosen, 1983).

In the intervals between REM phases we are in deep sleep with slow delta wave brain activity and apparently the brain continues search processes initiated sometime earlier in the day when we have been trying to remember something we have learnt in the past without success.

During REM we have theta wave activity as we do when falling asleep. When in REM sleep a *block* of information is retrieved from memory. This may be a dream, the solution to some problem that has been bothering us, or recall of the information we have been trying to remember.

3. MEMORY

Sometimes one can awake at the end of an REM phase and several 'items' may be in one's mind. There may be as many as about ten items, in fact, the capacity of the short-term memory, and it will be difficult to remember more than one or two of them.

It is during an REM phase, indeed, that we are most likely to get the message that some nocturnal relief for bladder pressure is needed and we wake up.

When we wake up with a dream or an idea in our minds it is in short-term memory and we need to write the idea down or we may forget it. Dunne suggests that at the end of the day the idea or dream can be recalled if we relax and make a conscious effort to remember it just before going to sleep, presumably reasoning that our brain will be in a similar state to that when we awoke with the dream or idea.

Perhaps any time during a quiet evening might be just as good a time to relax and try and remember the forgotten information.

Such schemes as Superlearning (Ostrander & Schroeder, 1979) are based on the idea of using baroque music and other measures to get the brain into a relaxed alpha mode in order to learn with high efficiency. The HEART routine for study described earlier in this chapter also relies on conscious efforts at relaxation at the outset.

The same relaxation and brain wave ideas are helpful to effective and creative thinking. Not surprisingly too, 'sleeping' on a decision or problem might be helpful, as recommended in Mohr's Laws of Decision at the close of Chapter 1.

CONCLUSION

Human memories are often laid down in a split second and remembered permanently yet others, especially most of those laboriously lectured to us at school, are quickly forgotten:

Education is what remains, if one has forgotten everything one learned in school.
Albert Einstein, *Out of My Later Years* (1950).

3. Memory

An understanding of memory processes can be some help in rectifying the situation, in turn contributing to better thinking.

An understanding of the information processing model of memory of Figure 3.1, for example, might help us improve our memory by conscious use of elaborative rehearsal.

In learning it is helpful to realize that interference occurs and that is often best to learn one 'block' of information at a time and then take a break to allow it to consolidate in long-term memory.

Figure 3.2 reminds us that deliberate learning requires some repetition and of why the repetitive nature of advertising is so successful.

In searching our minds for an idea some knowledge of the associative and categorical nature of memory might be helpful. So too might the realization that information higher in the hierarchical storage of Figure 3.4 is recalled quicker.

Relaxing without distraction can also be remarkably effective in getting ideas flowing at a steady trickle through a quiet evening. Indeed, sometimes ideas might come in a flood!

Finally, Krech's brilliant environmental enrichment experiments with rats remind us that thinking in a cozy study or a comfortable armchair might be even better than in his 'enriched' environment for lab rats.

Sadly the same cannot be said of palatial boardrooms:

No grand idea was ever born in a conference
but a lot of foolish ideas have died there.
F. Scott Fitzgerald, Notebooks N

no doubt a result of the Peter Principle mentioned in the first chapter (Peter & Hull, 1969).

3. Memory

Chapter 4

THINKING

THE TOOLS WE USE FOR THINKING

In Chapters 2 and 3 learning and memory were discussed. What we have learnt and can remember is basically what we have to think with. In other words, we can't think meaningfully about things we know nothing about.

Thinking uses four elements:

[1] Images.
We often use *visual imagery* in thinking. For example, we often find it easier to describe:
(a) The shape of something by sketching it.
(b) A physical operation by demonstrating it.

In connection with example (b) the term *muscular imagery* is sometimes used to describe the way in which we remember complex physical movements.

[2] Symbols.
Language involves the spoken and written use of symbols. These symbols can be words, mathematical formulae, pictures (including diagrams, maps and graphs) or gestures that represent either *objects, operations, relationships* and *qualities*.

Most obviously we use language to communicate with one another. Language also plays an important part in thinking, making it possible to perform mental processes such as analyzing, synthesizing, thinking abstractly and generalizing. For example, usually [not always!] we have to 'collect our thoughts' in deciding what to say to someone and this is a thinking process.

4. THINKING

[3] Concepts.

Concepts can be defined as categories that represent a class of objects, events or qualities wherein each item has a number of common features. A simple example is birds which 'mentally' are a concept and birds have common properties such as two legs, wings and the ability to fly and lay eggs.

Some birds, like the ostrich or emu that do not fly, do not fit this bird concept so well so that in the hierarchical structure of semantic memory we might store the concept of birds as a 'heading', associating with it the 'universal' features of two legs and feathers. Below this in the 'top-down' tree structure (i.e., really a root structure perhaps) may be storage locations for the two sub-categories of birds that fly and those that don't.

Such categorization is important for both efficient learning and memory storage, and efficient recall and thence thinking.

When driving, for example, when you see a set of traffic lights (a concept) you note which colour is 'on' and quickly decide (a thinking process) what action to take.

As noted, *natural concepts* like birds may involve atypical examples. More abstract concepts like 'bad' and 'nice' are even more 'fuzzy' and the criteria we each associate with such concepts vary considerably.

Learning of concepts is made easier by *transfer* when they are similar to already familiar concepts.

[4] Rules.

Rules involve connections between features of a concept and between different concepts.

In the case of traffic lights, for example, we should know the rules and have only to choose 'yes' or 'no' as to whether we follow the appropriate rule. Indeed, in a split second may be all we have time to do so.

The rule for traffic lights might be represented as

(green = go) OR (amber = slow down) OR (red = stop)

and the rule for driving might be written

4. Thinking

(accelerator = go) OR (no accelerator = slow) OR (brake = stop)

so to stop at a red light we have to connect the two rules, a process probably carried out in short term memory.

Here a good exercise would be to write BASIC coding to combine the two foregoing rules in the same way our brain might handle it. In a 'traffic light' segment of code an INPUT statement could read in numbers 1,2,3 to corresponding to green etc., using these to direct execution appropriately to a 'driving' code segment in which the 'flags' 1,2,3 determine which message of GO etc. is printed to the screen.

More complex rules might combine simple rules using the sort of embedding used by memory to store related text statements described in Chapter 3.

CREATIVE THINKING

Divergent thinking involves considering a number of alternatives, some of which may be new and/or impractical, rather than seeking a single logical solution.

Creative thinking involves finding novel but practical solutions to a problem or task using divergent thinking and may occur in three stages:

[1] Preparation: define the facts and materials needed for the new solution.

[2] Incubation: acquire further information, think about, and 'sleep on' the problem.

{3] Assembly: combine information to find the solution.

Creativity may be enhanced by 'undirected' or *autistic thinking*, as occurs in dreams, in which one's own 'personal' and unique concepts are freely associated. This is accomplished by *brainstorming* in which the mind is allowed to roam freely through as many ideas as possible.

4. THINKING

Creative people enjoy creating things, are assertive, have a risk taking approach, tend to be impulsive, dislike constraints, like a little complexity, are objective about their efforts (i.e., able to critically examine them) and accept feedback from others.

Among other characteristics, creative people may also be intuitive, perceptive, ingenious, industrious, persistent, independent, unconventional, courageous, uninhibited, moody, self-centred and eccentric.

PROBLEM SOLVING

Problems can be attacked in three stages:

[1] Defining the problem

At first this might involve realizing that a problem exists.

Then we need to determine:

(a) What is the initial situation, i.e., what is known about the problem?

(b) What is the goal?

(c) What are the restrictions or *constraints*?

(d) What moves or *operations* are required to reach the goal?

[2] Generating possible solutions

Solutions to a problem can be obtained by such *strategies* as:

(a) In the case of mathematics problems, for example, *algorithms* can be used to try large numbers of solutions on a computer.

(b) Use an existing *heuristic rule* or 'rule of thumb.'

(c) Redefine the problem, for example by breaking it down into stages and seeking a 'solution' for each stage. Such *means-end analysis* is sometimes more successful if the problem is examined by working backwards through these stages.

(d) Use a new arrangement of existing techniques or materials.

4. THINKING

(e) Invent new techniques or materials, i.e., use *insight learning*. This requires *creative thinking* which, as described earlier, often involves *incubation* periods.

Creative thinking can be inhibited by:

(i) *Functional fixedness,* the difficulty of imagining new uses for materials or devices.

(ii) *Mental set,* the difficulty in finding new strategies for approaching a problem. Set can be induced by recent experiences or old habits.

[3] Testing and evaluating the solutions

Alternative solutions are tested to see how well they work in relation to predetermined criteria.

Sometimes problems can be solved by *trial and error* so that trial solutions are repetitively adjusted until satisfactory.

Selection of the best solution from a number of alternatives should be done with a quantitative basis.

LATERAL THINKING

Edward de Bono proposed lateral thinking as an alternative to logical or *vertical* thinking. Some of the features of lateral thinking are:

➢ Steps can be jumped (and 'filled' later).

➢ Steps need not be 'correct' so long as the conclusion is correct and may be made in order to *generate* a new direction or branch, that is, an additional OR in the notation used earlier.

➢ Interpretation of task criteria and alternative solution properties can be changed and the process is not *finite,* that is it need not reach a conclusion in any given time.

➢ It is *probabilistic* so that less obvious solutions are considered so that the best solution is obtained (if a valid solution exists).

4. Thinking

De Bono (1982) recommends use of the word PO:

"PO is the laxative of language"

as an alternative to the words 'yes' and 'no' to emphasize that lateral thinking is not quick to say no to less obvious solutions and, rather than stop at obstacles to a solution, one should *go around* them by such means as those summarized above.

Whilst 'po' seems a somewhat trivial, if not absurd, idea, it may have some merit for many of us do indeed have a tendency to persist trying to solve some problems rather than 'go around' them.

Selecting the best candidate for a job is a good example. If this is done with lateral thinking:

[1] Some criteria might be ignored or downgraded in importance so that more candidates will be considered.

[2] Those that do not satisfy some criteria might remain under consideration.

[3] Candidates not at the top of the list are reevaluated.

Lateral thinking is better understood with reference to the decision trees described in the next chapter. In these lateral thinking might encourage us to consider branches that have lower probabilities of success.

The bottom line, however, is that lateral thinking simply involves considering more than one possible solution to a problem or task.

In this context the author uses the term 'bilemma' when one has difficulty deciding between two alternatives, and then the term 'trilemma' when there are three alternatives, viewing the latter as the preferred situation as he feels it fairly easy to knock out one of three alternatives.

As in Mohr's Law of Politics (vide chapter 17) deciding between two more equal alternatives is a good deal harder. In the farcical and outdated Westminster system, for example, the 2 main parties are relatively similar in policies, incompetence etcetera, so many a voter makes up their mind on which side of the political fence to place their vote only at the last minute.

4. Thinking

Sequential Thinking

In detective work, particularly solving 'cold cases', what might be called sequential thinking is useful. An example of this is my theory that MI5/6 and the CIA might have taken an interest in me on occasion. If so, a factor in this would surely have been my father (CBO) being one of the team that split that atom in Cambridge in 1931, at the same time becoming a socialist, and then being President of the Australia Soviet Friendship Society (ASFS) in the 1950s and 1960s – no doubt the reason for CIA interest in him, and for his never being able to obtain a visa to visit the USA, whereas he was treated like royalty when he toured USSR nuclear facilities in 1955.

CIA interest in myself, therefore, might have been initiated when I too went to Cambridge to do a PhD and, as my memoirs have recently been completed but not published, Table 4.1 shows key events related to this 'spooks' theory, the 2013 event in Table 4.1 suggesting that there may also have been a Cambridge-based vendetta against me.

This 'initiating event' and some of the other events during my lifetime that I deem suspicious are shown in Table 4.1 in chronological order. In the fashion of Likert scaling these are given scores in the final column of this table, the 'OUP heist' of 1992 scoring 10 and thus being a 'clincher'.

The final event in Table 4.1 is also a 'clincher', showing that the spooks farce continues, as evidenced by a 2 week chain of phone calls from half a dozen 'uncallable back' numbers initiated accidentally by ringing myself from a nearby booth to test a new TAM I had just bought, my message to my new TAM beginning with *"I have not gone to Cuba yet."*

No doubt the USA's Echelon base in Australia picked up this call because of the keyword 'Cuba.' The result was a farcical series of phone calls over 2 weeks, beginning with 5 calls in a couple of hours after my booth call, these from different "overseas" numbers, as my CID system announced loudly, numbers which one could not even get one ring on when trying to return the call. Fortunately, after a couple of weeks these 'spook calls' went back to their normal occasional occurrence rate of about once a week.

4. Thinking

Table 4.1. Scores for chronological 'spooks' events.

Year	Event	Who?	Score
1931 +	CBO, socialist nuclear physicist unable to obtain US visa (precursor to my history below).	CIA	10
1955	While CBO is touring USSR nuclear facilities a stranger briefly appears and stays next door – myself and a brother see him bedding my mother through a partly open blind.	ASIS	8
1975	A homo Don tries to pick me up in the Rose and Crown in Cambridge.	MI5	4
1976	A very drunk US journo visits the tiny R&C bar illegally open after midnight a few times.	CIA	4
1977	External examiner ('DA') tries to sink me at PhD 'viva' exam – I proved he (or his RS) had fiddled their results (mine were honest).		3
1979	CUP gets 'DA' (see 1977) to review my first (OK) FEM book – 1st review OK, DA's an insane rave. Bigger 'tome' asked – then knocked back in July 1980.	?	4
1980	CUP tells me to send 'tome' to MacMillan – another insane rave review sinks me.	?	4
1981+	CUP publishes FEM book by person who'd 'nominally' been my tutor in Churchill College. This weakish book gave a 'recipe' for the 9 df thin plate triangle (an important element) which fails for some common geometries.	?	3
1982	An MIT maths bod visits my dept in Auckland – he had coauthored a weak book on FEM. Said he was "on way to Canberra." Was he 'setting up' my downfall and promising my HOD payback later? - see 1984 and 1988.	CIA	5
1984	HOD (PhD Camb.) bullies me into resigning. I never get another job - with hindsight I realize he was backstabbing me as referee.	?	5
1985+	Extended/updated tome again rejected by CUP, along with a new book. CUP reject every book effort thereafter whereas in 1991 OUP & Springer accept the tome.	?	6

4. Thinking

Table 4.1 – continued.

Year	Event	Who?	Score
1988	Auckland HOD who bullied me into resigning ends sabbatical leave with a tour of US Universities – who paid for this? (see 1982).	CIA	6
1992	**20% of the copy-edited tome returning to OUP Oxford was stolen at Heathrow and leaflet headed "understanding private industry" left in its place.**	MI5	10
1993+	I often ring Cuban consulate in Sydney re my going to Cuba as a 'refugee' - suspect the calls always intercepted somehow.	ASIS	5
1997-2001	Cambridge VC sets AFP onto me and I am overtly spooked in St Kilda's streets for years.	AFP	9
2001	Watched by spook from small park opposite my house. He hid behind a fence for hours but I saw him when he stepped forward a bit.	ASIS	6
2001-2004	Overtly spooked in streets of Cheltenham by day and night when I move there.	AFP	9
2005	3 police cars converge on me while walking in Cheltenham – I set up this and other spook events by making phone calls.	VIC police	4
1995-2014	Regular 'spook' phone calls, many with suspicious silence and "Goodbye" at the end.	AFP	8
2012	Editor of a new book has a suspicious accident.	ASIS	6
2013	Taken to court for annoying a Cambridge secretary on phone – they say I left there on bad terms – hence their vendetta thereafter.	Cambridge U	9
2014	After release of book critical of work of 2 Cambridge people an internet scammer invades and searches my 3 PCs for hours.	?	5
2014	**Ringing myself from booth initiates 2 weeks of spook phone calls** + a Telstra van faces my house for an hour & leaves when it sees me leave. A relative is a private detective with a 'little black van' so I can work this out and CIA monitors phones calls globally via "Echelon". See text prior to this table for other details.	AFP/CIA	9

4. Thinking

Note that events in this table have different sources/causes, and some are 'doubtful'. Nevertheless, the table illustrates the 'detective thinking' involved and the spooks farce continues as the last row of Table 4.1 shows.

One fairly consistent connection, however, seems to be the Cambridge one, dating as it does back to my father's conversion to Socialism there at the same time as Kim Philby et al. were recruited in Cambridge by the KGB as double agents.

Many of us know that the CIA + MI6 have been fighting the red peril since England's SIS sank a Soviet ship at harbour in 1918 using two-man torpedo boats (Mohr, 2013b). They still are to protect the capitalist society they represent. Table 4.1 is an example of this, and targeting relatives of a target person is the theme of a plot I have planned for one of my spy-genre books, only one having been published thus far (Mohr, 2012c).

With China holding most of US debt, and many other countries somewhat 'left' politically, Anglo-American influence in world affairs seems likely to decline, there being more people in jail in the US than attending University, whilst there are literally millions of CCTV spy cameras in London, an outcome George Orwell would never have dreamed of in his worst nightmares that he might have had in coming up with the plot for his book *1984* (Abelson et al., 2008).

WORRYING

Earlier, three stages of creative thinking were mentioned, the second of these being *incubation*.

This implies a somewhat relaxed way of approaching things. In fact *worrying* about problems is a key part of how many people try to solve them.

Indeed, as I know from personal experience, people with a habit of developing ideas over the long term tend also to suffer some degree of anxiety over them, regularly worrying about how to improve them and find a final solution.

Newton, for example, used to awake with an idea and spend hours at his bedside getting it down on paper. Not surprisingly, he had three nervous breakdowns at Cambridge University, leaving at the age of 42.

4. THINKING

Perhaps Thomas Alva Edison, with 1093 patents to his name, perhaps thanks to a few years of home schooling, is a better example, having developed the habit of inventing things at an early age (Heyn, 1976).

Worrying about a problem might take place in various ways, for example:

[1] Tossing and turning in your sleep or walking the streets.

[2] Subconsciously worrying about them and perhaps waking at the end of an REM sleep phase with a possible answer.

[3] Writing notes about the problem, adding to these when additional ideas arise.

[4] Looking up books and asking other people to try and find the answer.

[5] Making a note of the problem somewhere such as in a diary or on the corner of a notice board.

As we must all have experienced sometimes, however, if we worry about the problem long enough we eventually see it a little more clearly and often come up with an answer.

SERENDIPITY

This word was invented in the 18th century by the English man of letters Horace Walpole when inspired by the Persian fairy tale "The Three Princes of Serendip" whose heroes often made discoveries by chance.

In their book *The Art of Insight, How to have more AHA! moments,* Charles Kiefer and Malcolm Constable (2013) say:

> *Insights, wisdom, and good judgment come from a clearheaded, calm, and focused state of mind.*

Serendipitous ideas, however, are unpredictable. Sure, they may come after weeks, months, or even years of working on some problem. But they may come when awakening from a dream in an REM stage of sleep when the brain is 'reorganizing' itself, or at almost any other time of day when the some thought passes through the brain which is perhaps related to the problem in question.

4. Thinking

There is no doubt, however, that those who have a habit of trying to come up with new ideas will have more serendipitous moments, and no doubt Edison's 1093 patents came about as a result of his having his own home laboratory in his teenage years (Heyn, 1976).

Perhaps one of the best examples of serendipity was the discovery of penicillin as a result of a lab door being left open accidentally, contaminating a Petri dish on the floor below.

Another was Henri Bequerel's discovery that fluorescent radium salts produced good photographic images on bad weather days without much light. Repeating his experiments in a dark room confirmed this result, and he gave the task of finding the source of the radiation and explaining it to Marie Curie as the topic of her doctoral thesis (Maccinis, 2009).

Conclusion

In a book entitled *Elementary Thinking* the reader might expect this chapter to have been the key chapter. In fact we are in the early stages of the journey thus far and the usual somewhat 'woolly' discussions of the elements of thinking, creative thinking, problem solving, and lateral thinking are of little use.

The discussion of thinking thus far, however, may be considered as a simple formal introduction. In following chapters, diagrams, tables, numbers and matrices will appear to put a little meat on the bones of these early chapters.

Chapter 5

CRITICAL THINKING

CRITICAL THINKING

Many of the tools used for critical thinking, such as decision trees and tables, are usually prepared by one or two people for presentation to a group of people at a meeting.

'Decision theory' is a somewhat imprecise term sometimes used to refer to techniques for making business decisions. Critical thinking also refers to the process of examining one or more alternative ideas or proposals and deciding which, if any, to choose.

Critical thinking to determine the best of a number of alternative solutions to a problem typically involves such steps as:

[1] Define the problem and the criteria that a solution must meet.

[2] Compare alternative solutions to these criteria.

[3] Evaluate which solution best satisfies the criteria.

[4] Revue this decision.

Benefit-cost analysis, which is discussed later in the present chapter, is a good example of critical thinking based mainly on financial considerations.

5. CRITICAL THINKING

DECISION MATRICES

An example is the 'prisoner dilemma matrix' where two prisoners are interrogated separately. What happens if neither, one or both confess?

Prisoner B		Prisoner A	
		Confess	Don't
	Confess	Both - 20 years	A Life B 10 years
	Don't	A 10 years B Life	Both - free

The table shows that the best option is clearly that neither should confess, giving a simple example of how it is usually best to seek advice on, and involve others in important decisions.

DECISION TABLES

A good example is the following table of the performance of three categories of stocks and shares under boom, steady and slump market conditions.

	Boom (a)	Steady (b)	Slump (c)
Gilt edged (x)	5 %	5	5
Speculative (y)	20	0	-10
Unit trusts (z)	10	5	0

What then is the best mix of shares to buy?

The *deterministic solution* is as follows. For a 10 year cycle time in business conditions assume $a = 1$, $b = 6$ and $c = 3$. Then the profit (%) from each of the three share types is:

x: 5 + 30 + 15 = 50
y: 20 - 30 = -10
z: 10 + 30 = 40

so that one should buy x or z but not y (unless boom conditions are assured for a known period).

5. Critical Thinking

Selection of the best solution from a number of alternatives should be done with a quantitative basis, preferably using a process of summing *weighted attributes.*

Table 5.1.
Job candidate selection using weighted attribute scores.

Attribute	Weight	Score Tom	Score Dick	Score Harry	Weighted score Tom	Weighted score Dick	Weighted score Harry
Qualifications	2	8	5	3	16	10	6
Experience	3	5	7	6	15	21	18
Age	1	5	5	8	5	5	8
Interview	2	3	5	8	6	10	16
Referees	1	5	5	5	5	5	5
Total					46	51	53

A good example is the task of selecting the 'best' of three candidates Tom, Dick and Harry, for a job using the *decision table* of Table 5.1.

Here five attributes: qualifications, experience (relevant), age (or total experience), impression made at interview and strength of recommendations made by referees, are used and each of these is given a weight in the second column.

Then the three candidates are given a score out of ten for each attribute by each member of the selection panel and the results averaged (to the nearest round number for simplicity here), giving the results shown in columns 3,4,5.

Finally, these scores are multiplied by the weights, giving the results of columns 6,7,8 and these figures are summed to give the totals shown.

The final result indicates Harry as the best candidate.

In practice, however, it is best to include other considerations such as:

[1] Who top scored in the most important attributes?

[2] If the candidate is an existing employee (in another position) has there been any bias?

5. CRITICAL THINKING

In this sort of analysis the choice of attributes is crucial, as is their weighting, so that such factors can also be reviewed before making a final decision.

PARETO'S LAW

Pareto's Law (Slaybaugh, 1967) is:

In most situations a relatively small percentage of certain objects contributes a relatively high percentage of output.

This is the basis of *contribution-by-value analysis* (also called ABC analysis).

For instance 15-30 percent of the population contributes 70-90 percent of the tax revenue, 20 percent of the employees in an office may do 60 percent of the work, or 20 percent of the items in inventory may account for 60 percent of the sales.

As an example of ABC analysis, the percentage of total dollar annual sales for each product are calculated and tabulated in descending order. Then the cumulative percentage contribution is added as a final column to show how much, say, the first 20% of products contributes.

PROBABILITY TREES

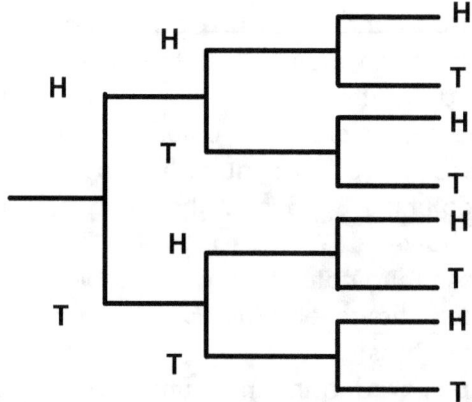

Figure 5.1. Example of a probability tree.

5. CRITICAL THINKING

The simplest example is that of tossing a coin three times. All possible outcomes are shown in Figure 5.1.

This is a special case of the *binomial distribution* and, for example, the probability of three successive heads is

P(H/H/H) = (1/2)³ = 1/8

and the answer follows from Figure 5.1 because P(H) = P(T).

Probability trees are of little use but the idea can be incorporated with that of a decision tree to assist in important business decisions.

DECISION TREES

Decision trees are sometimes a useful way of depicting business strategies. A simple example is that of a manufacturer asked by a supermarket chain to make a 'home brand' version of its product, a decision tree for which is shown in Figure 5.2.

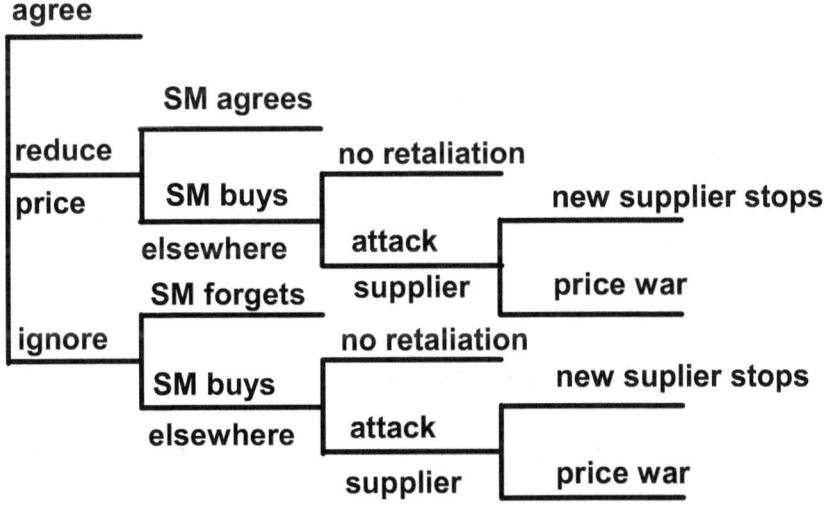

Figure 5.2. Example of a decision tree.

As another example Figure 5.3 considers the problem of deciding whether to launch a rocket at a certain time or not, attaching probabilities and profit figures to the decision tree.

5. CRITICAL THINKING

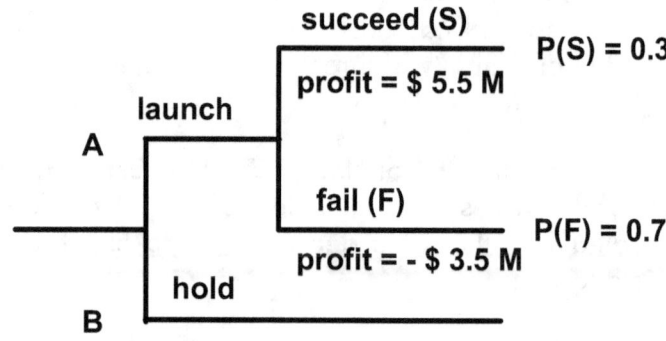

Figure 5.3. Decision tree with probabilities and financial outcomes.

Then the Expected Monetary Value (EMV) of a launch is 0.3(5.5) - 0.7(3.5) = - $0.8M so we should decide to hold.

With more optimistic figures, for example P(S) = 0.7 and P(F) = 0.3, the EMV of **A** is $2.85M and the launch decision is much more favourable, though perhaps still not certain.

BENEFIT-COST ANALYSIS

As an example of this widely used procedure consider the problem of developing a road repairs program for which the costs of the various levels of repairs or reconstruction are shown in Table 5.2.

Table 5.2. Cost of road operations.

Operation	$k /lane km
P Patching	10
T Topseal (25 mm)	20
S Reseal (50 mm)	50
F First two courses	100
R Reconstruction	200

5. Critical Thinking

Table 5.3 shows the various types of road works to be carried out and the years of service provided by the treatments of Table 5.2.

Table 5.3. Required works and longevity of the options.

Road type	Lane km to repair	Years of service				
		P	T	S	F	R
A Residential	30	2	5	10	20	50
B Residential feeder	20	1.5	4	8	15	45
C Signaled arterial	10	1	3	5	10	30
D Freeway	5	0.5	2	3	5	10

Then the years of service in Table 5.3 (the benefit or return r) are divided by the corresponding costs c of Table 5.2 to give the *benefit-cost ratio* or r/c results of Table 5.4.

Table 5.4. r/c ratios for the various options.

Road type	Operation				
	P	T	S	F	R
A (30)	0.20	0.25	0.20	0.20	0.25
B (20)	0.15	0.20	0.16	0.15	0.225
C (10)	0.10	0.15	0.10	0.10	0.15
D (5)	0.05	0.10	0.06	0.05	0.05
c	(10)	(20)	(50)	(100)	(200)

The 'best' construction program is formed by giving priority to those activities with the greatest r/c ratios.

Then, choosing the larger r/c ratios in Table 5.4 the construction program is determined, as shown in Table 5.5.

For the first step of the program the two largest r/c ratios (both 0.25) are considered, that is the A/T and A/R options (where A = row and T = column) in Table 5.4.

5. Critical Thinking

For these the increment in total cost or δC values are given by multiplying the figures in brackets for the appropriate rows and columns in Table 5.4. Then the increment in total benefit or δQ values are given by multiplying the 'km' and 'Years of service' values in Table 5.3.

Then the A/R option is rejected as too costly, so that stage 1 of the program is A/T.

Table 5.5. Works program selection.

Stage	Option	δC	δQ	C	Q
1	A/T	600	150	600	150
	A/R	6,000	1,500		
2	B/R	4,000	900		
	B/T	400	80	1,000	230
3	C/T	200	30	1,200	260
	C/R	2,000	300		
4	D/T	100	10	1,300	270
	D/S	250	15		

Next we choose the B/R and B/T options, respectively with r/c = 0.225 and 0.20, finally selecting the second, the first being too costly.

Now, assuming we desire a spread of activity over all types of road (A - D), we next compare C/T and C/R, both with r/c = 0.15, choosing the cheaper option again for stage 3. Now requiring a D component for stage 4 we select D/T with the maximum r/c value for this road type.

Figure 5.4 shows the benefit-cost curve for the program selected in Table 5.5 and this takes the required form (that is, the slope diminishes gradually).

Such approaches may seem relatively tedious and mathematically trivial at first sight but in practice the data of Tables 5.2 and 5.4 is generally constant, the main variable being the quantities or work required in Table 5.3.

5. Critical Thinking

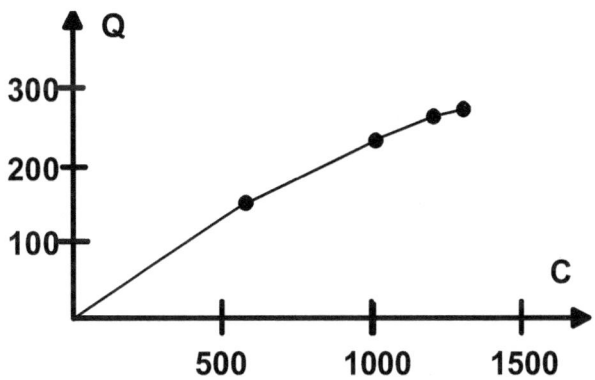

Figure 5.4. Benefit-cost curve for the program of Table 5.5.

Conclusion

Decision trees, especially if they have probabilities and costs attached, are useful tools in the decision making process.

Decision tables are also useful, especially if they have weighted quantities to enable a total score to be given to the alternatives under consideration.

Benefit-cost analysis has been included here as it is, essentially, a decision table method, albeit once involving a number of (consecutive) decisions or selections.

Finally, we should always remember that, as the 2010 book *Bozo Sapiens* seeks to remind us, "to err is human" (Kaplan & Kaplan, 2010). Nevertheless, critical thinking using such methods as those discussed in the foregoing chapter should help avoid making bad decisions.

5. Critical Thinking

Chapter 6

Group Thinking

Meetings

Meetings take many forms from the formal board or political meeting to the informal process of talking to one or more people in the office over a problem.

They are, however, an important way of getting ideas and solving problems. In other words they are an important part of the human thinking process.

Indeed, it is safe to assume that animals think and the conditioning of flatworms with only 400 brain cells described in the second section of Chapter 1 is evidence that even the lowliest of animals do.

Meetings, however, are a particular feature of human 'group thinking' where our language and writing skills play an important part.

Formal meetings

In business, as in politics, meetings are an important part of the process. As in parliament, standard procedures should be followed in calling, running and reporting meetings.

To publicize an impending meeting an agenda paper is distributed, for example:

BULLDUST ASSOCIATION OF VICTORIA

Annual General Meeting to be held at 1, Spring St at 8:00 p.m. on Thursday 10/8/2014.

6. Group Thinking

BUSINESS

1. Chairperson's opening remarks.
2. Apologies.
3. Minutes of the AGM held on 13/7/2014.
4. Business arising out of the minutes.
5. Correspondence.
6. Business arising out of the correspondence.
7. President's report (AGM only).
8. Treasurer's report.
9. Election of new members.
10. Subcommittee reports/Reports from delegates.
11. Election of office bearers:
President, Vice-president(s) (1 or 2), Chairperson, Secretary, Treasurer,
Committee (circa 5)
12. Election of auditor.
13. Guest speaker: Mr. J.C. Smith, former Prime Minister, on "Politics Today."
14. Motions on notice:
a. Mr. Jones to move, "That the secretary be granted an honorarium of ten dollars ($10)."
b. Mrs. Brown to move, "That the Government be requested to reduce the sales tax on bull dust."
15. General business.
16. Notice of motions.
17. Date of next meeting.
18. Close.

During such a meeting the secretary will keep notes and these are used to prepare the *minutes* of the meeting, copies of which are sent to members and other interested parties prior to the next meeting.

These should cover such items as: Present; Apologies; 1. Minutes of previous meeting; 2. Financial report; 3. Issue A: report on discussion, suggestions, resolutions etc.; 4. Issue B: report on etc.; 5. General business, discussion etc.; 6. Next meeting: date/time. "The meeting then closed." Signed . . . ., Chairperson &/or President.

6. Group Thinking

In the matter of meetings of businesses and associations the following additional subjects are worth consideration:

Chairperson. The chairperson's duties are simply to ensure that the agenda is followed and to deal with motions.

Motions. A motion is a proposed *resolution*. It may be:
a. Procedural, for example "That the meeting adjourn."
b. Substantive, for example "That ABC's account be paid."

A motion is dealt with as follows:

Mover: states (preferably in writing) the motion and explains it. Seconder: (called by the chairperson) speaks for the motion.

Speaker(s): alternatively speak against/for the motion.

Mover: summarizes the case for the motion.

Chairperson:
> "The motion is that - - -."
> "The question is that the motion be agreed to."
> "Those in favour?"
> "Those against?"
> "I declare the motion carried/lost."

Note that motions can be:
1. In parts (a), (b) etc.
2. Amended.
3. Rescinded.
4. Foreshadowed.

Procedural motions. These generally have two functions:
a. To dispose of business, for example "That the meeting adjourn" or "That the speaker be no longer heard."
b. To deal with business, for example to vary the order of business or to call for a vote ("That the motion be put").

"Point of order". This exclamation to the Chairperson is a complaint, for example, that the speaker has taken too long, is out of order (poor language) or is not speaking on the subject.

Voting methods: These include
(1) Voices/show of hands.
(2) Division.
(3) Poll or ballot (which may be secret).

6. GROUP THINKING

Constitutions: Associations, companies etc. should have a constitution that contains usually standard clauses governing behaviour of the company and its members, the running of meetings and other matters requiring rules. Some of the most common clauses are:

Name, objectives, membership and subscription clauses.

Meetings, committee, elections and quorum clauses.

Finance, dissolution, voting and amendments clauses.

Interpretations, delegations, open/closed meetings and expulsion clauses.

Standing orders: These are the rules for the procedure of meetings, for example setting time limits for meetings and stating the procedure for putting motions.

Election systems: Prior to an election such matters as the following should be considered:
1. A call for nominations.
2. Provision for postal or proxy votes.
3. Appointment of a returning officer.
4. Method of election, for example:
a. First past the post, or
b. Preferential/proportional/points systems.

On matters such election systems the reader may require a little further reading to learn more detail but, generally, so far as meetings are concerned, it is also a good idea to attend one or two properly run ones.

There are also a few rare books on procedure for meetings. I remember buying one over 30 years ago (Renton, 1972) and taking great delight in moving "That the speaker be no longer heard until he can speak to the meeting properly prepared" (the chap kept fumbling through pages of his proposal and changing his mind when asked any question).

I am sure they had never heard of such a motion. Anyway it was carried and the offender gave me dirty looks around the institution for weeks afterwards.

6. GROUP THINKING

GROUP BRAINSTORMING

The practice of meetings for group brainstorming has been widely practiced with success and several factors have been found to improve results:

[1] People tend to have twice as many ideas in the group situation because of the more stimulating environment, 'cross fertilization' of ideas and arousal of competitive spirit.

[2] Scheduled alternation of individual and group thinking improves results.

[3] As more ideas are produced they tend to improve.

[4] Second sessions a few days later improve results because of 'incubation' etc.

[5] Screening of the results by a second group.

As discussed in Chapters 4 and 5, creative thinking to produce new ideas and solutions should be followed by critical thinking to evaluate them.

MIND MAPS

Mind mapping was created by Tony Buzan (Norcan, 1999) and is sometimes a useful way of getting ideas down on paper.

A mind map begins with map title (title branch) at the centre of a blank page, typically a project to be undertaken. To this thoughts are added as *child branches*. Typically these will be actions or tasks that need to be done to complete the project. Some, if not all, of these tasks will involve several smaller tasks and in this way a mind map grows out from the central title.

Advantages of mind maps are:

[1] That they can be written down quickly as only key words are used to describe each element of the map.

[2] They are easy to read and are ideal for presenting ideas on a board to an audience.

6. GROUP THINKING

[3] They are a good way of getting an overview of a project or proposal.

[4] They lend themselves to 'evolution' as new ideas are added.

Mind maps can be used for:
- Group brainstorming sessions
- Presentations
- Decision-making
- Note-taking
- Planning
- Summarizing projects or proposals.

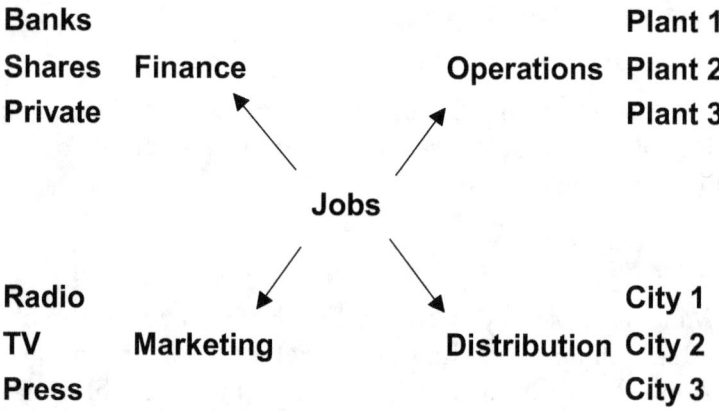

Figure 6.1. Mind map of company activities.

Figure 6.1 shows an example of a mind map for the CEO of a small manufacturing company. This reminds him of the four basic functions of finance, manufacturing, marketing and distribution.

These four items are then broken down further and additional information such as the names of the personnel responsible for each of the activities could easily be added to the map.

6. GROUP THINKING

CONCLUSIONS

Meetings are, of course, a good way of getting ideas.

An alternative idea is to circulate a folder containing blank forms around an office to collect ideas. For best results the folder would be circulated more than once.

Boxes to collect suggestion slips are another commonly used way of collecting complaints and suggestions for improvement.

Group brainstorming sessions are much used, for example, in the advertising industry to come up with ideas for advertising campaigns.

It should be noted, however, that it is sometimes possible to do a little brainstorming on one's own. Under the right conditions sometimes one can rapidly produce a flood of ideas in just a few minutes.

Collecting ideas for a book, perhaps about a subject of which you have long experience, is an excellent example. At first ideas for chapter titles might come slowly but, with a little bit of luck, within something like an hour of thought in a relaxed quiet atmosphere the ideas will come gradually, sometimes 'bunches' of ideas flooding into one's mind.

At the end of the thinking session you might feel like saying something like: "I've got a book!"

Sometimes the same sort of thing can happen in a group brainstorming session.

6. Group Thinking

Chapter 7

CORPORATE THINKING

BUSINESS POLICY

The first goal of corporate thinking is to establish business policy (BP). Perhaps the four basic elements of business policy formulation are *environment, resources, constraints* and *objectives*.

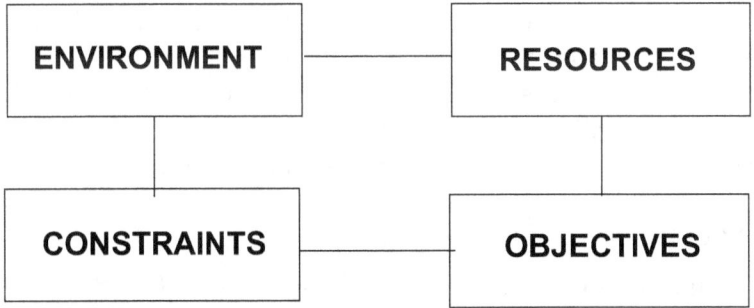

Figure 7.1. Fixed element analysis model.

These four elements are shown in the fixed element analysis model of Figure 7.1. With each of these there are both *qualitative* and *quantitative* matters to consider. Briefly considering each of these in turn:

Environment

Quantitative considerations include market size, scale of operations, capital requirements.

Qualitative considerations include who are the competitors in the marketplace, product differentiation, patents and product distribution.

7. CORPORATE THINKING

Resources

Quantitative resources might include available finance, material and human resources.

Qualitative resources might include corporate strategy and tactics, a company structure and/or role model.

Constraints

Quantitative constraints will include finance limits, human limitations and resistance, material and human resource limits, and market size.

Qualitative constraints will include legal restrictions as well, of course, as union work restrictions.

Note that there are *internal constraints* such as work force size and *external constraints* such as laws.

Objectives

Quantitative objectives might include maximum sales and maximum profit.

Qualitative objectives might include good corporate image, customer loyalty, product quality, and personnel loyalty.

In this context the term *Management by Objectives* (MBO) is worth note and this simply refers to management styles which focus primarily on such objectives as the 'bottom line.'

CONTROLLABLE ELEMENT ANALYSIS

Once the fixed elements of Figure 7.1 are fully defined attention can turn to considering the controllable elements of business policy. These include:
- Corporate goals and objectives: these should include both short and long-term plans.
- Corporate structure: what is the most efficient structure for the company?
- Finance policies: target operating margins, profits and return on capital. Levels of debt and equity.
- HRM policies: types of people required and levels of remuneration.
- Manufacturing policies: location of plants and processes to be used.

7. Corporate Thinking

- Marketing policies: product pricing and market positioning. Forms of advertising and advertising budget.
- Distribution policies: mode of distribution.
- Accounting policies.
- R&D policies: what percentage of profits will be put back into R&D? Are joint R&D ventures possible?

Once these business policies have been established they should be reexamined to check such things as:

[1] Is the company well enough differentiated from others in the same marketplace?

[2] Are the products well enough differentiated from competing products?

[3] Are the finance, marketing, distribution and other policies sufficient to ensure ongoing operations and adequate sales?

[4] Are there contingency plans should any problems occur?

Clearly establishing detailed business policy, therefore, is no easy matter and a good deal of thought is required, usually from a number of people in the case of a large organization.

Corporate structure

Corporate structure is the hierarchical structure and communication channels giving rise to the chain of command and response in a company or organization. Some of basic types of corporate structure are:

[1] **Functional structure.** This is the usual structure for small companies and corresponds to one division of type (2) below.

[2] **Divisional structure.** For a corporation with just two divisions this is of the form of Figure 7.2.

7. Corporate Thinking

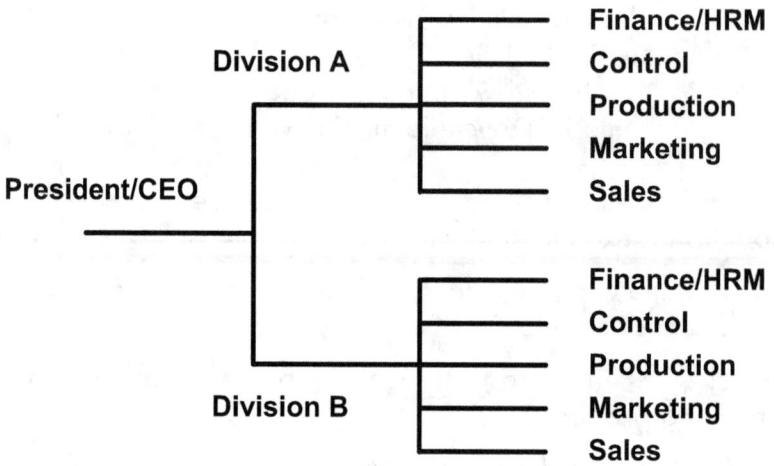

Figure 7.2. Divisional corporate structure.

[3] Matrix Structure

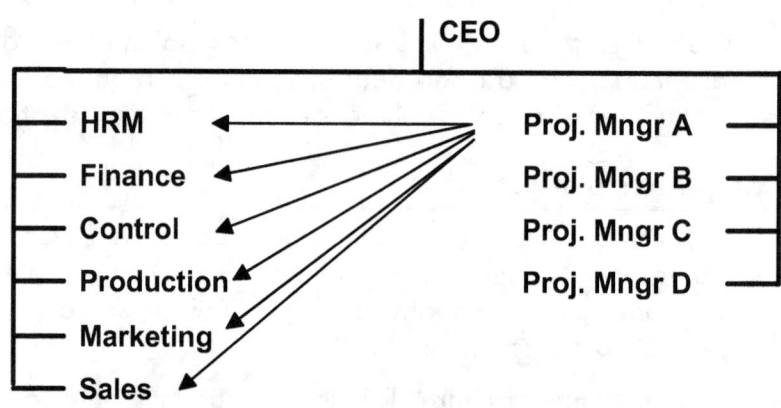

Figure 7.3. Matrix organization structure.

Note that in Figure 7.2 Finance and HRM are combined into one group, but not in Figure 7.3. Similarly, marketing and sales might often be one group. In a very small business, of course, the boss or owner is HRM/control/marketing, finance is the bank a few doors away, and the few employees may be production and sales.

7. CORPORATE THINKING

[4] Ring structure.

This is typical of political parties and voluntary organizations. Such structures can be described as follows:

Centre = president/CEO
Inner ring = secretary/treasurer/vice presidents etc.
+ presidents of committees for finance/membership/PR etc.
+ chairpersons of branches
Outer ring 1 = clusters of members of each committee
Outer ring 2 = clusters of members of each branch

In the outer rings the 'clusters' are like satellites (at the same radius) and each is another group of members which in turn holds local meetings and the committee presidents and branch chairpersons report back to the inner ring or *board* or *central committee.*

Thus committee chairpersons and branch presidents have to attend two lots of meetings, as will some branch members when these are delegates from the branches, as is often the case.

In the case of political parties the central committee is the elected members of the party in parliament. These 'politicians' often have to attend committee and branch meetings, as well as those of parliament, and are therefore often busier than we sometimes imagine.

Some additional aspects of such corporate structures are:

a. Hierarchical or 'one to one' structure as shown on the left in Figure 7.4.

b. A mixture of hierarchical and group structure is shown on the right in Figure 7.4.

c. Responsibilities of members may overlap, for example project manager A in Figure 7.3 is involved in two groups, that is with the group comprising the CEO and the other project managers and with the managers of the finance, HRM etc. divisions.

d. It is usually in the interests of middle level members that lower levels do not know the chain of command.

e. It is usually in the interests of both higher and lower levels that the chain of command is known.

7. CORPORATE THINKING

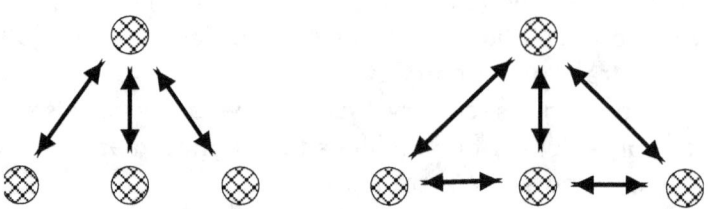

Figure 7.4. Hierarchical and group structures.

Generally, for example, case (b) is a more efficient structure than (a).

In case (d) middle level members are more empowered by ignorance of the chain of command by their subordinates. Whether this situation is in the interests of the company, however, is very doubtful and, indeed, it usually is not.

Such comments are merely a beginning in looking at the nuances of command structures. Further aspects of communication are considered elsewhere in the present book.

Finally, it should be noted that managers should be seeking to ensure that *effective communication* occurs throughout the corporate structure and it is not difficult to personally check that information has been properly passed on from time to time. That the information is understandable and is being given to people capable of understanding it is a matter that should also be given some consideration.

LEADERSHIP AND GROUP PERFORMANCE

Formal communication within a company will tend to follow the corporate structure. Effective communication can considerably improve productivity and morale.

Figure 7.5 shows the results of a study of the relationship between mean or average performance (or productivity) and amount of contact with the group supervisor. Clearly relatively frequent and regular management contact improves productivity as we would expect.

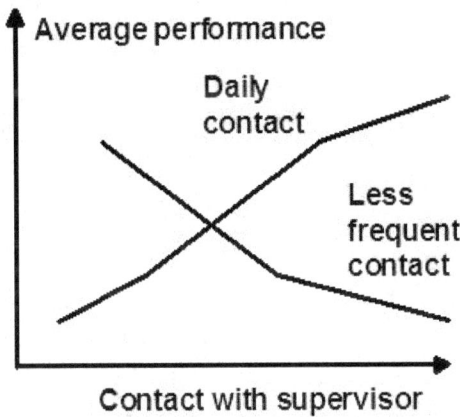

Figure 7.5. Communication with management.

Figure 7.6 shows the type of result obtained in a correlation of worker performance and group loyalty, indicating that productivity improves if group loyalty is high. In part this improvement results from the (necessary) emergence of 'team leadership'.

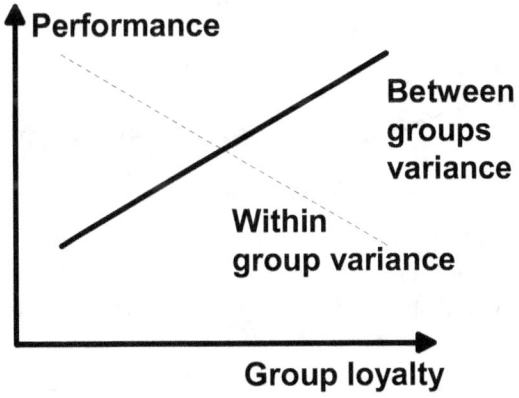

Figure 7.6. Performance and communication with boss vs. group loyalty.

7. Corporate Thinking

The study of Figure 7.6 also found that correlation between the proportion of workers who took their complaints to the boss and group loyalty took the same form (that shown).

In addition, the correlation between how easy the group found communication with the boss and group loyalty also took the same (ascending) form shown in Figure 7.6.

Effective communication (and hence loyalty) within the group and with the supervisor, therefore, both lead to improved productivity. In addition group loyalty improves communication with the supervisor, that is, the factors of group loyalty, amount of supervisor communication, quality of supervisor communication, and productivity are all interwoven in such a way as to suggest that if communication is optimized considerable improvements in productivity might result.

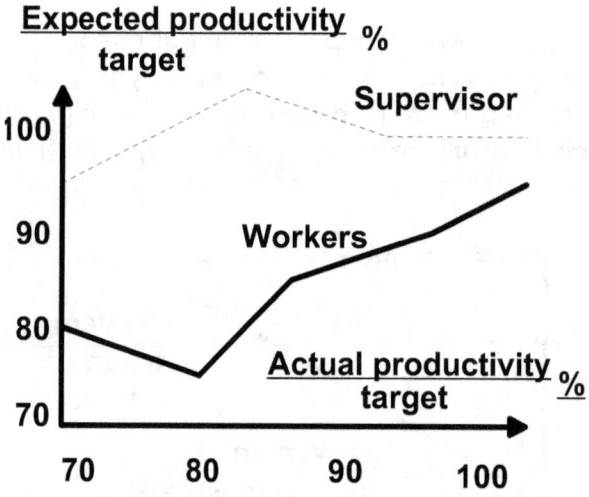

Figure 7.7. Expected vs. actual productivity

Figure 7.7 shows expected productivity compared to actual productivity for both the supervisor and the workers. Clearly the expectations of the supervisor are greater than those of the workers and are always fairly close to the target productivity.

7. Corporate Thinking

The expectations of the workers, on the other hand, are for improvement when productivity is low and for slowing down when productivity is high, and are perhaps more realistic.

Unfortunately, however, there is no data from this study on the correlation between supervisor and worker expectations though this, of course, would depend on communications and, in any case, productivity variation is our main concern.

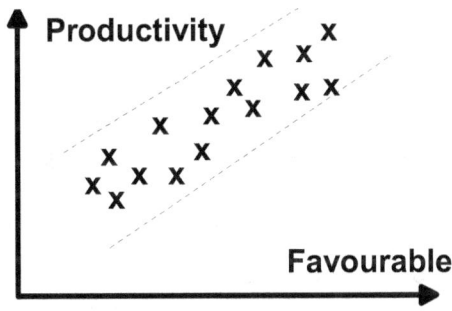

Figure 7.8. Dependence of productivity on supervisor attitude.

Figure 7.8 shows the results of a study of the effect of attitude of supervisor on productivity. There was a considerable spread in the results but there was sufficient correlation to support the finding that the more favourable the attitude of the supervisor (to both the workers and the job) the greater the productivity, as we might expect.

We might also expect that favourable supervisor attitude resulted in more favourable worker attitude and that the latter also results in greater productivity.

Figure 7.9 shows the relationship of peer group loyalty to productivity when motivation is towards accepting versus rejecting company goals. Clearly peer group loyalty towards company goals results in greater productivity as we would expect.

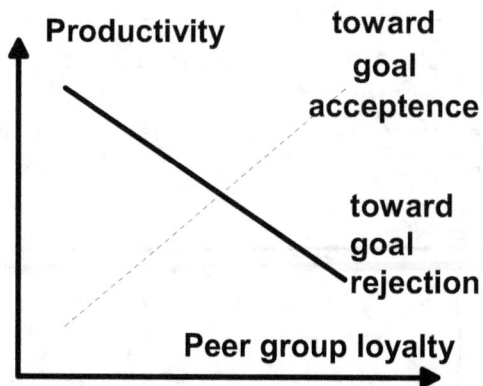

Figure 7.9. Loyalty towards company goals vs. productivity

The results of Figure 7.9 are related to those of Figure 7.6, showing that group loyalty is a very important factor in productivity.

Conclusion

Besides those conclusions already made in the foregoing discussion, the following recommendations are suggested as worthwhile by the results of Figures 7.5 - 7.9:
[1] There should be effective communication of productivity goals.
[2] There should be thorough assessment of productivity results.
[3] Groups and tasks with low productivity should be identified.
[4] Group loyalty should be encouraged and groups should be motivated to accept new staff and 'loners' in a group.
[5] Leadership audits should be used.
[6] Supervisors should exhibit favourable attitude and communicate frequently and regularly with their staff.
[7] Group loyalty toward company goals should be sought.
[8] Supervisors should make themselves freely available to staff with complaints and other feedback and make themselves easy to communicate with.

7. Corporate Thinking

Generally, therefore, good leadership involving sufficient efficient communication of goals and team attitudes is likely to result in very considerable improvements in productivity.

It is also important, however, that measurements are made of productivity, group loyalty and management efficiency. The results will then be useful in identifying problems requiring correction and productivity results when favourable, for example, can be used as motivational information for supervisors and their groups.

Conclusions

The crucial thinking in setting up a company is formation of the four fixed elements of business policy. In order the major initial decisions are:
- Environment: product choice(s), marketing.
- Resources: finance, start-up personnel.
- Constraints: finance, personnel and time limitations.
- Objectives: initial break-even and thence survival.

In larger organizations an effective corporate structure is required to communicate business policy and maintain day-to-day operations.

As shown in Figs 7.5 to 7.9 effective communication that improves productivity will:

[1] Be regular.

[2] Promote communication and thence loyalty between workers.

[3] Communicate realistic production targets.

[4] Project a positive management attitude to both the work and the workers.

[5] Promote worker loyalty to the company and thence acceptance of company goals.

As a bottom line, developing detailed business policy requires a lot of thought and the ongoing operation of a company requires a good deal of communication and, in turn, much thought about feedback etc.

7. Corporate Thinking

Chapter 8

Surveys of Public Opinion

Introduction

Surveys are the only effective way of gauging public opinion and are much used in market research.

On a smaller scale, questionnaires can be used to gauge student opinions in schools and Universities or customer satisfaction with a small business.

A special case, perhaps, elections are the cornerstone of parliamentary democracy. At the beginning of Chapter 1 Aristotle's views on so-called democracy actually being oligarchy in his time were quoted, the point being that real democracy would allow us to vote on every major issue rather the have politicians do it for us (Buchanan & Tullock, 1965).

Voting, however, is a simple form of survey and is used to reach decisions on company boards and at meetings of shareholders to elect board members.

In this chapter we consider market research and examples of survey techniques.

Market research

The purpose of market research is to collect data upon which to base marketing decisions which may range from ad hoc decisions on how to market a new product to fine tuning the operational routine for long term advertising of a product. Some of the stages of a market research campaign and the techniques that may be employed in these stages are:

8. Surveys of Public Opinion

[1] Problem awareness and conceptualization. This may include monitoring of trade press, appraisal of current marketing practice, feedback from marketing efforts and 'related-area' reading in newspapers and magazines.

[2] Hypothesizing and qualitative problem refinement. This may include:
- Group discussions
- Motivational research
- Unstructured interviews
- Recorded observations
- Laboratory experiments
- Consumer 'clinics'

[3] Validation and quantification of marketing program. This may include:
- Market surveys
- Retail audits
- Consumer panels

Considering these in order:

Market surveys

Market surveys are to determine the situation in a market at present, the performance of the competitors in the market and likely future trends. This may involve:
- Collecting existing data ('desk research').
- Collecting new data, for example official figures such as trade statistics.
- Usually a census of part of the relevant population is conducted.
- Structured questionnaires may be used and the results collated to provide a final report.
- Reports should include details of the sample, the time and the method by which the survey was conducted.

Retail audits

These involve regularly checking stock levels at selected sites to give a measure of the effectiveness of distribution and sales for these sites.

8. Surveys of Public Opinion

Consumer panels

These are representative groups of people who provide continuous data, for example via a diary provided for this purpose. This approach is often used to test brand loyalty and switching.

MARKET RESEARCH SAMPLING

Sampling may be by characteristics such as gender or variable features such as weight where matters of diet are concerned, for example. Some of the simple procedures of selection commonly used include:

- Random sampling using random numbers, for example when the sample size is 1,000 out of a total population of 100,000 then the chance of selection is 1/100.
- Systematic sampling, for example every n^{th} person is chosen, for example from the phone book.
- Stratified sampling where a quota for each stratum of the population, for example for middle and low incomes, is set.
- Cluster sampling. An example of this would be choosing a street at random and then interviewing everybody in it.

Accuracy

If we are seeking data on population age distribution, for example, the preferred source would be birth records but generally verbal data is gathered for such purposes and this may involve error and bias.

Sampling errors

These diminish with the size of the sample (whereas bias does not) and are measured by the *standard deviation* or error S (which is the square root of the variance) which is calculated as

$$S = \sqrt{\Sigma(x - x_{av})^2/(n-1)} = \sqrt{(\Sigma x^2 - (\Sigma x)^2/n)/(n-1)}$$

the second formula being called the *raw score formula*.

8. SURVEYS OF PUBLIC OPINION

MEASUREMENT OF ATTITUDES

Psychophysical scaling, or the measurement of reactions to a stimulus, is sometimes referred to as 'stimulus-person scaling'. This is related to the 'CAB' mechanism introduced in Figure 2.4 and is not to be confused with *psychometrics* or 'person scaling' which deals with IQ and like tests.

Scales of measurement

First it is useful to consider different types of scales of measurement that might be used to measure attitudes:

- 'Nominal' measurement. This simply differentiates items, for example the numbers given to members of a sporting team.
- Ordinal measurement. Here, for example, we simply establish an order such as A > B > C. Such scales can be subjected to a *monotonic transformation* when the relative positions on the scale are altered but they remain in the same order.
- Interval scales. For these a *unit* is needed. When such scales undergo *linear transformation*, for example, the values on the scale might, say, be doubled, but points on the scale remain in the same relative positions.
- Ratio scales. For these we need a fixed origin relative to which points are some ratio to each other.

Ordinal scales are much used in measuring attitudes and sometimes, once these are established, interval scales can be formed.

Psychophysical scaling

Some of the more notable techniques developed for psychophysical scaling include (Eagly & Chaiken, 1993):

[1] **Method of successive intervals.** This was proposed by Thurston in 1937 and involves assuming reactions to stimuli are equivalent to a distance on the 'psychological scale' which assumes normally distributed responses and measures distance on this scale in terms of the standard deviation S.

8. Surveys of Public Opinion

[2] Method of equal-appearing intervals.

This was proposed by Thurston in 1929. In this approach responses are divided into 11 intervals each of size one. Then respondents are asked to place an item, for example the statement "I like - - " or item A, into one of the intervals. If the interval 5 is chosen this gives a score of 5 for A. Then the mean score for the item A is its scale value.

This procedure establishes a scale which is then used to measure attitudes by using a subset of the items scaled by the first (scaling) pool of judges. These items are presented in random order to persons to be tested and they are asked to place them on the scale, not according to their attitude, but according to their view of the score deserved by the item. Then the resulting test score is the sum of the scale values selected and this can be compared to the 'standard' values selected by the first pool of judges to measure the attitude of individual persons.

[3] Method of paired comparisons.

This approach was proposed by Thurston in 1928. In this approach the statements or stimuli are presented in pairs and placed in order. Hence the process is comparable to a 'bubble sort' and results in an ordinal scale. Then the number of times options A, B, C etc. were favoured is summed for each and the resulting score yields a scale. This process, however, requires very large numbers of judgments and is impractical except for a relatively small number of items requiring scaling.

[4] Guttman scaling.

This approach gives stimulus-person scaling simultaneously and results in a matrix of data called the *Guttman scalogram*. As an example, imagine that we have five rods of from 5 to 7 feet in length (the exact lengths are not known). Then we ask each judge or respondent to place a one in the Guttman scalogram matrix shown for the raw data in Table 8.1. This is then reorganized to give the result in Table 8.2.

8. Surveys of Public Opinion

Table 8.1. Guttman scalogram for raw data.

	Stimuli (rods)				
Persons	C	E	B	D	A
2 (Jim)*	1	1	1	1	0
4	0	1	0	1	0
3	1	1	0	1	0
6	0	0	0	0	0
5	0	1	0	0	0
1	1	1	1	1	1
* e.g. Jim is taller than C, E, B, D but not A					

Table 8.2 is obtained by placing the column with least ones at the left, the column with the most ones at the right, and so on. Then the row with the maximum number of ones is placed at the top (this is for Bill in our example and hence he is the tallest person) and that with the least ones is placed at the bottom.

Table 8.2. Reordered Guttman scalogram.

Persons	Stimuli (rods)					Score
	A	B	C	D	E	
1	1	1	1	1	1	5
2	0	1	1	1	1	4
3	0	0	1	1	1	3
4	0	0	0	1	1	2
5	0	0	0	0	1	1
6	0	0	0	0	0	0

The result is an upper diagonal matrix, as shown in Table 8.2, and this results in a score for each person shown on the right side in Table 8.2. Then the fact that this matrix can be reproduced entirely from these scores testifies that we have indeed achieved the required scaling.

8. Surveys of Public Opinion

The preceding example of Guttman scaling was for physical stimuli, when a perfect upper triangular matrix resulted. Generally, however, this is not the case then attitudinal stimuli are considered.

Table 8.3. Bogardus' social distance scale.

	Acceptance level					
	Would marry	As a friend	Would give a job	Allow as citizen	OK as visitor	No contact
Armenians						
Bulgarians						
Canadians						
etc.						

An example is Bogardus' social stimulus scale, illustrated in Table 8.3, in which respondents are asked to judge how closely they would relate to people of various nationalities or races.

Such attitudinal stimuli do not yield a perfect upper triangular matrix but it has been suggested that when about 90% of the non-zero entries do appear on or above the diagonal that this *coefficient of reproducibility* value is acceptable.

Conclusion

Attitude scaling requires a certain amount of care, for example stimuli should not be ambiguous or irrelevant and responses to them should approximate a 'parabola distribution'. In psychological research electricity, light and sound have been used as stimuli. As we have noted, however, it is attitudinal stimuli of the type shown in Table 8.3 which provide the greatest challenge and which are most relevant in market research.

Of the methods of scaling discussed here the Guttman scalogram is appealing in nature whilst the rather obvious method of equal-appearing intervals is satisfactory for most purposes.

8. Surveys of Public Opinion

Person scaling

Unlike stimulus-person scaling techniques, person scaling techniques make no attempt to locate responses on a scale and they are classified *a priori* as either favourable or unfavourable toward the attitude object. Then the location of persons on the attitude dimension is determined by the number of stimuli with which they agree and the extent of their agreement.

These person scaling methods are derivatives of the psychometric model traditionally much used for ability or IQ tests in which responses to items are viewed as indicators of a common latent ability.

Likert's *method of summated ratings* was designed to be much easier to use than the method of equal-appearing intervals but to be at least as reliable. In this approach a large pool of items which are chosen intuitively for their relevance to the attitude object is used. These items usually consist of statements of belief, but statements about behaviours or affective reactions can also be used.

Typically, in Likert scaling each item is presented to respondents in a multiple-choice format such as:

1. Strongly disagree.
2. Disagree.
3. Undecided.
4. Agree.
5. Strongly agree.

Then the response to each item is given a score such as 5 for strongly agree.

Then, for example, a survey on attitudes towards women might contain questions like:

(a) Swearing is more objectionable from a woman.
(b) Intoxication in women is worse than in men.

With scores from 1 - 5 given to each of perhaps a dozen or so such questions the total score is then obtained for each respondent.

8. SURVEYS OF PUBLIC OPINION

Such a survey is much simpler than Thurston's method of equal-appearing intervals but usually the initial pool of items should be pilot tested on a group of people to eliminate ambiguous and nondiscriminating items which tend to result in neutral responses. This can be done by examining the *item-total score correlations*, each of which correlates the respondents' scores on an item with their scores summed over all the items. Then a good item will have a positive correlation and generally better items have higher correlations.

Likert scaling, in addition to the method of equal-appearing intervals and Guttman scaling are all of interest and the reader will probably recognize at least the description of Likert scaling.

EXAMPLE OF LIKERT SCALING

The following table gives an example of a type of questionnaire which the author found useful over two decades ago for class evaluation of teaching. The approach is, in fact, reminiscent of Likert scaling and students enjoyed the revenge [in advance] of giving a mark out of 100, especially as I asked them to also give marks (with different colour pen or ringed etc.) to the HOD who shared teaching of the subject with me. He scored pretty badly!

Though it looks a little formidable this survey worked well and I was pleased with the results.

In hindsight, however, I should point out that in most cases only a few questions should be used and perhaps never more ten, and preferably five for most purposes. In the case of Table 8.4, however, I had a captive class happy to fill out the longish questionnaire as a change from the usual lecture scenario.

8. SURVEYS OF PUBLIC OPINION

Table 8.4. Questionnaire using Likert scaling.

Circle the appropriate number:	Very good	Good	Average	Fair	Poor
Rate your lecturer's:					
1. Choice of material	5	4	3	2	1
2. Performance generally	5	4	3	2	1
3. Explanations of the theory	5	4	3	2	1
4. Use of practical examples	5	4	3	2	1
5. Development of theory	5	4	3	2	1
6. Stressing important points	5	4	3	2	1
7. Choice of tutorial examples	5	4	3	2	1
8. Time given to individuals	5	4	3	2	1
9. Choice of lab. experiments	5	4	3	2	1
10. Helping understand subject	5	4	3	2	1
11. Useful in its own right	5	4	3	2	1
12. Teaching report writing	5	4	3	2	1
How well does the lecturer do in:					
13. Getting you interested	5	4	3	2	1
14. Knowledge of subject	5	4	3	2	1
15. Motivating you	5	4	3	2	1
16. Giving clear explanations	5	4	3	2	1
17. Lecturing at followable rate	5	4	3	2	1
18. Giving good lecture notes	5	4	3	2	1
Other:					
19. Are the tests useful?	5	4	3	2	1
20. Course relevant to needs?	5	4	3	2	1
Add the numbers you circled:	Score/100:				

8. Surveys of Public Opinion

Conclusions

Market research campaigns require a good deal of planning if the results are to be meaningful, let alone accurate.

Attitude measurement or psychophysical scaling plays an important role in market research and the Guttman scalogram is an appealing method for this.

Likert scaling is a simple and widely used method of 'person scaling,' that is, determination of people's attitudes to a product or service.

8. Surveys of Public Opinion

Chapter 9

MATHEMATICAL LOGIC

THE ALGEBRA OF SETS

A set is a collection of objects or elements, each having some common property which defines membership of the set. The set is defined by a list of members or by a rule which unambiguously defines membership.

Two simple examples are

$S = \{$ Tom, Dick, Harry $\}$
$N = \{\, n \mid n$ is a positive integer $\}$

where braces are used to enclose a listed set and the symbol '$\mid$' precedes the definition of a *limit* and thus may be read as 'subject to the limit(s)/restriction(s)'. Here S is a *finite set* and N is an *infinite set*.

The number 3 is a member of the set N which is written as $3 \in N$ whereas the number π is not which is written as $\pi \notin N$.

A set which has no members is called the *null set*, denoted as $\emptyset$. If two sets A and B contain precisely the same elements they are said to be equal, denoted as $A = B$, and the conditions

If $x \notin A$ then $x \notin B$, or $x \notin A \rightarrow x \notin B$
If $x \notin B$ then $x \notin A$, or $x \notin B \rightarrow x \notin A$

apply, where $\rightarrow$ is the *conditional* and may be read as 'implies that'. If all elements of set A are also elements of set B (but not necessarily vice-versa) then A is a *subset* of B, denoted as $A \subset B$ or $A \subseteq B$ if equality of the two sets is possible.

Then if $A \subset B$ and $B \subset C$ then $A \subset C$.

9. MATHEMATICAL LOGIC

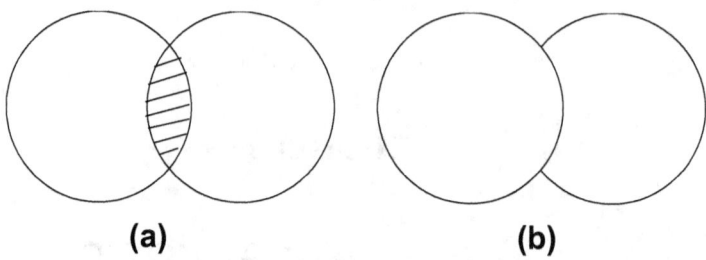

Figure 9.1. Intersection and union of sets.

Figure 9.1(a) illustrates the *intersection* of two sets, denoted as A∩B, using a *Venn diagram*. Thus A∩B comprises the common elements of the two overlapping sets.

Figure 9.1(b) illustrates the *union* of two sets, denoted as A∪B and consisting of all the elements of both sets with the proviso that the common elements in (A∩B) are counted only once (Copi, 1968).

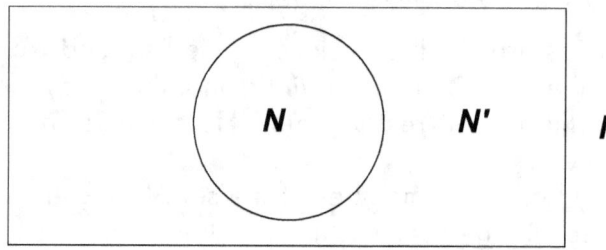

Figure 9.2. Universal set, a set, and its complement.

If we define a *universal* set *I* as the set of all things under consideration and take this to be all real numbers, then for the set of integers *N* we can define the *complement* of this set, denoted *N'*, as the set of all non-integer real numbers and this is everything outside this set (but within the universal set) as shown in Figure 9.2.

Set algebra obeys a number of basic laws such as:
(i) The associative law for intersection
X ∩ (Y ∩ Z) = (X ∩ Y) ∩ Z

9. MATHEMATICAL LOGIC

(ii) The associative law for union
$$X \cup (Y \cup Z) = (X \cup Y) \cup Z$$

(iii) The distributive law of intersection over union
$$X \cap (Y \cup Z) = (X \cap Y) \cup (X \cap Z)$$

and these laws can be proved using Venn diagrams to 'build up' both sides of these equations in steps.

A basic idea of sets, subsets and the intersection and union of sets is worthwhile and useful later in this chapter but detailed knowledge of the algebra of sets is not needed.

SWITCHING CIRCUITS

The theory of switching circuits has important application in telephony and electronics. In terms of *thinking* it is possible, conceptually at least, to have switches in the decision trees of Chapter 5 to allow or disqualify a particular branch.

Two switches connected *in series* as follows

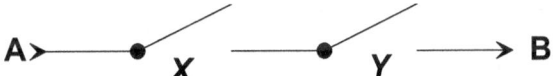

we denote as $X \otimes Y$.

If we denote $X = 1$ as closed (or true) and $X = 0$ as open (or false) for switch X we can construct a *truth table* for all possible switching combinations:

X	Y	$X \otimes Y$
0	0	0
0	1	0
1	0	0
1	1	1

9. MATHEMATICAL LOGIC

Two switches connected *in parallel* as follows

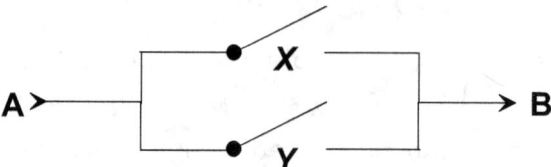

we denote as $X \oplus Y$.

The truth table for these parallel switches is

X	Y	$X \oplus Y$
0	0	0
0	1	1
1	0	1
1	1	1

Now consider an object a and two sets X and Y. If $a \in X$ denote this as $X = 1$ or if $a \notin X$ denote this as $X = 0$. Then for intersection of X and Y, that is $X \cap Y$, the truth table is

X	Y	$X \cap Y$
0	0	0
0	1	0
1	0	0
1	1	1

because only if a belongs to both X and Y does it belong $X \cap Y$. This table has the same outcomes as that for two series switches.

Similarly, the truth table for $X \cup Y$ has the same outcomes as that for two parallel switches.

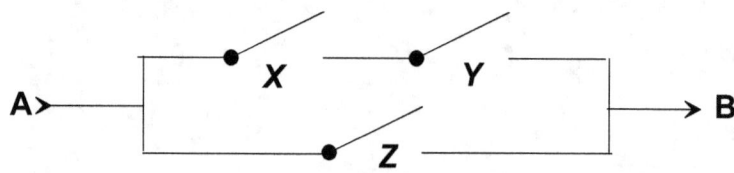

Figure 9.3.

9. MATHEMATICAL LOGIC

Considering the combined switch of Figure 9.3 which can be represented by

$$T = (X \otimes Y) \oplus Z \text{ or } T = (X \cap Y) \cup Z$$

We can use the distributive law of set algebra to transform this:

$$T = Z \cup (X \cap Y) = (Z \cup X) \cap (Z \cup Y)$$

The last expression represents the combined switch

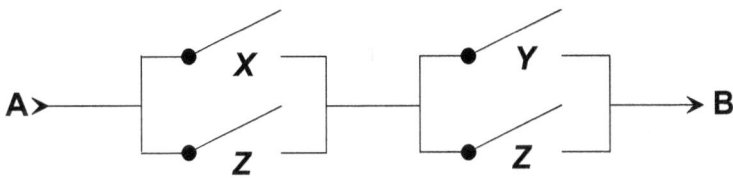

which is equivalent to that of Figure 9.3, as can be verified by the following truth table:

X	Y	Z	$(X \cap Y) \cup Z$	$(Z \cup X) \cap (Z \cup Y)$
0	0	0	$0 \cup 0 = 0$	$0 \cap 0 = 0$
1	0	0	$0 \cup 0 = 0$	$1 \cap 0 = 0$
1	1	0	$1 \cup 0 = 1$	$1 \cap 1 = 1$
1	0	1	$0 \cup 1 = 1$	$1 \cap 1 = 1$
0	1	1	$0 \cup 1 = 1$	$1 \cap 1 = 1$
1	1	1	$1 \cup 1 = 1$	$1 \cap 1 = 1$

The same outcomes are obtained for each combined switch and they are therefore equivalent, in fact because both Z switches must be open or closed at the same time.

As in set theory, in switching theory we can have a switch X' which is the complement or *negation* of the switch X and thus X' is closed when X is open and vice-versa.

Finally, note that the correspondence between sets and switching circuits arises because we have treated each switch as a small set with only two elements, zero or unity.

9. MATHEMATICAL LOGIC

PROPOSITIONAL CALCULUS

In propositional calculus we define a proposition to be a statement which is either true (T) or false (F), for example:
(a) *It is raining,* which we shall denote as p.
(b) *I am wearing my raincoat,* which we shall denote as q.
(c) *I shall get wet,* which we shall denote as r.

Such statements as
(d) Hurry up
are not propositions.

Propositions can be connected by:
[1] The *conjunction* 'and', denoted as $\wedge$.
[2] The *disjunction* 'or', denoted as $\vee$.
[3] The *conditional* 'if ... then ... ', denoted $\rightarrow$.
[4] The *biconditional* 'if and only if', denoted $\leftrightarrow$.

The connective $\rightarrow$ is sometimes called implication and $\leftrightarrow$ is sometimes called mutual implication.

The combined truth tables for *negation*, denoted as $\sim$, and the connectives [1] - [4] are:

p	q	$\sim p$	$p \wedge q$	$p \vee q$	$p \rightarrow q$	$p \leftrightarrow q$
T	T	F	T	T	T	T
T	F	F	F	T	F	F
F	T	T	F	T	T	F
F	F	T	F	F	T	T

For $p \rightarrow q$ the truth table is not as might be expected by the verbal interpretation 'if ... then ...' and the truth results follow more easily from the interpretation 'implies' so that in results row 3 q = T does not negate the 'implication' that q = T when p = T.

Note that here $\vee$ is the *inclusive disjunction* or 'either, possibly both' which is written as $(p \vee q) \wedge (p \wedge q)$
and the *exclusive disjunction* or 'either, not both' is written as
$$(p \vee q) \wedge \sim (p \wedge q)$$

9. Mathematical Logic

Then using the statement definitions (a), (b) and (c) the compound statement

If it is raining & I am not wearing my raincoat, I shall get wet
  p   q = am wearing   q

can be written symbolically as $(p \wedge \sim q) \to r$

Propositional calculus has the same working rules as set algebra (whose rules are the same as those for switching circuits), for example:

[1] Commutative law:
(a) $p \vee q \leftrightarrow q \vee p$
(b) $p \wedge q \leftrightarrow q \wedge p$

[2] Associative law:
(a) $p \vee (q \vee r) \leftrightarrow (p \vee q) \vee r$
(b) $p \wedge (q \wedge r) \leftrightarrow (p \wedge q) \wedge r$

[3] Distributive law:
(a) $p \wedge (q \vee r) \leftrightarrow (p \wedge q) \vee (p \wedge r)$
(b) $p \vee (q \wedge r) \leftrightarrow (p \vee q) \wedge (p \vee r)$

The correspondence between switching circuits, sets and propositional calculus can be summarized by the following table:

Set algebra	Switching	Propositional calculus
$\cap$	$\otimes$	$\wedge$
$\cup$	$\oplus$	$\vee$
′	′	$\sim$
=	=	$\leftrightarrow$

113

9. Mathematical Logic

Application to logical thinking

Logical thinking is deliberate and goal-oriented and involves two forms of reasoning:

[1] Inductive reasoning

Inductive reasoning involves extrapolating or generalizing from information available to draw a conclusion. This is usually illustrated by examples like: "I have four apples which are all red, therefore all apples are red."

Writing a similar example of inductive reasoning in simple notation

a, b, c, d all have properties P and Q
a, b, c all have the property R
Therefore d has the property R

perhaps makes this process clearer.

As another example:

Scandinavians (S) have fair hair or property F
Bill (B) has fair hair
Therefore Bill is Scandinavian or $B \in S$

Note that the argument of the latter example is not correct. For it to be correct the first statement would have to be *only* Scandinavians have fair hair. Alternatively, if the first statement was: Negroes do not have fair hair, then a correct conclusion would be that Bill is not a Negro.

[2] Deductive reasoning

Deductive reasoning examines whether an argument consisting of a sequence of statements is true (T) or false (F), for example the two simple statements

Apples are red, or statement p
Oranges are red, or statement q

can be used to form the compound statement

$$p \wedge q$$

114

9. MATHEMATICAL LOGIC

A *truth table* can then be used to examine the four possible outcomes for this:

p	q	p ∧ q
T	T	T
T	F	F
F	T	F
F	F	F

and in our example the second result row applies so that the compound statement is false.

A better example which has a sequence of statements is

If Anthony got the job, then he went to Brisbane, or $A \to B$
If he went to Brisbane, then he met Charlie, or $B \to C$
If he met Charlie, he also met Dave, or $C \to D$
Anthony did not meet Dave, or $\sim D$
Either Anthony got the job or someone else did, or $A \vee E$
Therefore someone else got the job, or $\therefore E$

The truth table for this example takes 32 lines but the result can be deduced by reading backwards through the first four lines to deduce that Anthony did not get the job, when the fifth line gives the conclusion E.

As a final example consider the compound statement

*If it is raining and I am not wearing my raincoat,
I shall get wet*

p = raining q = am wearing r = get wet

which is written symbolically as $(p \wedge \sim q) \to r$

The truth table for this is

p	q	r	~q	p ∧ ~q	(p ∧ ~q) → r	(p ∧ ~q) ↔ r
T	T	T	F	F	T	F
T	T	F	F	F	T	T
T	F	T	T	T	T	T
T	F	F	T	T	F	F
F	T	T	F	F	T	F
F	T	F	F	F	T	T
F	F	T	T	F	T	F
F	F	F	T	F	T	T

9. MATHEMATICAL LOGIC

so that the compound statement is only proved false if

*It is raining and I am not wearing my raincoat,
I shall not get wet*

If, on the other hand, the biconditional is used for this compound statement then half the outcomes prove the statement false, as shown in the final column of the truth table.

CONCLUSION

Switching and set algebra are both types of *Boolean algebra*. Our interest here, however, is primarily the symbolic logic of propositional calculus as an aid to thinking in terms of logical arguments.

Even those of us less than enthusiastic with maths might prefer symbolic logic to trying to unravel the logic, if any, of long paragraphs of argument.

The present author, for example, has throughout his adult life used the symbol → in writing informal notes as an abbreviation for 'implies' or 'if ... then it follows that ...'

A notation for propositional calculus that might be preferred for mnemonic reasons can be borrowed from BASIC coding by using the notation:

.AND. for the conjunction
.OR. for the inclusive disjunction
.XOR. for the exclusive disjunction
IF ..... THEN for the conditional
= for the biconditional.

and 'computer logic' is discussed in the following chapter.

Chapter 10

COMPUTER PROGRAMMING

FLOW DIAGRAMS

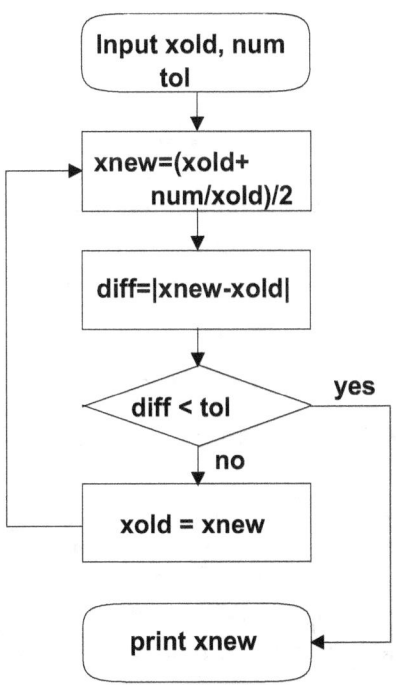

Figure 10.1. Flow diagram for short program.

Figure 10.1 shows the flow diagram for a short BASIC program that uses Newton's method for finding the root of a number in which the root is given by iterating the recursion relation $x_{new} = (x_{old} + num/x_{old})/2$

where num = number for which the square root is required
x_{old} = initial estimate of the square root

10. Computer Programming

Using a tolerance number 'tol' as a termination criterion the QBASIC program is:

```
INPUT xold, num, tol
lab1: xnew = (xold + num/xold)/2
diff = ABS(xnew-xold)
IF diff<tol GOTO lab2
xold = xnew: GOTO lab1
lab2: PRINT xnew
```

and to test the program typical input is 1,4,0.001 to obtain an approximate result for $\sqrt{4} = 2$.

Note that ABS( ) is the function for absolute value and that lab1 and lab2 are 'labels' in place of line numbers to allow direction of GOTO statements.

Flow diagrams are useful for planning very large programs, typically each item representing a subroutine.

Most programs given in this and later chapters are in QBASIC which was free with DOS 5 and reads easily into Visual Basic (VB). Most of these use line numbers for didactic purposes.

Programming mathematical logic

Both QBASIC and VB provide the Boolean operators

NOT, AND, OR, XOR, EQV, IMP

and in VB Boolean variables have the values 'True' or 'False' whilst in QBASIC the value true = -1 and false = 0.

These Boolean operators simply return values corresponding to their truth tables from pairs of statements as in the following VB example:

```
Sub main()
A = 10: B = 8: C = 6: 'Initialize variables
Result = A > B Imp B > C: Debug.Print Result: ' Returns True
Result = A > B Imp C > B: Debug.Print Result: ' Returns False
Result = B > A Imp C > B: Debug.Print Result: 'Returns True
End Sub
```

10. Computer Programming

The following problem was discussed in Chapter 9:

If Anthony got the job, then he went to Brisbane, or $A \to B$
If he went to Brisbane, then he met Charlie, or $B \to C$
If he met Charlie, he also met Dave, or $C \to D$
Anthony did not meet Dave, or $\sim D$
Either Anthony got the job or someone else did, or $A \vee E$
Therefore someone else got the job., or $\therefore E$

This can be coded in the same way as we would solve it by inspection, that is to work backwards from the fourth line, and the following VB program does this, for simplicity writing results to the Debug window (QBASIC only simulates Boolean operations with 1 = True and 0 = False).

```
Sub main()
Dim a, b, c, d, e As Boolean
d = False: Debug.Print "d = ", d
If d = False Then c = False
If c = False Then b = False
If b = False Then a = False
 e = Not (a): Debug.Print "e = ", e
End Sub
```

Here the condition 'd = False' acts like the single *boundary condition* or datum required in Finite Element Method (FEM) models of DC and other networks that are discussed in Chapter 13. Indeed, some preliminary research was done by the author to try and solve this problem using Linear Programming (LP) which is also used to optimize distribution networks.

Generally, however, such logic problems are best solved by 'inspection' where, as in the present example, finding an appropriate 'entry condition' and applying the conditions in an appropriate order will often quickly solve the problem.

10. COMPUTER PROGRAMMING

DYNAMIC PROGRAMMING

Dynamic programming is a process of *recursive optimization* in which steps toward the optimum solution are taken using information from previous steps, typically for time dependent problems.

The general procedure used in dynamic programming is:

[1] Divide the problem into stages, a process referred to as *decomposition*.

[2] At each stage decisions are made based on an optimization objective. This objective is called the *recursion equation*.

[3] The results are combined to yield a solution, a process referred to as *composition*. Sometimes the 'summation' of decisions made at each stage may be said to form a *policy*.

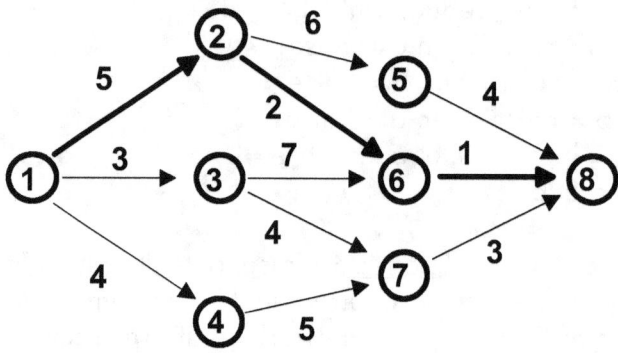

Figure 10.2. Shortest route problem.

Figure 10.2 shows the shortest route or 'stagecoach' problem. Here the nodes are towns and the distances between them are shown on the arrows between nodes. We seek to determine the shortest route systematically and this can be done using a tabular dynamic programming approach.

In this we conduct a *forward pass* to form a table in which all the cumulative route lengths to each node are calculated, noting the shortest route lengths to each node.

10. Computer Programming

Then we conduct a *backward pass* in which we work backwards through the table choosing the shortest stage lengths for a sequence of nodes to obtain the shortest route.

Table 10.1. Precedence table for shortest route problem.

Node	Route lengths (nodes)	Node for least RL
1	0 (-)	0
2	5(1)	1
3	3(1)	1
4	4(1)	1
5	11(2)	2
6	7(2), 10(3)	2
7	7((3), 9(4)	3
8	15(5), 8(6), 12(7)	6

The *precedence table* for the problem of Figure 10.2 is given in Table 10.1. Here the backward pass identifies node 6 as the node which has the shortest route length (RL) to node 8. Next node 2 is identified as that with the shortest stage length to node 6, leaving only the first node to define the shortest route as being 1-2-6-8 with length = 5+2+1 = 8 units.

The following QBASIC program for the shortest route problem reads the number of nodes (Z) and the number of links between them (E) at line 20. Then the node number pairs and distances for each of these links or elements are read in line 30.

The data included in lines 180 - 200 is for the problem of Figure 10.2 and the output (from line 160) will simply be the node numbers of the shortest route in reverse order (excluding node 1), that is 8, 6 and 2.

```
5 REM Program for Shortest Route Problem
10 DIM N(20, 20), D(20), T(20), P(20, 3), B(20)
20 READ Z, E: PRINT "Shortest route is:"
30 FOR I = 1 TO E: READ N(I, 1), N(I, 2), D(I): NEXT
40 FOR I = 1 TO E: FOR J = 1 TO 3: P(I, J) = 0: NEXT: NEXT
50 FOR K = 1 TO E: J = N(K, 2): I = 1
```

10. Computer Programming

```
60 FOR M = 1 TO 3: IF P(J, M) = 0 THEN 70
65 I = I + 1: NEXT
70 P(J, M) = K: NEXT
80 FOR I = 1 TO Z: B(I) = 0: T(I) = 100: NEXT: T(1) = 0
90 FOR K = 1 TO E: I = N(K, 1): J = N(K, 2): T2 = T(I) + D(K)
100 IF T2 < T(J) THEN T(J) = T2
105 NEXT
110 FOR K = Z TO 1 STEP -1: F = 100
120 FOR M = 1 TO 3: IF P(K, M) = 0 THEN 150
130 L = P(K, M): N1 = N(L, 1): N2 = N(L, 2): T2 = T(N1) + D(L)
140 IF T2 < F THEN B(N2) = N1: F = T2
150 NEXT: NEXT: K = Z
160 PRINT K: K = B(K): IF K = 1 THEN END
170 GOTO 160
180 DATA 8,11
190 DATA 1,2,5, 1,3,3, 1,4,4, 2,5,6, 2,6,2
200 DATA 3,6,7, 3,7,4, 4,7,5, 5,8,4, 6,8,1, 7,8,3
```

A *precedence matrix* is formed in lines 50 to 70 and this stores the element numbers leading to each node. Then a *forward pass* is used in lines 80 to 105 to find the shortest distance to the nodes.

Then a *backward pass* is carried out in lines 110 to 150. Here the precedence matrix is used to find and store the node which gives the shortest distance to each node in array B( ).

Finally, in line 160 the shortest route is output. Such programs, of course, are a more attractive approach to dynamic programming problems than tables such as Table 10.1, which, except for the simplest of problems, quickly become rather cumbersome.

Gauss-Mohr Reduction

This is a modification of Gauss-Jordan reduction, a method of inverting matrices (of numbers). Gauss-Jordan reduction is, in turn based on Gauss reduction, the classical way of solving simultaneous algebraic equations of the form

$$A \{ x \} = \{ b \}$$

10. Computer Programming

It does this by working through the equations in order in a *forward reduction* to eliminate one additional variable from each successive equation. The result is an upper triangular matrix with zeroes below the leading diagonal.

Gauss reduction is a method of *direct solution* of matrix equations, that is, a solution is obtained without calculating the inverse of the connecting matrix A. This method is also called *triangular elimination* because it reduces the matrix A to an 'upper triangular' matrix. The operations required to achieve this are exactly the same as in Gauss-Jordan reduction except that the 'row subtraction' operations are only carried out below the leading diagonal of the matrix.

Table 10.2. Example of Gauss reduction (pivots underlined).

(a) forward reduction				
		Matrix A		{b}
	$\underline{2}$	2	2	12
	2	3	4	20
	2	4	3	19
r1* = r1/pivot	1	1	1	6
r2 - 2 x r1*	0	$\underline{1}$	2	8
r3 - 2 x r1*	0	2	1	7
OK	1	1	1	6
r2*= r2(last)/pivot	0	1	2	8
r3(last) -2 x r2*	0	0	$\underline{-3}$	-9
OK	1	1	1	6
OK	0	1	2	8
r3(last)/pivot	0	0	1	3
(b) back substitution				
$b_3 = x_3 = 3$				
$b_2 - 2x_3 = x_2$ or $8 - 2(3) = 2$				
$b_1 - x_2 - x_3 = x_1$ or $6 - 2 - 3 = 1$				

Table 10.2 performs Gauss reduction to solve the problem of determining the unknown coefficients { x } in the equations A {x} = {b} with the matrix A and the *vector* { b } shown at the top of the table.

10. Computer Programming

Here in the forward reduction to reduce matrix A to upper triangular form the same operations are carried out on the vector { b }, moving through the rows in turn to:
(a) Divide each row by its diagonal entry or pivot.
(b) Multiply this row by the entries below its pivot and subtract the result from the rows below to produce zeroes below the pivot.

Then *back substitution* yields the solution of the matrix equation A { x } = { b } in reverse order as

$$x_i = b_i - \sum_{j=i+1}^{3} a_{ij} x_j$$

and this operation is equivalent to inverting the upper triangular matrix to which A was reduced and premultiplying the RHS vector by it (it must be as it yields the solution!). Inversion of triangular matrices, therefore, is a very simple exercise numerically.

Gauss-Jordan reduction applies the same operations as Gauss reduction, but only to the matrix A, and both above and below the diagonal, to form its inverse.

Gauss-Mohr reduction performs the same operations as Gauss-Jordan reduction but applies these to the RHS vector {b} at the same time and approximately halves the number of operations required by operating only to the right of the 'pivots' a_{ii} on the diagonal (so that A^{-1}, which we do not require, is not obtained).

Gauss-Mohr reduction is demonstrated by solving a simple DC network problem in Chapter 13.

Mohr's Code

Codes and ciphers abound through history and, for example, Julius Caesar had a personal one (and probably needed it) as did many others in his line of work. Modern examples that are household names are Morse code and Pitman shorthand which one excellent secretary I knew personally was very good at, Pitman shorthand having originally being intended as a code.

10. COMPUTER PROGRAMMING

In the digital age, however, codes for the purposes of encryption have become increasingly important and some are "unbreakable" according to Abelson et al. (2008).

Table 10.3. Cipher for a simple code

	M	A	D	B	A	S	T	A	R	D
M	a	b	c	d	e	f	g	h	i	j
A	k	l	m	n	o	p	q	r	s	t
D	u	v	w	x	y	z	a	b	c	d
B	e	f	g	h	i	j	k	l	m	n
A	o	p	q	r	s	t	u	v	w	x
S	y	z	a	b	c	d	e	f	g	h
T	i	j	k	l	m	n	o	p	q	r
A	s	t	u	v	w	x	y	z	*	*
R	*	*								
D										

I try very hard to please so if I you are having trouble understanding this great book *Mohr's Code* might be a little help. Table 10.3 is the key to a simple code of a type once quite popular because of the ease with which it can be changed (by using a new key word or phrase which might also be included in a message).

In the table the top row and LH column the phrase (madbastard) is the *keyword* for the code. Then the letter *a* is represented by *ss, og* or *no* by using the first letter as the row in the table and the second as the column.

Notice that the alphabet has been written three times (sufficient) and the following * entries are positions used to denote the end of a word (that is *a3r, a3d, rm* and *ra*).

Then the reader can verify that the code

ma3mmda1ma2 mm1 a1bmrmd1ma2 mbmmda2

translates into 'have a nice day' if the numbers indicate which 'a' to use and you have been told to select the first available entry given by the two or three letter/number combination.

125

10. Computer Programming

Such a code can be complicated a little further by including a further key number, say 7, when every seventh letter of the coded message is ignored. Then, with regular changing of the keyword, a not too simple code is obtained.

CONCLUSIONS

Flow diagrams are useful for planning large programs and projects.

Logic, however, is best dealt with by symbolic logic and not coding.

The shortest route problem provides a good thinking and coding exercise and is a good introduction to the Critical Path Method discussed in the next chapter.

Gauss-Mohr reduction is an efficient way of solving simultaneous algebraic equations and is used to solve a small Input-Output Analysis problem in Chapter 16. The very short matrix inversion and solution routine used for that purpose also proves useful in Chapter 13.

As for databases, even the task of specifying criteria for a *find* in a database to select particular entries from it and then produce a *report* is a computer applications exercise which requires skill and thought. Note also, that Appendix A gives a rudimentary introduction to BASIC (beginner's all-purpose symbolic instruction code) – including some small measure of introduction to dealing with databases, finding information in them, etcetera.

Finally, on the matter of codes, perhaps such word games as palindromes and Spoonerisms could play a part in these, though I doubt it (Augarde, 2003). I do recall, however, that 'The Goons' (Spike Milligan etc.) called the latter Roonerspisms.

Codes are the be-all and end-all of computing, however, the Hollerith card system used on early computers being used by IBM German subsidiary Demohag to record the names of Jews in Germany prior to WW2 (Black, 2001), whilst today ASCII remains the most widely used character code.

Chapter 11

Planning and Scheduling

Flow-line production

The flow-line method of production scheduling is the basis of assembly line production. The method is easily understood by considering three contrasting production systems.

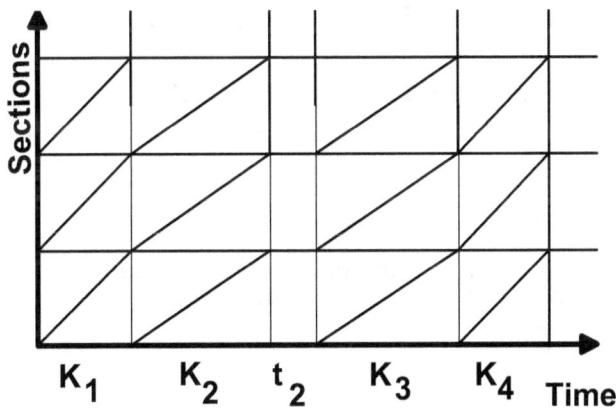

Figure 11.1. Parallel production.

Figure 11.1 illustrates production in which all products are made at the same time. For parallel production the total project time is given by

$$T_p = \Sigma (K_i + t_i)$$

where K_i is called the *production module* for steps i and t_i are waiting times (for holidays etc.). In the case where all rates are the same the total production time when there are m steps and no waiting times is

$$T_p = K m$$

This approach gives the shortest total time but requires maximum usage of resources but is only practical in one-off situations

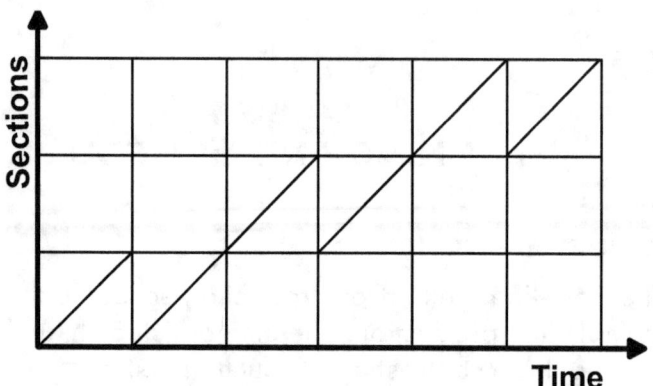

Figure 11.2. Sequence production.

Figure 11.2 illustrates sequence production in which each sub-project is completed before starting the next. This gives the total project time as

$T_s = n \Sigma (K_i + t_i)$

when there are n sections or sub-projects. When the modules for the steps in these are equal and there are no waiting times the total time is given by

$T_s = K m n$

where we have $m = 2$ and $n = 3$ in the example of Figure 11.2.

This approach results in the longest total time and delaying one activity does not affect others. This again represents an extreme situation in relation to the flow-line approach and both Figures 11.1 and 11.2 are of little practical value except as an introduction to the flow line model.

Figure 11.3 shows an example of flow-line production where in car manufacture, for example, line A might be for engine assembly, B for body building, C for drive system and D for final assembly.

11. PLANNING AND SCHEDULING

Then for flow-line production the total production time is given by

$$T_f = K(m + n - 1)$$

where the production modules or rates are equal, as must be the case to prevent lines interfering (unless there are gaps between the lines and still only a temporary difference in the 'general' rate is permitted as flow lines cannot cross).

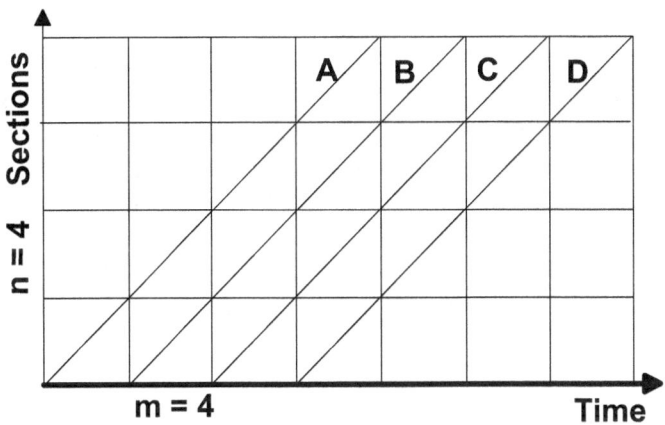

Figure 11.3. Flow-line production.

Then in Figure 11.3 the time until all lines are in operation is given by

$$K(m - 1)$$

and this is called the *running in time* and is equal to the *running out time*, that is the time for cessation of production after the first line finishes.

Hence the *time of full production* can be calculated as

$$K(m + n - 1) - 2K(m - 1) = T_{full} = K(n - m + 1)$$

and in practice it is desirable to maximize the ratio

$$T_{full}/T_f = K(n - m + 1)/K(m + n - 1)$$

so that the larger the number of sections the more efficient the process, for example in mass production where $n \gg m$.

11. Planning and Scheduling

The flow-line method is an important tool for production scheduling and can also be used elsewhere when a number of similar projects are undertaken or when a project can be broken into sections of similar nature, as in construction of a multistory building, for example. Then, as the flow-line method emphasizes, the work on these sections should be overlapped as much as possible to maximize the efficiency of operations.

Group technology

Group technology is an approach more suited to such applications as engineering manufacture where grouping components into families by identifying common manufacturing requirements is more important than an assembly line approach. In this approach some of the key considerations are:

[1] Group technology is directed at *batch production* and more emphasis is placed on dealing with *components*.

[2] Components are grouped into families in which they have similar manufacturing requirements to other family members.

[3] Machines or production units are grouped into *production cells* which deal with *component families*.

[4] These production cells are the approximate equivalent of a flow-line in assembly line models and the component families are comparable to the sections or 'sub-projects' in flow-line production.

For each component a *Component-Process-Routing* (CPR) program can be established. Then, where grouping of components into families is not obvious, comparison of their CPR programs to determine whether they visit similar sequences of production cells may help in component grouping.

Sometimes a component's CPR program may be 'all over the place' and this may be indicative of a need to rearrange the factory layout.

11. PLANNING AND SCHEDULING

In designing an efficient production system component quantities and production cell capacities must be balanced approximately and some manipulation of component families and grouping of facilities may be needed to achieve a reasonable balance.

In some cases physical layout corresponding to the product flow may require rearrangement to improve overall efficiency.

Table 11.1. Travel chart.

r/c	Opn	1	2	3	4	5	6	7	8	r
5	1		20	10	5	5	10			50
1.6	2	5		10	10	5			10	40
1	3				5	5	15			25
1.2	4	5		5		5	10			25
0.5	5				→→ TO		5	5		10
0.8	6		5		From			15	15	35
0.6	7					5			10	15
0.14	8						5			5
	c	10	25	25	20	20	45	25	35	

Using the CPR program data the *travel chart* shown in Table 11.1 can be constructed for the component flows for a period of time.

Then for flow-line assembly Table 11.1 should yield an upper triangular matrix. To improve the sequencing we sum the row and column entries, as shown, and then calculate the ratio of these sums on the left side of Table 11.1.

Then operations with high values of this ratio should be placed earlier in the sequence and operations with low values placed later. Such rearrangement will maximize in-sequence movement and minimize 'backtracking.'

Observing the extreme left column of Table 11.1 the required order of operations is:

Operation sequence: 1, 2, 4, 3, 6, 7, 5, 8

and the travel chart provides a convenient means of improving the sequencing. Note, however, that the criterion for this must be the ratio of the row and column totals and not the individual totals.

In addition, a limitation of the travel chart is that it cannot take into account the possibility of 'U-lines', for example, where shortcuts alter the situation considerably.

For certain types of production, typically engineering manufacturing of a range of related products, the group technology approach is useful. A good deal of judgment is required in grouping products and processes but the travel chart is one of many techniques which assist in obtaining a more efficient production operation.

LINE-OF-BALANCE SYSTEMS

Line-of-balance (LOB) systems are useful for manufacturing situations where emphasis is based on *assembly* of a product from components. The lines of production of the various components are drawn backwards from the LOB to schedule the operations on these (Enrick, 1965).

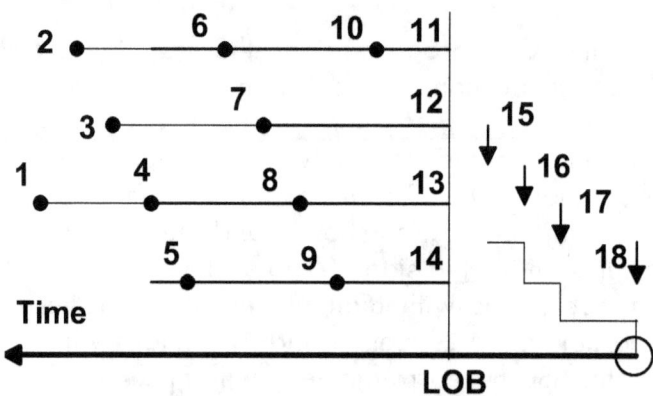

Figure 11.4. LOB flow chart.

Figure 11.4 shows an example of an LOB flow chart, time originating at the extreme right hand side.

11. PLANNING AND SCHEDULING

Flow lines for four components are drawn back from the LOB, the nodes in these corresponding to completion of some stage of their manufacture.

Then, to the right of the LOB the assembly stages are scheduled, as shown, completion occurring at point 18 (in FEM parlance we might term this a 'node').

The LOB approach corresponds to parallel production and, as in that method, breaks can easily be introduced into LOB flow charts.

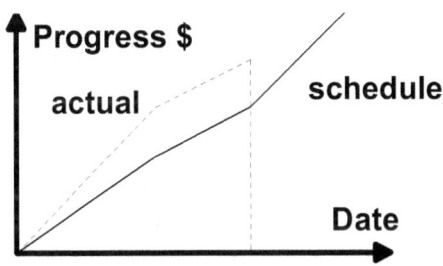

Figure 11.5. LOB production schedule.

As shown in Figure 11.5 progress (here as a dollar value) at any stage can compared with the LOB schedule.

LOB flow charts are a very simple means of scheduling and are particularly appropriate where emphasis is on assembly of a product.

THE CRITICAL PATH METHOD (CPM)

Figure 11.5 shows a critical path network of elements (identified by a letter) with durations shown. Note the dummy element G* (with zero duration) inserted to enforce a precedence.

The longest or *critical path* can be found using the same tabulation as in Table 10.1, except that now the longest times to each node are sought.

11. PLANNING AND SCHEDULING

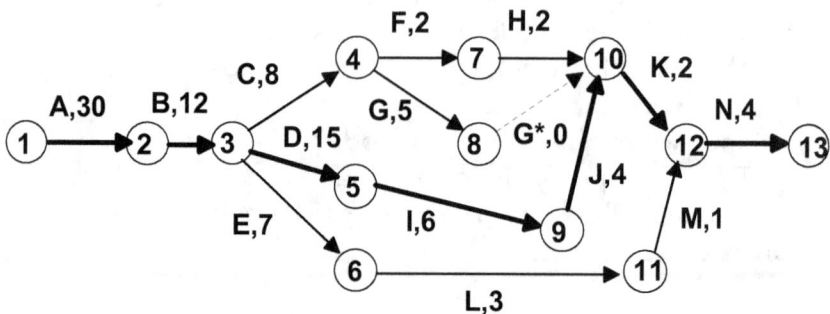

Figure 11.5. Critical path network.

The problem is programmed as in the shortest route program given in Chapter 10 and the precedence matrix P(,) has a column for each node and a loop through the element node number pairs collects the numbers of the elements feeding into each node in this matrix. Then a *forward pass* through the elements calculates the earliest start (ES) time for each element (stored in S1( )) and its earliest finish time (EF) is given by adding its duration (and stored in F1( )). The longest time to each node is also calculated during the forward pass and stored in matrix T( ).

Finally the longest path time to the last node is the duration of the project and a *backward pass* works back through the elements and calculates their latest finish times (LF, stored in F2( )) as the longest times (in T( )) for their end nodes and subtracts their durations from these to obtain their latest start (LS) times (stored in S2( )). Then for elements on the critical path ES = LS and EF = LF.

The data is for the problem shown in Figure 11.5, the first line being the number of nodes and elements. The remaining lines each give the pair of node numbers and the duration for each element in order.

11. Planning and Scheduling

```
5 REM CRITICAL PATH METHOD PROGRAM
10 DIM N(20, 2), D(20), C(20), W(20), T(20), P(3, 20)
20 DIM S1(20), F1(20), S2(20), F2(20)
30 A$ = "        ": READ Z, E: REM Input # of nodes & elements
40 FOR I = 1 TO 3: FOR J = 1 TO 10
50 P(I, J) = 0: NEXT: NEXT: REM Initialize precedence matrix
60 FOR I = 1 TO E
70 READ N(I, 1), N(I, 2), D(I): REM ,C(I),W(I);Rem I/P Element data
80 NEXT: REM Elements must be in numerical order
90 Q = 0: Q2 = 0: REM Initialize total project costs
100 FOR K = 1 TO Z: T(K) = 0: NEXT: REM Initialize LF times for nodes
110 FOR K = 1 TO E: J = N(K, 2): I = 1
120 FOR M = 1 TO 3: IF P(M, J) = 0 THEN GOTO 140
130 I = I + 1: NEXT M: REM Collect preceding element
140 P(I, J) = K: NEXT K: REM Numbers for each node
150 FOR K = 1 TO E: REM COMMENCE FORWARD PASS **********
160 I = N(K, 1): J = N(K, 2): S1(K) = T(I): REM S1(K)=ES time for element
170 F1(K) = T(I) + D(K): REM F1(K)=EF time for each element
180 IF F1(K) > T(J) THEN T(J) = F1(K): REM + node LF time if necessary
190 Q = Q + D(K) * C(K): Q2 = Q2 + D(K) * C(K) * W(K)
200 NEXT: REM END FORWARD PASS        **********
210 PRINT "JOBTIME = ", T(Z): PRINT "JOBCOST = ", Q:
PRINT "PESSIMISTIC COST VARN = ", Q2
220 FOR I = 1 TO E: F2(I) = 1000: NEXT: REM Initialize LF times
230 FOR K = 1 TO E: REM COMMENCE BACKWARD PASS %%%%%%
240 R = E - K + 1: I = N(R, 1): J = N(R, 2): REM Move back thru elements
250 IF J = Z THEN F2(R) = T(Z): REM LF time for last element
260 S2(R) = F2(R) - D(R): REM LS = LF - element duration
270 FOR M = 1 TO 3: S = P(M, I): IF S = 0 THEN GOTO 290
280 IF F2(S) > S2(R) THEN F2(S) = S2(R): REM LF of prec. eles =ele LS
290 NEXT
300 IF S1(R) = S2(R) THEN F = F + D(R) * W(R): REM + to project delay
310 NEXT: REM END BACKWARD PASS     %%%%%%%%
320 PRINT "PESSIMISTIC JOB DELAY = ", F
PRINT "    Element    "; "ES"; A$; "EF"; A$; "LS"; A$; "LF"
330 FOR K = 1 TO E: PRINT USING "##########"; K; S1(K); F1(K);
S2(K); F2(K): NEXT
340 END
500 DATA 13,15
510 DATA 1,2,30, 2,3,12, 3,4,8, 3,5,15, 3,6,7
520 DATA 4,7,2, 4,8,5, 8,10,0, 7,10,2, 5,9,6, 9,10,4, 10,12,2
530 DATA 6,11,3, 11,12,1, 12,13,4
```

11. Planning and Scheduling

Provision for a cost C( ) per unit time and a 'wastage' W( ) or tolerance on the duration for each element is not used in this listing of the program.

Output gives the ES, EF, LS and LF times for each element (they are input in 'alphabetical' order and output in the same order) and these will correspond to the critical path shown by heavy lines in Figure 11.5.

The output is given in the following table:

Element	A	B	C	D	E	F	G	G*	H	I	J	K	L	M	N
ES	0	30	42	42	42	50	50	55	52	57	63	67	49	52	69
EF	30	42	50	57	49	52	55	55	54	63	67	69	52	53	73
LS	0	30	54	42	58	63	62	67	65	57	63	67	65	68	69
LF	30	42	62	57	65	65	67	67	67	63	67	69	68	69	73

Then we see that the critical elements A, B, D, I, J, K, and N, do indeed have ES = LS and EF = LF and the dummy element has ES = EF and LS = LF.

Elements not on the critical path are said to have *float*, an amount of time by which they can be delayed without delaying completion of the project.

Conclusions

The flow-line method is a simple but important method of production planning that illustrates the principles of assembly line production well.

Group technology is a good example of logically reorganizing a workshop, for example, so that different products flow more efficiently through the various processes they require.

The line-of-balance technique is a very simple method of scheduling manufacture and assembly of the components for a product.

11. Planning and Scheduling

The critical path method (CPM) is widely used in the building and other industries and, with the inclusion of upper and lower tolerances on element durations is called the Program Evaluation and Review Technique or PERT (Federal Electric Corporation, 1963).

A useful QBASIC program is given for CPM which uses the same precedence matrix approach as used in the shortest route program given in Chapter 10.

11. PLANNING AND SCHEDULING

Chapter 12

Linear Programming

The Simplex Method

The Simplex Method of solving Linear Programming (LP) problems was developed by Danzig circa 1947. In this slack variables y are added to inequality constraints and the problem is written

$$\text{Min/Max} \quad z = \{c\}^t [x] \quad (12.1)$$

$$\text{subject to} \quad A\{x\} + I\{y\} = \{b\} \quad (12.2)$$

where I is a unit matrix (=1 on leading diagonal). Applying Gauss-Jordan reduction to Equation 12.2, premultiplying both sides by a matrix B which is equal to the inverse of A, we obtain

$$\{x\} + A^{-1}\{y\} = A^{-1}\{b\} \quad (12.3)$$

where we write A^{-1} symbolically only. In fact this applies strictly only when the constraints are all equality constraints equal in number to the number of variables $\{x\}$ so that A is a square and hence invertible matrix, when the solution is the RHS of Equation 12.3.

Generally, however, there are some inequality constraints to which slack variables must be added. Then there are usually more variables than there are constraint equations and the solution procedure must determine which are the 'critical' or *active* constraints and solve to determine the optimum solution in terms of these.

This means that, in practice, we replace A^{-1} in Equation 12.3 by a matrix B which is a matrix that *reduces* the augmented matrix [A, I] partially using Gauss-Jordan reduction on a column by column basis.

12. LINEAR PROGRAMMING

Then variables which take a non-zero value at any point in the solution process are said to be in the *basis,* noting that generally some variables will be zero, in particular slack variables associated with constraints intersecting at the optimum point.

As an example of the Simplex Method consider the two variable problem

Maximize $z = 5x_1 + 4x_2$ (12.4)

subject to the constraints

$2x_1 + x_2 \leq 6$ (12.5)
$4x_1 + 5x_2 \leq 20$ (12.6)

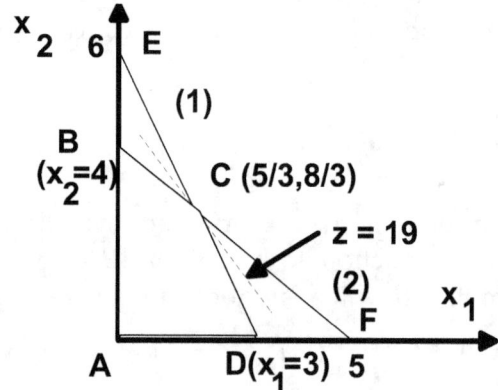

Figure 12.1. LP problem with 2 variables.

Including two slack variables there are four variables and the optimum solution will involve non-zero values of two of these so that the number of possible solutions is $^4C_2 = 4!/(2!2!) = 6$, these being the points A, B, C, D, E, F shown in Figure 12.1, that is the intersections of the constraints and/or the axes, which are also constraints as all variables must be positive.

12. Linear Programming

The simplex *tableau* for the problem is:

Table 12.1. Simplex tableau for Equations 12.4 - 12.6 (pivots underlined).

<u>2</u>	1	1	0	6	
4	5	0	1	20	
5	4	0	0	0	
1	1/2	1/2	0	3	
0	<u>3</u>	-2	1	8	
0	3/2	-5/2	0	-15	
1	0	5/6	-1/6	5/3	$x_1 = 5/3$
0	1	-2/3	1/3	8/3	$x_2 = 8/3$
0	0	-3/2	-1/2	-19	$z = 19$

The problem is solved by using the *pivot* selection rule:

[1] The pivot column is chosen as that with the maximum positive cost. When no positive cost remains (in the bottom or objective function row) the required maximum has been obtained.

[2] The pivot row is then chosen as that with the minimum value of b/a, b being a RHS value for a constraint and a being a coefficient in the pivot column.

Then in Table 12.1 the first tableau has max $c = 5$ and min $b/a = 3$, giving the underlined pivot = 2 shown. Using Gauss-Jordan reduction (see Chapter 10) to reduce this column to 'unit' form with zeroes for all but the pivot position and the bottom cost row, we obtain the second tableau shown.

Then in the second tableau the max $c = 3/2$ and the min b/a for this column is 8/3, giving the underlined pivot shown (= 3). Then GJR with this pivot yields the third tableau shown. As no positive costs remain this gives the solution for the maximum, $z = 19$ with $x_1 = 5/3$ and $x_2 = 8/3$.

Note that choosing the row using the 'min b/a' rule is equivalent to moving along the axis for this variable (for the pivot column) until a constraint is first encountered, the resulting pivot choice being the 'safest', ensuring that we remain in the feasible region.

12. LINEAR PROGRAMMING

Reversed constraints

In the latter exercise we have only dealt with $\leq$ constraints (by adding slack variables). To deal with $\geq$ constraints the constraint is simply reversed in sign and once again we add slack variables.

Equality constraints

Equality constraints must be enforced. One way of ensuring this is adding an *artificial variable* y^* and ensure that a pivot is chosen in the row for this constraint to force y^* out of the basis (i.e., to zero). Pivots must thereafter be disallowed in the column for y^*.

An alternative approach is to replace each equality constraint by a pair of $\leq$ and $\geq$ constraints, reversing the signs for the $\geq$ constraint as described above.

DISTRIBUTION PROBLEMS

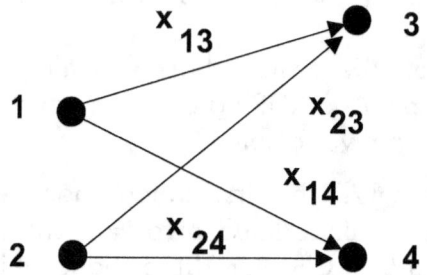

Figure 12.2. Distribution network.

Figure 12.2 shows a distribution network with two supply points S_1 and S_2 and two demand points D_1 and D_2. The flows between the points are the x_{ij} values shown and the costs per unit for these flows are shown in Table 12.2 where the supplies and demands generated by the four points are also given.

12. LINEAR PROGRAMMING

Table 12.2. Distribution problem data.

Origin	Destination 3	4	Supply
1	2	1	30
2	1	2	60
Demand	40	50	90/90

Then the *distribution* (or *transportation*) *problem* is the optimization problem

Minimize $z = \Sigma \Sigma c_{ij} x_{ij}$ (12.7)

subject to the constraints

$x_{13} + x_{14} + 0 + 0 = 30$ (12.8a)
$0 + 0 + x_{23} + x_{24} = 60$ (12.8b)
$x_{13} + 0 + x_{23} + 0 = 40$ (12.9a)
$0 + x_{14} + 0 + x_{24} = 50$ (12.9b)

where Equations 12.8 are the supply constraints and Equations 12.9 are the demand constraints.

The problem can be solved by the Simplex Method when the last constraint is omitted. This makes allowance for the fact that the sum of the demands equals the sum of supplies so that this last constraint is not required. The data for the problem of Figure 12.2 is included in the program given in the following section.

PROGRAM FOR SEQUENTIAL MIN + MAX

The following program uses the 'worst -b & min c/-a' rule to find the minimum solution, a negative coefficient 'a' being chosen to eliminate the infeasible negative 'b' on the RHS. This is the dual pivoting dual to the standard 'max c & min b/a' rule that is used to find a maximum solution.

Note that the program uses similar coding to that in the short Gauss-Mohr reduction routine given in the first section of Chapter 16 to *partially* reduce the matrix for each pivot choice.

12. LINEAR PROGRAMMING

The data is read in simply as a line giving the number of constraints (N), the total number of variables (M) and Q = 1,2,3 (see line 10 for explanation), followed by the constraints (in ≤ form and including their columns for slack variables and their RHSs) and finally the 'cost row', that is, for simplicity the full simplex tableau is read in.

```
10 REM Q=1 for MAX, Q=2 for MIN & Q=3 for MIN then MAX
30 DIM A(10, 15): T = 10 ^ -6: READ N, M, Q
40 FOR I = 1 TO N + 1: FOR J = 1 TO M + 1: READ A(I, J): NEXT: NEXT
50 C1 = 0: FOR J = 1 TO M: C2 = A(N + 1, J)
60 IF C2 > C1 THEN C1 = C2: C = J
NEXT
70 IF C1 = 0 THEN 250
80 F = 0: B1 = 10 ^ 10
90 FOR I = 1 TO N
100 IF A(I, M + 1) < 0 THEN F = 1
110 IF ABS(A(I, C)) < T THEN 150
120 B2 = A(I, M + 1) / A(I, C)
130 IF B2 < 0 THEN 150
140 IF B2 < B1 THEN B1 = B2: R = I
150 NEXT I
160 IF F = 1 THEN GOSUB 330
170 IF F = 0 AND Q >= 2 THEN 250
180 X = A(R, C)
190 FOR J = 1 TO M + 1: A(R, J) = A(R, J) / X: NEXT
200 FOR I = 1 TO N + 1
210 IF I = R THEN 230
215 X = A(I, C)
220 FOR J = 1 TO M + 1: A(I, J) = A(I, J) - X * A(R, J): NEXT
230 NEXT I
240 GOTO 50
250 PRINT "Z = ", -A(N + 1, M + 1)
260 FOR I = 1 TO N: FOR J = 1 TO M
270 D = ABS(A(I, J) - 1)
280 IF D < T AND ABS(A(N + 1, J)) < T THEN K = J
NEXT J
290 PRINT "X"; : PRINT USING "##"; K; : PRINT " = ";
PRINT USING "######.###"; A(I, M + 1)
300 NEXT I
310 IF Q = 3 THEN Q = 1: GOTO 50
320 END
330 B1 = 0: FOR I = 1 TO N
340 B2 = -A(I, M + 1): IF B2 < 0 THEN 360
```

12. LINEAR PROGRAMMING

```
350 IF B2 > B1 THEN B1 = B2: R = I
360 NEXT I
370 C1 = 10 ^ 10
380 FOR J = 1 TO M
390 IF ABS(A(R, J)) < T THEN 430
400 IF A(R, J) > 0 THEN 430
410 C2 = -(A(N + 1, J) / A(R, J))
420 IF C2 < C1 THEN C1 = C2: C = J
430 NEXT J
440 RETURN
DATA 6,10,3
DATA 1,1,0,0,1,0,0,0,0,0,30
DATA -1,-1,0,0,0,1,0,0,0,0,-30
DATA 0,0,1,1,0,0,1,0,0,0,60
DATA 0,0,-1,-1,0,0,0,1,0,0,-60
DATA 1,0,1,0,0,0,0,0,1,0,40
DATA -1,0,-1,0,0,0,0,0,0,1,-40
DATA 2,1,1,2,0,0,0,0,0,0
```

The dimensioning limits to nine constraints and fourteen variables (line 30) and data is included for the distribution problem of Figure 12.2 using the 'split constraint artifice to deal with the equality constraints. The minimum solution is

$$x_{14} = 30, \quad x_{23} = 40, \quad x_{24} = 20$$

so that the minimum total transportation cost is
$$z = 30(1) + 40(1) + 20(2) = 110.$$
The maximum solution is

$$x_{13} = 30, \quad x_{23} = 10, \quad x_{24} = 50$$

giving the maximum total cost $z = 170$.

With a little additional coding the program can be modified to store only the matrix A of Equation 12.2, the RHS vector and one additional column matrix to store the new column formed in the 'I' (unit) part of the augmented matrix when a column is reduced in matrix A. This new column then replaces the reduced column (to 'unit form' with a unit entry and the rest zeroes) in the matrix A, keeping a record of which variables have entered the *basis* by storing their ordinal numbers in another 1D array.

12. LINEAR PROGRAMMING

DIRECT LP METHOD PROGRAM FOR DISTRIBUTION PROBLEMS

The following program uses the 'direct' method of Mohr (2000) to solve distribution problems. In this a pivot is taken in each (constraint) row in turn in the column with the minimum value of $c_j/|a_{ij}|$ and Gauss-Jordan reduction applied to this column, yielding an initial *infeasible* solution to the problem. The minimum solution is then obtained by choosing pivots using the 'worst -b, min c/-a' rule (again note $a < 0$ to eliminate the infeasible negative b on the RHS) and printed.

Next the maximum solution is obtained (in lines 210 - 270) using the 'max c, min b/a' rule and when we require this to be printed line 140 alters to 140 IF I=0 THEN 210.

```
10 REM Distribution Problem Program - for MAX
20 REM RESTORE 500
30 DIM A(20, 20), B(20), NV(20): READ NC, NX: REM Read data
40 FOR I = 1 TO NC + 1: FOR J = 1 TO NX: READ A(I, J): NEXT: READ B(I): NEXT
50 FOR I = 1 TO NC: C = 10 ^ 6
60 FOR J = 1 TO NX: IF ABS(A(I, J)) < .000001 THEN 80
70 F = A(NC + 1, J) / ABS(A(I, J)): IF F < C THEN C = F: COL = J
80 NEXT J
90 GOSUB 350: NEXT I
100 I = O: C = 0: FOR K = 1 TO NC: IF B(K) < C THEN I = K: C = B(K)
105 NEXT
110 C = 10 ^ 6: FOR J = 1 TO NX: IF A(I, J) >= 0 THEN 130
120 F = A(NC + 1, J) / ABS(A(I, J)): IF F < C THEN C = F: COL = J
130 NEXT
140 IF I = 0 THEN 280
190 GOSUB 350
200 IF I > 0 THEN 100
210 C = 0: FOR K = 1 TO NX: IF A(NC + 1, K) > C THEN J = K: C = A(NC + 1, K)
215 NEXT
220 IF J = NX + 1 THEN 280
230 T = 10 ^ 6: FOR K = 1 TO NC: IF A(K, J) <= 0 THEN 250
240 F = B(K) / A(K, J): IF F < T THEN I = K: T = F
250 NEXT: IF C = 0 THEN 280
260 COL = J: GOSUB 350
270 GOTO 210
```

12. Linear Programming

```
280 FOR J = 1 TO NX
290 C = 0: FOR I = 1 TO NC: IF ABS(A(I, J)) < .000001 THEN C = C + 1
295 NEXT
300 IF C <> NC - 1 THEN 320
310 FOR I = 1 TO NC: IF ABS(A(I, J)) = 1 THEN K = I
315 NEXT: NV(K) = J
320 NEXT J
330 FOR I = 1 TO NC + 1
335 PRINT "  X"; : PRINT USING "##"; NV(I);
336 PRINT " = "; : PRINT USING "##########"; B(I): NEXT
340 END
350 P = A(I, COL): B(I) = B(I) / P
360 FOR J = 1 TO NX: A(I, J) = A(I, J) / P: NEXT
370 FOR K = 1 TO NC + 1: IF K = I THEN 410
380 M = A(K, COL): B(K) = B(K) - M * B(I)
390 FOR J = 1 TO NX
400 A(K, J) = A(K, J) - M * A(I, J): NEXT J
410 NEXT K
420 RETURN

430 DATA 5,9
440 DATA 1,1,1,0,0,0,0,0,0,110
450 DATA 0,0,0,1,1,1,0,0,0,160
460 DATA 0,0,0,0,0,0,1,1,1,150
470 DATA 1,0,0,1,0,0,1,0,0,140
480 DATA 0,1,0,0,1,0,0,1,0,200
490 DATA 5,10,10,20,30,20,10,20,30,0

500 DATA 8,20
510 DATA 1,1,1,1,1,0,0,0,0,0,0,0,0,0,0,0,0,0,0,0,90
520 DATA 0,0,0,0,0,1,1,1,1,1,0,0,0,0,0,0,0,0,0,0,75
530 DATA 0,0,0,0,0,0,0,0,0,0,1,1,1,1,1,0,0,0,0,0,35
540 DATA 0,0,0,0,0,0,0,0,0,0,0,0,0,0,0,1,1,1,1,1,25
550 DATA 1,0,0,0,0,1,0,0,0,0,1,0,0,0,0,1,0,0,0,0,40
560 DATA 0,1,0,0,0,0,1,0,0,0,0,1,0,0,0,0,1,0,0,0,35
570 DATA 0,0,1,0,0,0,0,1,0,0,0,0,1,0,0,0,0,1,0,0,70
580 DATA 0,0,0,1,0,0,0,0,1,0,0,0,0,1,0,0,0,0,1,0,30
590 DATA 1.5,6.4,1.8,4,3.5,1.6,2.6,1.9,3.1,5.8,5.3,3.5,2.4,1.3,2.2
600 DATA 50,50,50,50,50,0
```

12. Linear Programming

```
605 DATA 8,20
610 DATA 1,1,1,1,0,0,0,0,0,0,0,0,0,0,0,0,0,0,0,0,51
620 DATA 0,0,0,0,1,1,1,1,0,0,0,0,0,0,0,0,0,0,0,0,80
630 DATA 0,0,0,0,0,0,0,0,1,1,1,1,0,0,0,0,0,0,0,0,119
640 DATA 0,0,0,0,0,0,0,0,0,0,0,0,1,1,1,1,0,0,0,0,100
650 DATA 0,0,0,0,0,0,0,0,0,0,0,0,0,0,0,0,1,1,1,1,20
660 DATA 1,0,0,0,1,0,0,0,1,0,0,0,1,0,0,0,1,0,0,0,60
670 DATA 0,1,0,0,0,1,0,0,0,1,0,0,0,1,0,0,0,1,0,0,97
680 DATA 0,0,1,0,0,0,1,0,0,0,1,0,0,0,1,0,0,0,1,0,118
690 DATA 50,51,62,80,55,50,51,62,59,55,50,51,63,59,55,50,70,69,68,67,0
```

Note that the RESTORE statement in the second line of the program chooses which set of data to use (with REM before it the first set of data is used).

The first set of data (lines 420 - 490) is for the distribution problem of Figure 13.2 for which the minimum and maximum solutions have total costs 6,700 and 8,850.

The second set of data (lines 500 - 600) is for the distribution problem of Table 15.5, giving min. and max. solutions of 1651 and 2162.

The third set of data (lines 605 - 690) is for the inventory problem posed as a distribution problem given in Chapter 15, for which the min. and max. solutions are 18,939 and 22,441.

Conclusion

Linear programming is often used for 'mix problems' in which the variables are quantities of ingredients in a product or parts of a project and the objective function will typically involve the costs of these parts and seek to minimize the total cost.

Here we have considered distribution problems and given two useful programs for LP, one being a 'direct' method for distribution problems. The data included with the latter is for three problems considered in following chapters.

Chapter 13

FINITE ELEMENT NETWORKS

DC NETWORKS

The Finite Element Method (FEM) was developed by Argyris et al. in the 1940s in Germany to analyze the aircraft structures (Argyris, 1965).

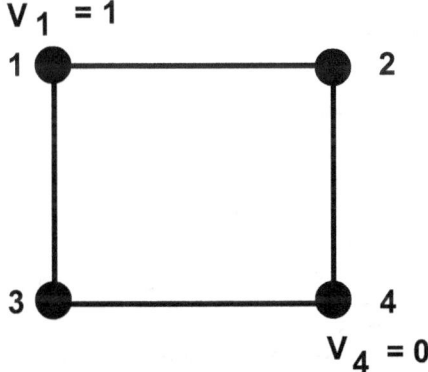

Figure 13.1. FEM model of simple DC network
Resistances 12, 13, 24, 34 all = 1.
Potential at node 1 is 1 and at node 4 it is 0.

As a simple example of FEM Figure 13.1 shows a direct current (DC) network with four resistance *elements* connecting four *nodes* and this corresponds to the simple *precedence memory model* of Figure 3.5 if each node is taken to be a group of neurons storing a memory item.

13. FINITE ELEMENT NETWORKS

The numerical FEM model for this 'structure' is obtained by summing matrices for each element formed by using Ohm's Law to write the current flow in each element ij as

$$Q_{ij} = (V_i - V_j)/R_{ij}$$

where V_i and V_j are the voltages at nodes i and j at each end, and R_{ij} is the *resistance* of the element.

Then writing the two equations for current flow at each end of the element as a matrix we obtain the element equations

$$\begin{Bmatrix} Q_{ij} \\ -Q_{ij} \end{Bmatrix} = (1/R_{ij}) \begin{bmatrix} 1 & -1 \\ -1 & 1 \end{bmatrix} \begin{Bmatrix} V_i \\ V_j \end{Bmatrix} = k \begin{Bmatrix} V_i \\ V_j \end{Bmatrix}$$

Doing this for each element and writing the entries from their *element matrices* k in a *system matrix* K in positions corresponding to the node numbers for each element we obtain the system equations:

$$\{Q\} = \begin{Bmatrix} Q_1 \\ Q_2 \\ Q_3 \\ Q_4 \end{Bmatrix} = \begin{bmatrix} G_{12}+G_{13} & -G_{12} & -G_{13} & 0 \\ -G_{12} & G_{12}+G_{24} & 0 & -G_{24} \\ -G_{13} & 0 & G_{13}+G_{34} & -G_{34} \\ 0 & -G_{24} & -G_{34} & G_{24}+G_{34} \end{bmatrix} \begin{Bmatrix} V_1 \\ V_2 \\ V_3 \\ V_4 \end{Bmatrix} = K\{V\}$$

where $G_{12} = 1/R_{12}$ is the reciprocal of the resistance, or *conductance,* of element 12.

This *assembly* process for the system matrix is easily done by a computer program and the matrix problem can be solved using the same Gauss-Mohr routine as that in the program of for Input-Output Analysis in the first section of Chapter16.

As it stands there are no 'loads' on the RHS in $\{V\}$ because currents at a node must sum to zero so that there is no 'leakage' (this is known as Kirchhoff's current law). Therefore, either input or output currents must be specified at some nodes to 'force' current flows. Alternatively, voltages are specified for at least two nodes, one of these being a 'datum' potential equal to zero.

13. Finite Element Networks

Here this is done in the program by calculating equivalent current 'loads' by multiplying the columns in the system matrix for 'specified voltage nodes' by the voltage specified at them and adding the result to the load matrix { Q } which is represented by array V( ) in the following program.

Then the problem is solved to determine the nodal voltages or potentials and the element currents are calculated using

$$Q_{ij} = (V_i - V_j)/R_{ij}$$

A QBASIC short program that assembles and solves this problem is given below. Here key notation is

NN(,)	matrix storing the element node numbers
R( )	matrix storing the element resistances
C(,)	the system matrix
V( )	the nodal voltages
NP	number of nodes
NE	number of elements
NS	number of nodes with specified voltage
a$, b$	format specifier strings
X, S	temporary numbers

The program reads the data in lines 3, 5 and 9, 'deploying' the element matrices into the system matrix in lines 6 and 7 and modifying the RHS 'load' vector V( ) for the specified voltages in line 11.

Then only lines 14 to 20 are required to solve the problem using Gauss-Mohr reduction.

Here X is first used to store the *pivot* for 'row division' operations (line 14) and then used to store the 'row multiplier' (line 17) for the row subtraction operations (line 19) and doing these on the RHS vector V( ) (line 17) as well yields the solution.

Note that the RHS line numbers are for reference purposes only and are not part of the program and must be removed before it can be run.

13. Finite Element Networks

```
DIM NN(20, 2), R(20), C(20, 20), V(20)               1
a$ = "###": b$ = "######.###"                        2
READ NP, NE, NS                                      3
FOR K = 1 TO NE                                      4
READ I, J, R: NN(K, 1) = I: NN(K, 2) = J: R(K) = R   5
C(I, I) = C(I, I) + 1 / R: C(I, J) = C(I, J) - 1 / R 6
C(J, I) = C(J, I) - 1 / R: C(J, J) = C(J, J) + 1 / R 7
NEXT                                                 8
FOR K = 1 TO NS: READ N, S                           9
FOR I = 1 TO NP                                     10
C(N, I) = 0: V(I) = V(I) - S * C(I, N)              11
C(I, N) = 0: NEXT I                                 12
V(N) = S: C(N, N) = 1: NEXT                         13
FOR I = 1 TO NP: X = C(I, I): V(I) = V(I) / X       14
FOR J = I + 1 TO NP: C(I, J) = C(I, J) / X: NEXT    15
FOR K = 1 TO NP: IF K = I THEN GOTO NEXK            16
X = C(K, I): V(K) = V(K) - X * V(I)                 17
FOR J = I + 1 TO NP                                 18
C(K, J) = C(K, J) - X * C(I, J): NEXT J             19
NEXK: NEXT K: NEXT I                                20
PRINT " Node   Voltage"                             21
FOR I = 1 TO NP                                     22
PRINT USING a$; I; : PRINT USING b$; V(I): NEXT I   23
PRINT " Element  Current"                           24
FOR K = 1 TO NE: I = NN(K, 1): J = NN(K, 2)         25
Q = -(V(J) - V(I)) / R                              26
PRINT USING a$; I; J; : PRINT USING b$; Q: NEXT     27
DATA 4,4,2                                          28
DATA 1,2,1, 1,3,1, 2,4,1, 3,4,1                     29
DATA 1,1, 4,0                                       30
```

The data appended to the program (lines 28 - 30) is for the problem of Figure 13.1 for which the solution is $V_2 = V_3 = 0.5$ and currents = 0.5 for each element.

13. FINITE ELEMENT NETWORKS

FINITE ELEMENT DISTRIBUTION MODELS

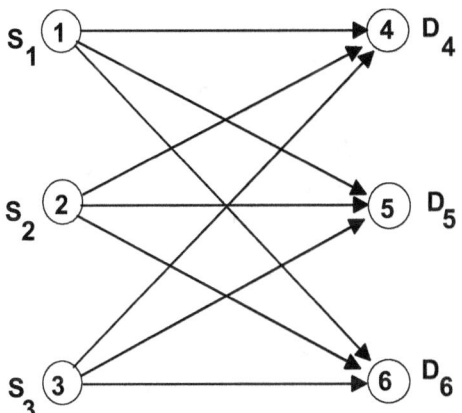

Figure 13.2. Distribution network.

Fig 13.2 shows a distribution network for which the data is given in Table 13.1.

Table 13.1. Distribution problem data.

Unit costs			Supplies
5	10	10	110 [1]
20	30	20	160 [2]
10	20	30	150 [3]
140 [4]	200 [5]	80 [6]	
Demands			

Using the 'direct' Linear Programming (LP) program given in the penultimate section of Chapter 12 the optimum solution (giving minimum total transportation cost, $T = 6700$) is found to have route flows:

$$15 = 110,\ 25 = 80,\ 26 = 80,\ 34 = 140,\ 35 = 10 \tag{13.1}$$

and the number of non zero route flows
= number of supply points + number of demand points −1
as is always the case in this type of problem.

13. FINITE ELEMENT NETWORKS

Using this solution to write the supply and demand constraints Σflows in/out = node supply/demand in matrix form as

(13.2) $\quad A\{q\} = \begin{bmatrix} 1 & 0 & 0 & 0 & 0 \\ 0 & 1 & 1 & 0 & 0 \\ 0 & 0 & 0 & 1 & 1 \\ 0 & 0 & 0 & 1 & 0 \\ 1 & 1 & 0 & 0 & 1 \\ 0 & 0 & 1 & 0 & 0 \end{bmatrix} \begin{Bmatrix} q_{15} \\ q_{25} \\ q_{26} \\ q_{34} \\ q_{35} \end{Bmatrix} = \begin{Bmatrix} 110 \\ 160 \\ 150 \\ 140 \\ 200 \\ 80 \end{Bmatrix}$

each route flow can be expressed, using Mohr's First (flow) Law of Distribution, as a function of the 'potentials' V_i, V_j at each node,

$$q_{ij} = (V_i - V_j)/c_{ij} \qquad (13.3)$$

Taking all $c_{ij} = 1$, we can write the *basis transformation*

$$\{q\} = \begin{Bmatrix} q_{15} \\ q_{25} \\ q_{26} \\ q_{34} \\ q_{35} \end{Bmatrix} = \begin{bmatrix} 1 & 0 & 0 & 0 & -1 & 0 \\ 0 & 1 & 0 & 0 & -1 & 0 \\ 0 & 1 & 0 & 0 & 0 & -1 \\ 0 & 0 & 1 & -1 & 0 & 0 \\ 0 & 0 & 1 & 0 & -1 & 0 \end{bmatrix} \begin{Bmatrix} V_1 \\ V_2 \\ V_3 \\ V_4 \\ V_5 \\ V_6 \end{Bmatrix} = T\{v\} \quad (13.4)$$

Substituting Equation 13.4 into Equation 13.2, first reversing the signs of the bottom three rows of A (note that now $A = T^t$), we obtain $K\{V\} = A T\{V\} =$

$$\begin{bmatrix} 1 & 0 & 0 & 0 & -1 & 0 \\ 0 & 2 & 0 & 0 & -1 & -1 \\ 0 & 0 & 2 & -1 & -1 & 0 \\ 0 & 0 & -1 & 1 & 0 & 0 \\ -1 & -1 & -1 & 0 & 3 & 0 \\ 0 & -1 & 0 & 0 & 0 & 1 \end{bmatrix} \begin{Bmatrix} V_1 \\ V_2 \\ V_3 \\ V_4 \\ V_5 \\ V_6 \end{Bmatrix} = \begin{Bmatrix} 110 \\ 160 \\ 150 \\ -140 \\ -200 \\ -80 \end{Bmatrix} = \{Q\} \quad (13.5)$$

13. FINITE ELEMENT NETWORKS

which is exactly the same result (for K) as is obtained by summing element matrices of the form

$$k_{ij} = (1/c_{ij})\begin{bmatrix} 1 & -1 \\ -1 & 1 \end{bmatrix} \qquad (13.6)$$

(with all $c_{ij} = 1$) for the optimum network (i.e., with only the five flows of Equation 13.1).

So it transpires that we can use the program given for DC networks to model distribution problems simply by replacing resistance R by route unit cost c_{ij}. Then the 'loads' are the nodal supplies and demands (with inflow taken as positive) specified as such for each node and the boundary condition is simply $V = 0$ at the last node (6 here) as a datum for V.

Modelling the optimum network (5 routes) it is found that the routes can now have any unit costs and the flows remain the same. If all $c_{ij} = 10$ the nodal potentials are

$$V_1 = 300, V_2 = 1600, V_3 = -600, V_4 = -2000, V_5 = -800, V_6 = 0 \qquad (13.7)$$

(the latter being the boundary condition) and the 'reaction' at node 6 = -80, as expected. That we can have any costs here corresponds to a *statically determinate structure* in structural mechanics. Here we shall call it a *minimum system*.

Table 13.2. Route flows in FEM distribution model

	4	5	6
1	23.4	77.9	8.7
2	52.3	56.9	50.8
3	64.3	65/2	20.5

If all 9 original routes (with the costs of Table 13.1) are included, however, the solution is that shown in Table 13.2, with total cost $T = 7313$ (Mohr, 2000).

We now have a very useful means of modelling distribution problems, and using the steepest descent method they can then be optimized, as shown in Chapter 15.

13. FINITE ELEMENT NETWORKS

Indeed, the FEM model can be used to obtain 'better than optimal' solutions. In Figure 13.1 using only the routes of Equation 13.1 and increasing supply at node 1 by 20 units, we obtain route flows

$$15 = 130, 25 = 60, 26 = 100, 34 = 140, 35 = 10$$

and total cost T is still = 6700, a more efficient result.

Note that the here the boundary flow at node 6 increases to 100 to take this supply increase. Alternatively, if we specify demand of 160 at node 4, the solution has a 'back flow' and is

$$15 = 130, 25 = 80, 26 = 80, 34 = 160, 35 = -10$$

Here, then, we have here an important but simple new application of the powerful finite element method.

FINITE ELEMENT TRAFFIC FLOW MODELS

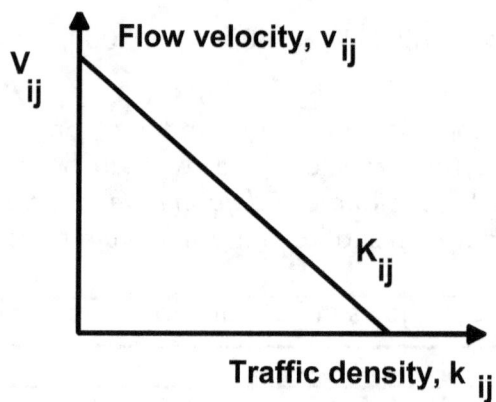

Figure 13.3. Linear traffic flow law.

The classical linear flow rule for traffic flow illustrated in Figure 13.3 is

$$v_{ij} = V_{ij}(1 - k_{ij}/K_{ij}) \tag{13.8}$$

where v_{ij} and k_{ij} are the element traffic velocity and density and V_{ij} and K_{ij} are respectively the element *free flow velocity* and *jam density*.

13. FINITE ELEMENT NETWORKS

The flow in the element is given by $q_{ij} = k_{ij} v_{ij}$ so that the equations for each element are

$$\begin{Bmatrix} q_i \\ q_j \end{Bmatrix} = (K_{ij} V_{ij}/L_{ij}) \begin{bmatrix} 1 & -1 \\ -1 & 1 \end{bmatrix} \begin{Bmatrix} P_i \\ P_j \end{Bmatrix} \qquad (13.9)$$

where q_i, q_j are the inflows at each end, L_{ij} is the route length and P_i, P_j are arbitrary potentials at the element nodes.

Thus the problem is analogous to that of a DC network, where now $L_{ij}/(K_{ij} V_{ij})$ plays the role of the element resistance, and to model a network the element matrices are deployed according to their node numbers to form a system matrix for the network.

Figure 13.4 shows a simple example network with the nodal flows shown, positive flows being inwards. The same free flow velocity $V_f = 60$ is assumed for all elements. A single boundary condition $P = 0$ is set at the last node as a datum and the in and out flows are the 'load' data. The system equations are solved to determine the nodal potentials P_i from which the element flows are calculated using

$$q_{ij} = R_{ij} (P_i - P_j), \text{ where } R_{ij} = K_{ij} V_f / L_{ij} \qquad (13.10)$$

Then solving the quadratic equation

$$q_{ij} = k_{ij} v_{ij} = k_{ij} V_f (1 - k_{ij}/K_j) \qquad (13.11)$$

two roots k_a and k_b and their corresponding velocities v_a and v_b are obtained. In the present work the feasible root is the larger velocity v_b and, using this, the total travel time in the network is calculated as

$$T = \Sigma \, |q_{ij}| \, L_{ij}/|v_b| \qquad (13.12)$$

13. FINITE ELEMENT NETWORKS

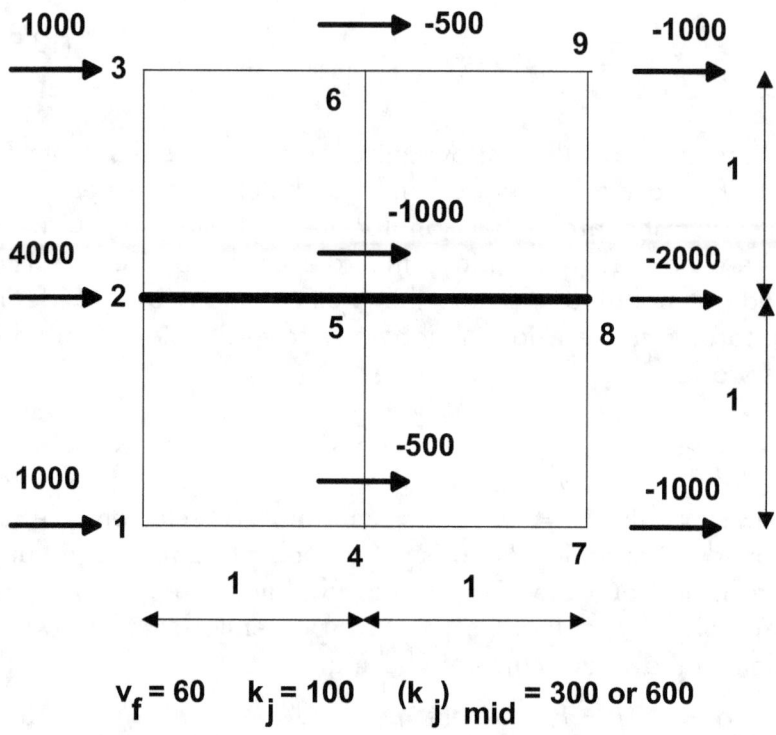

Figure 13.4. Traffic flow network.

The results are shown in Table 13.3. In case (b) we have upgraded the centre routes 25, 58 (by increasing their jam densities from 300 to 600) and the flow changes are as expected, the flows in these centre routes increasing and the total travel time in the system decreasing significantly.

13. Finite Element Networks

Table 13.3. Solutions for the route flows in Figure 13.4.

Route	(a) mid k_i = 300			(b) mid k_i = 600		
	Flow	k_2	v_2	Flow	k_2	v_2
12	-178.6	3.07	-58.16	60.4	1.02	59.39
23	178.6	3.07	58.16	-60.4	1.02	-59.39
14	1178.6	26.85	43.89	939.6	19.44	48.34
45	-142.9	2.44	-58.54	-192.3	3.32	-58.01
36	1178.6	26.85	43.89	939.6	19.44	48.34
56	142.9	2.44	58.54	192.3	3.32	58.01
25	3642.9	84.54	43.09	4120.9	79.11	52.09
58	2357.1	46.49	50.70	2736.3	49.73	55.03
47	821.5	16.37	50.18	631.9	11.96	52.82
69	821.5	16.37	50.18	631.9	11.96	52.82
78	-178.6	3.07	-58.16	-368.1	6.57	-56.06
89	178.6	3.07	58.16	368.1	6.57	-56.06

Total travel time   234.63 hours   213.44 hours

Conclusion

The Finite Element Method is a powerful method of modelling widely used in engineering, mathematics and physics. Its application has been extended to distribution problems (Mohr, 1999a), input-output analysis (Mohr, 1999b) and traffic flow networks (Mohr, 2004b). In these latter applications such models help *decisions* to be made about alteration or removal of elements of a system, in other words quite literally an exercise in 'elementary thinking'.

DC networks are probably the simplest possible application of FEM and the simple problem of Figure 13.1 may be likened to the proposed precedence memory model of Figure 3.5.

13. FINITE ELEMENT NETWORKS

Using the flow rule of Mohr's First Law of Distribution, product distribution networks can be modelled in the same way as DC networks with the supplies at supply points specified as inflows to the network and the demands at demand points specified as outflows from it.

Distribution problems are usually optimized using Linear Programming and this eliminates almost half the supply routes. This is not always practical and it is much more important to model the distribution network as we have here so that we can then model the effect of changes in supplies and demands.

Traffic flow networks can also be modelled using FEM in much the same way as DC networks, perhaps the most important advance in the relatively new field of traffic engineering.

In the next chapter two general optimization techniques, one of them new, which can be applied to FEM distribution and traffic flow models are discussed.

Chapter 14

OPTIMIZATION TECHNIQUES

THE STEEPEST DESCENT METHOD

The method of steepest descent is one of the most fundamental methods available for nonlinear optimization problems. This is a *first order gradient method* which is based on allowing a *perturbation*

$$|\delta x| = \sqrt{(\Sigma\ \delta x^2)} \qquad (14.1)$$

in the vector of (design) variables, resulting in the *objective function* altering by an amount

$$\delta f = \Sigma\ (\partial f/\partial x_i)(\delta x_i) + \lambda(\Sigma(\delta x^2 - \Delta^2) \qquad (14.2)$$

where Δ is the optimum perturbation, that is, that for which

$$\partial(\delta f)/\partial(\delta x_i) = 0 = \partial f/\partial x_i + 2\lambda\ (\delta x_i) \quad i = 1 \to n \qquad (14,3)$$

from which it follows that

$$\{\delta x_i\} = -\{\partial f/\partial x_i\}/2\lambda = -\ (\text{constant})\{g\} \qquad (14.4)$$

so that the greatest change in the objective function results from search in the direction of the *gradient vector* $\{g\}$.

In practice numerical methods are usually used to calculate the gradient vector approximately, perturbing each variable in turn by an amount δx_i and noting the change in the objective function δf_i. Then the gradient vector is estimated by the first order *finite difference* approximations

$$\{g\} = \{\delta f_i/\delta x_i\} \qquad (14.5)$$

this being a simple example of the 'vector search methods', many of which use a combination of $\{g\}$ and the vector normal to it as a search direction.

As a simple example of the steepest descent method suppose we wish to minimize the function

$$F = (x_1 - 2)^2 + (x_2 - 1)^2 \qquad (14.6)$$

The minimum is very obvious but assuming otherwise the steepest descent search procedure is written using a step length S as

$$\left\{\begin{array}{c} x_1 \\ x_2 \end{array}\right\}_n = \left\{\begin{array}{c} x_1 \\ x_2 \end{array}\right\}_{n-1} - S \left\{\begin{array}{c} \partial f/\partial x_1 = 2x_1 - 4 \\ \partial f/\partial x_2 = 2x_2 - 2 \end{array}\right\} \qquad (14.7)$$

where here the required partial derivatives are known explicitly (but in general would be calculated by the perturbation process of Equation 14.5).

Then beginning at the point (3,3) with $S = 0.2$ Equation 14.7 becomes:

$$\left\{\begin{array}{c} x_1 \\ x_2 \end{array}\right\} = \left\{\begin{array}{c} 3 \\ 3 \end{array}\right\} - 0.2 \left\{\begin{array}{c} 2 \\ 4 \end{array}\right\} = \left\{\begin{array}{c} 2.6 \\ 2.2 \end{array}\right\} \qquad (14.8)$$

yielding $f = 1.80$. Continuing with gradually increased step lengths the results shown in Table 14.1 are obtained.

Table 14.1. Results for steepest descent example.

S	x_1	x_2	f
0	3	3	5
0.2	2.6	2.2	1.8
0.4	2.2	1.4	0.2
0.6	1.8	0.6	0.2
0.8	1.4	-0.2	1.8
0.5	2	1	0

14. Optimization Techniques

Here with $s = 0.6$ we might suspect something but we proceed with $s = 0.8$ just to make sure. Now it is clear that a turning point has been passed, if not earlier, and *bisection* is used with $S = 0.5$ which in this case yields the correct solution.

Though this problem appears trivial it makes a useful computer exercise if the gradient vector is calculated numerically using perturbations in x_1 and x_2.

In this simple example only one search direction was needed but generally several must be used successively.

Constrained nonlinear problems

Constrained nonlinear optimization problems can be solved using Fiacco and McCormick's SUMT or *Sequence of Unconstrained Minima Technique* in which constraints are factored by *penalty factors* and added to the objective function. Then search techniques are used with a gradually increased value of the penalty factor to locate the optimum solution with increasing accuracy.

Exterior point methods

In these calculations begin from an exterior point (from the feasible region) and we seek to minimize the function

$$F(x) = f(x) + \beta \Sigma \mid c_i(x) \mid^2 + \beta \Sigma [e_j(x)]^2 \qquad (14.9)$$

where here | | denotes a *step function* which is zero when the inequality constraints $c_i(x)$ are not violated, $e_i(x)$ denotes an equality constraint and β is a penalty factor.

Then the SUMT technique involves solving the problem as though it were unconstrained using, for example, the steepest descent method with a sequence of gradually increasing values of the penalty factor.

If we begin with $\beta = 0$, for example, we would first obtain the unconstrained minimum. Then as β approaches infinity the constraints will take control of the solution if appropriate (in view of the use of a step function for the inequality constraints).

14. OPTIMIZATION TECHNIQUES

Interior point methods

With these SUMT is first applied to the task of minimizing

$$C = \Sigma s_i + \Sigma [e_i(x)]^2 \qquad (14.10)$$

where s_i are slack variables associated with the inequality constraints. This finds a feasible point and then we seek to minimize the function

$$F(x) = f(x) + \beta \Sigma[1/c_i(x)] + \beta^{-1/2} \Sigma \ |e_i(x)|^2 \qquad (14.11)$$

and now the inverted form of the term for the inequality constraints provides a *response surface* which prevents access to infeasible regions.

Many such slight variations of the SUMT approach have been suggested but we shall restrict attention to the basic form of Equation 14.9.

STEEPEST DESCENT EXAMPLE

As an example we use SUMT to tackle the problem

$$\text{Min. } f = (x_1 - 3)^2 + (x_2 - 3)^2 + (x_3 - 3)^2 \qquad (14.12)$$

subject to the constraints

$$1 + (x_1 - 1)^2/2 + (x_2 - 2)^2/2 - x_3 \geq 0 \qquad (14.13a)$$

$$6 - x_1 - x_2/2 - x_3 = 0 \qquad (14.13b)$$

$$3 + x_1 x_2/4 - x_3 \leq 0 \qquad (14.13c)$$

Equations 14.12 and 14.13 can be differentiated to obtain explicit expressions for the gradients of the augmented (by the constraints multiplied by the penalty factor) objective function. These gradients can then be used to obtain solutions by trial search (with additional programming this can be automated).

Better results are obtained (Table 14.2) by using perturbations of each *design variable* in turn (by about 1 to 5%) and calculating approximate gradients from the *finite difference* approximations $g_i = (F_2 - F_1)/\delta x_i$ for each variable i.

14. OPTIMIZATION TECHNIQUES

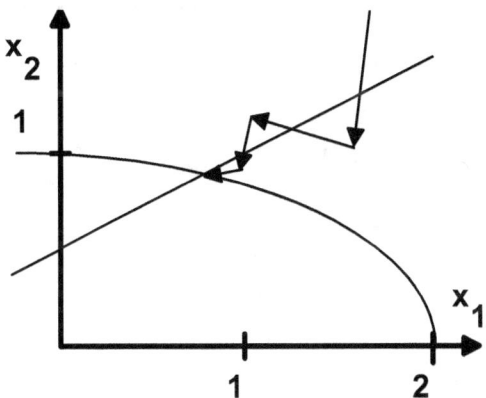

Figure 14.1. Typical progress of steepest descent method.

Plotting the progress of the solution for two variables the steepest descent method gives a 'criss-cross' result like that shown in Figure 14.1 and the methods such as the *conjugate gradient method* seek to obtain a 'more direct' solution.

CONJUGATE GRADIENT METHOD

Many 'compound' gradient methods have been developed. One of the earliest examples of these was the *conjugate gradient method* in which the modified gradient vector is given by

$$\{g\}^* = \{g\} - \{g\}^t\{g\}\{h\}/\{h\}^t\{h\} \qquad (14.14)$$

where $\{h\}$ is the gradient vector used in the previous search.

First, Table 14.2 shows the results obtained for the problem of equations (14.12) and (14.13) using the method of steepest descent, starting at point (1,1,1) and using *move limit* $M = 1.01$ to obtain a reasonably good approximate solution (with $M = 1.1$ only five searches were needed but the result was less accurate).

14. Optimization Techniques

Table 14.2. Results for problem of Equations 14.12 - 14.13.

β	S	x_1	x_2	x_3	F
Steepest descent					
1	0.14	2.3796	1.8907	3.1658	4.2631
	0.10	2.6412	1.9222	2.9720	3.6909
100	0.58	2.3891	0.5509	3.0373	23.8181
	0.22	2.5046	0.5330	3.2666	7.3386
	0.095	2.5056	0.5084	3.2512	6.9825
	0.21	2.4943	0.4925	3.2510	6.9281
	0.83	2.4840	0.4751	3.2756	6.7697
Conjugate gradient					
1	0.14	2.3796	1.8907	3.1658	4.2631
	0.10	2.6132	1.9041	2.9281	3.7179
100	0.61	2.4244	0.4941	3.1196	14.2246
	0.20	2.5036	0.5550	3.2548	7.9206
	0.074	2.5027	0.5243	3.2330	7.3565
	0.52	2.4889	0.4757	3.2775	6.7516
'Exact'	β = 10^5	2.4839	0.4604	3.2859	6.7977

The 'exact' solution was the average solution obtained using exact gradients, alternative starting points, move limit M = 1.01 and β = 10^n, n = 1,2,3,4,5, resulting in a process of 20 or more searches. This solution satisfies Equation 14.13b and almost Equations 14.13a and 14.13c as equalities so that using x_2 = 0.4604 in Equations 13.14a and 13.14c as simultaneous (=) equations gives the other values of this 'exact' solution. Note that the F value for this solution was for β = 10^5, not β = 100, and thus this is a good result.

The approximate solution is satisfactory and note in passing that the solution (3,0,3) satisfies the constraints, giving F = f = 9, a good example of an approximate solution which might be useful in practice.

Next the results using the conjugate gradient method of Equation 14.14 are given. The early results are similar and a good approximate solution is obtained with one less search.

14. Optimization Techniques

The QBASIC coding for this solution is:

```
10 N = 3: DIM X(N), G(N), H(N): REM SUMT program
15 M = 1.01
20 FOR I = 1 TO N: READ X(I): NEXT: DATA 1,1,1
30 INPUT "i/p B", B: D = M - 1: IF B = 99 THEN END
35 FOR I = 1 TO N: H(I) = 0: NEXT
40 S1 = 0: F1 = 0: GOSUB CALC: FA = F
45 REM Gosub EXACT:Goto 65
50 FOR I = 1 TO N: X(I) = X(I) * M: GOSUB CALC
60 X(I) = X(I) / M: G(I) = (F - FA) / (X(I) * D): NEXT
65 GOSUB CONJG
70 INPUT "i/p S ", S: IF S = 0 THEN 40
75 IF S = 99 THEN 30
77 S = S / B
80 FOR I = 1 TO N: X(I) = X(I) + (S1 - S) * G(I): NEXT
90 GOSUB CALC: DF = F - F1: PRINT X1, X2, X3, " f,df = ", F, DF
100 S1 = S: F1 = F: GOTO 70: END
110 CALC: X1 = X(1): X2 = X(2): X3 = X(3)
120 C = 1 + (X1 - 1) ^ 2 / 2 + (X2 - 2) ^ 2 / 2 - X3: IF C > 0 THEN C = 0
130 E = 6 - X1 - X2 / 2 - X3
140 L = 3 + X1 * X2 / 4 - X3: IF L < 0 THEN L = 0
150 U = (X1 - 3) ^ 2 + (X2 - 3) ^ 2 + (X3 - 3) ^ 2
160 F = U + B * (C * C + E * E + L * L): RETURN
170 EXACT: G(1) = 2*(X1 - 3) + 2*B*(X1 - 1)* C - 2 * B * E + B * X2 * L / 2
180 G(2) = 2 * (X2 - 3) + 2 * B * (X2 - 2) * C - B * E + B * X1 * L / 2
190 G(3) = 2 * (X3 - 3) - 2 * B * C - 2 * B * E - 2 * B * L
200 RETURN
210 CONJG: X = 0: Y = 0
220 FOR I = 1 TO N: X = X + G(I) * G(I)
230 Y = Y + H(I) * H(I): NEXT
240 IF Y = 0 THEN 260
250 FOR I = 1 TO N: G(I) = G(I) - X * H(I) / Y: NEXT
260 FOR I = 1 TO N: H(I) = G(I): NEXT
270 RETURN
```

The coordinates of the starting point and value of M are set in the program. Computation starts with request for the penalty value B, followed by search length S. Gradually increasing values of S are input until a turning point is passed, when the approximate value of S for the turning point is input, followed by a zero S to terminate the search, except where this is to be the last search with the current B value, when S = 99 is input.

Then to terminate the program S = 99 and B = 99 are input.

Note that by omitting line 65 (by inserting REM after the line number) the first steepest descent results of Table 14.2 are obtained. Note also that a subroutine to compute the exact gradients is included.

OPTIMALITY CRITERION METHODS

In *Optimality Criterion Methods* (OCM) analysis to determine the values of the variables of a mathematical model is iterated, adjusting chosen parameters of the model according to some *optimality criterion*. Generally, such methods do not obtain an optimum solution in the mathematical sense but they do yield improved solutions which are often close to the optimum solution and, in some cases, may prove to be a more practical result.

Fully stressed design

In cost-benefit analysis the criterion of constant ratio of benefit r_i and cost c_i for all components i of a plan of operations is well known.

Similar results apply elsewhere in mathematics, for example the pioneering paper by Michell (1904) in which it is shown that optimal building truss structures will have all their components equally stressed. The optimal solutions obtained by Michell involved structures consisting of orthogonal sets of curves intersecting at right angles, but it has since been shown that with relaxed boundary conditions the solutions are trusses with straight members as generally used in practice.

Then in other types of structures this criterion is often used, this process being called *Fully Stressed Design* (FSD), and after each analysis of the structure to determine the member stresses the sizes of the members are adjusted according, for example, to the ratio

$$t_{i+1} = t_i \, (S_i/S^*) \tag{14.15}$$

where t_i is the element thickness (the adjusted dimension) in the ith iteration, S_i its stress in this iteration and S^* is the upper stress limit. Then, in many problems convergence to an approximately optimal solution is obtained after a few iterations.

This same approach is useful in many other contexts, but retaining the FSD case as an example, the steps are:

[1] Establish an optimality criterion. In FSD this is that stress S = force/cross section area (for the example of a rod in tension or compression) should be approximately equal to some limiting value S^* for safety, in every part of the system.

[2] Analyze the structure and determine the stress in every member. Then:
(a) Where member stress > S^* increase the member cross section
(b) Where member stress < S^* decrease the member cross section

[3] Continue, repeating step (2) until member stresses are all approximately equal to S^* and/or the structure 'weight' $W = \Sigma \, A_i L_i$ stops changing (converges), here denoting A_i = cross section areas of members, L_i = their length and omitting the (constant) material density.

This approach is sometimes called *stress ratio design* and with such methods of iterative solution many other slight refinements to help guide us towards a realistic and sensible solution can be included, such as the following:

[1] *Move limits* that limit the changes in member areas (in the FSD example) allowed in any one step.

[2] *Section limits* A_{min}, that is minimum and perhaps maximum allowed values of A.

[3] *Convergence factors* that multiply the amount by which a member area is changed (compared to the value suggested by calculation), these usually having a value circa 0.8.

With some types of iterative numerical method an *overconvergence factor* greater than one is used.

14. Optimization Techniques

Common values of this range from 1.2 to 1.8, for example making the change in member area in FSD 1.5 times the amount suggested by its stress ratio S/S^* with a view to speeding up the solution. In other rather more exceptional cases an *under convergence factor* less than one is used to prevent oscillation in the solution.

FRD FOR FEM DISTRIBUTION MODELS

The flow ratio design method (FRD) was devised by Mohr (2004b) to approximately optimize FEM distribution models iteratively. For these the element constitutive parameters are their unit costs and for minimization these are adjusted at each iteration using Mohr's second (optimality criterion) law of distribution

$$c_{ij}^* = c_{ij}(q_m / |q_{ij}|) \tag{14.16}$$

where q_m is the 'median' flow in the network:

$$q_m \approx q_{av}/2 \tag{14.17}$$

and q_{av} is the average flow in the network:

$$q_{av} = \Sigma Q / N \tag{14.18}$$

where ΣQ is the total flow in the network of N routes (and = sum of supply flows S_i = sum of demand flows D_i).

Then to obtain the minimum solution lower and upper route cost limits

$$c_L = c_{av}/40 - c_{av}/10, \quad c_U = 10^6 \tag{14.19}$$

where $c_{av} = \Sigma c_{ij}/N$, are used.

For maximization $c_{ij} = c_{ij}(|q_{ij}|/q_m)$ is used to adjust the element unit costs and the lower limit c_L is chosen from 10 to 100% of the value used for minimization and the upper limit is chosen in the range $5(c_{av})$ to $100(c_{av})$ using the value 100 in the examples studied in the present work.

In the *dual problem* c_{ij} is replaced by its inverse in Equation 14.16.

14. OPTIMIZATION TECHNIQUES

Observing these limits iteration proceeds and some routes vanish as their c_{ij} values approach c_U, flows $q_{ij} < 0.001$ being set to zero prior to calculating the total distribution cost

$$T_0 = \sum |q_{ij}|(c_{ij})_0 \qquad (14.20)$$

where $(c_{ij})_0$ are the initial unit costs for each route.

When sufficient routes have dropped out the solution for the total cost T_0 and the route flows do not change with further iteration and an approximate optimum solution has been obtained.

Note that the lower limit 0.001 for q_{ij} was used with 8 d.p. computation and a value of 0.01 gave the same results and might be needed with less accurate computation.

CONCLUSIONS

The Linear Programming (LP) method has limited application but can be used to obtain the exact MIN and MAX solutions for distribution problems and a 'direct' LP method for these was given in Chapter 12.

It is more important to model distribution systems, however, as is done using FEM in the previous chapter.

Then steepest descent or the new FRD method can be applied to these models and this is done in the next chapter.

More important, steepest descent and FRD can be applied to a wide variety of other problems. By applying perturbations in variables in a complicated spreadsheet, for example, it may be possible to optimize the 'bottom line' using a steepest descent approach.

FRD might be applied to any retail business, for example, to adjust the costs of items according to their 'flow' or sales rate in order to approximately optimize the overall sales results.

Finally, the steepest descent method is a very basic one and the conjugate gradient method involves little additional coding and should generally be more efficient, especially for larger problems.

# 14. Optimization Techniques

Chapter 15

OPTIMAL NETWORKS

OPTIMIZING FEM DISTRIBUTION MODELS

The FEM distribution models developed in Chapter 13 can be optimized using the method of steepest descent. The merit function is the sum of the route 'cost flows'

$$F = T = \Sigma\, c_{ij} q_{ij} \qquad (15.1)$$

Defining an *element access* parameter A_{ij}, with initially $A_{ij}^0 = c_{ij}$ at the beginning of each search, using perturbations of each A_{ij}^0 the gradient vector is given by

$$\{g_{ij}\} = \{\delta f/\delta A_{ij}\} \qquad (15.2)$$

where $\delta A_{ij} = (M - 1)A_{ij}$

with M a move limit for which the value 1.1 is used for the present application, solving the system equations $K\{V\} = \{Q\}$ at each perturbation to determine δf.

Then trial search is conducted with a gradually increasing *search length S*, using

$$A_{ij}' = A_{ij}^0 - S\{g\} \qquad (15.3)$$

seeking a turning point in f.

If during search a negative route flow is detected we set $c_{ij} = A_{ij} = 0$ for that route and omit it from the model, also setting a flag which returns to calculation of a new gradient vector, the model having changed. Note that such element omission is disallowed during calculation of the gradient vector using Equation 15.2.

15. Optimal Networks

Dual models and maximization

Now our simple model permits two immediate variations:
1. Simply by using a positive sign in Equation 15.3 we can obtain maximum solutions.
2. Simply by using c_{ij} in place of $(1/c_{ij})$ as the constitutive parameter for the element matrices we obtain the *dual model*.

Now we can obtain both MIN and MAX solutions for primal distribution models and for dual distribution models as well.

Table 15.1. Distribution problem data.

Unit costs			Supplies
5	10	10	110 [1]
20	30	20	160 [2]
10	20	30	150 [3]
140 [4]	200 [5]	80 [6]	
Demands			

The results of FEM analysis of the distribution problem of Table 15.1 were given in Table 13.2. Analysis of the dual model (that is, with c_{ij} in place of $1/c_{ij}$) gives the route flows shown in Table 15.2, these having a total cost $T = 7930$.

Table 15.2. Route flows in dual FEM distribution model.

	4	5	6
1	29.3	51	29.7
2	68.7	80.3	11
3	42	68.7	39.3

In place of the nodal voltage values we have 'nodal currents' (that is, dual variables of the 'voltage/resistance' type). The values for the dual of the optimum primal network corresponding to Equations 13.1 are

$$\{ C^* \} = \{ 12.333, 4, 1.833, -12.167, 1.333, 0 \} \quad (15.4)$$

for which the route flows are calculated using Equation 13.3 with c_{ij} replaced by its inverse, giving the expected values:

$15 = 110$, $25 = 80$, $26 = 80$, $34 = 140$, $35 = 10$

15. OPTIMAL NETWORKS

Thus the nodal current values at nodes 2 & 5 are given by
$$C^*_2 = C^*_6 + q_{26}/c_{26} \qquad (15.5a)$$
$$C^*_5 = C^*_2 - q_{25}/c_{25} \qquad (15.5b)$$
and so on.

The four possible optimum results for the problem of Table 15.1 are compared with the exact solutions obtained by linear programming in Table 15.3. Note that some flows are midway between the two possible 'exact' MIN and MAX solutions.

Table 15.3. Solutions for primal & dual problem of Table 15.1.

Primal MIN					
S^*	0		0.4	0.7	0.7*
T	7,313		7198	6981	6700
flows	0, 110, 0 / 45, 35, 80 / 95, 55, 0				
Exact	0, 110, 0 / 0, 80, 80 / 140, 10, 0				6700
Dual MIN					
S^*	0		0.3	0.9	0.6*
T	7930		7792	7226	6700
flows	0, 110, 0 / 69.3, 10.7, 80/ 70.7, 79.3, 0				
Exact	0, 110, 0 / 80, 0, 80 / 60, 90, 0				
Primal MAX					
S^*	0		2.0	2.7	1.9	1.6*
T	7317		7335	7770	7570	8850
flows	110, 0, 0 / 0, 160, 0 / 30, 40, 80				
Exact	110, 0, 0 / 30, 130, 0 / 0, 70, 80				8850
Dual MAX					
S^*	0		0.4	0.7	1.1*
T	7930		8112	8495	8850
flows	110, 0, 0, 27.1, 132.9, 0/2.9, 67.1, 80				
Exact	110, 0, 0 / 0, 160, 0 / 30, 40, 80				

Note that the last search lengths in Table 15.3 (shown with an asterisk) should be done twice to 'smooth' the route flow results.

15. Optimal Networks

Use of FEM, of course, allows much more general models to be studied. If in the problem of Table 15.1 additional (one-way) routes 12, 21, 23, 32, 45, 54, 56, 65 are included with unit cost of 5, the resulting minimum solution obtained using search lengths

$S^* = 0, 0.15, 0.20, 0.30, 0.30, 0.30, 0.80, 0.01$

is shown in Figure 15.1.

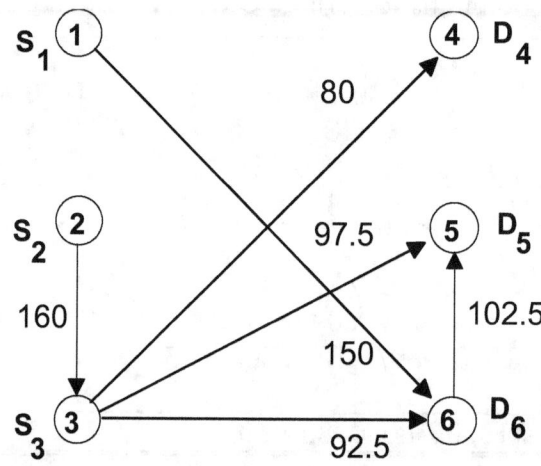

Figure 15.1. Solution for modified network.

Here points 3 and 6 have become *transfer points* to avoid the more costly direct routes from node 2. The total cost is reduced to 5050 (from 6700), an excellent example of the use of FEM models to obtain alternative solutions.

Program for Optimization of FEM Models

The solutions of Table 15.3 were obtained using the following program, an extension of that given in Chapter 13 for DC networks.

The element matrices are assembled to form the system matrix in lines 155 and 165. Boundary condition 'reactions' and the nodal 'loads' are added to the 'RHS' vector V( ) in lines 180-220.

15. OPTIMAL NETWORKS

Perturbation of variables occurs in lines 80 and 82 and the gradient vector is calculated in line 90. In line 115 search is conducted by simply using gradually increasing trial search lengths.

Element flows are calculated in line 355 and when an element is omitted (for having negative flow) this is signaled by an additional output line (giving the value of total cost TC) and we know to begin a new search. When no more members can be omitted, that is, we have a *minimum system,* the solution will not change with further search.

Key program variables are

NP,NE,NS # of nodes, elements & boundary condition nodes
M   perturbation magnitude for gradient calculation
         (= 1.1 in line 10)
RC( )   element unit costs
RA( )   element 'access' parameters = unit costs at start of search
C( )   system matrix
Q( )   nodal 'loads'
V( )   nodal 'potentials' (after solution)
IB( )   boundary condition flags =1 for boundary condition node
NN( )   element node numbers
SPEC( ) specified potentials for boundary condition nodes
         (here = 0 for last node)
G( )   gradient values for each element
         (determined by steepest descent)
TC   total cost for the network flows

```
5 REM FEM model of distribution networks
10 M = 1.1: Y = .1: REM Lines 115, 152 & 352 are 'case change' lines
15 DIM C(20, 20), V(20), IB(20)
20 DIM RC(20), NN(20, 2), RA(20), SPEC(20), Q(20), G(20)
25 REM RESTORE 1000
30 READ NP, NE, NS
35 FOR K = 1 TO NE
40 READ I, J, R: RC(K) = R: RA(K) = R
45 NN(K, 1) = I: NN(K, 2) = J: NEXT
50 FOR I = 1 TO NS: READ N, S: SPEC(N) = S: IB(N) = 1: NEXT
55 READ NQ, F: IF NQ = 0 THEN GOTO 65
```

15. Optimal Networks

```
60 Q(NQ) = F: GOTO 55
65 S1 = 0: FOR I = 1 TO NE: RA(I) = RC(I): NEXT
FLAG = 0: GF = 1: S = 0
70 cflag = 1: GOTO 135
72 F1 = TC: PRINT TC: Z = 0
75 Z = Z + 1: IF Z > NE THEN GOTO 102
77 IF RA(Z) = 0 THEN GOTO 100
80 RA(Z) = RA(Z) * M: cflag = 2: GOTO 135
82 RA(Z) = RA(Z) / M
90 G(Z) = (TC - F1) / ((M - 1) * RA(Z))
100 GOTO 75
102 GF = 0
105 PRINT "I/P S": INPUT S: IF S = 99 THEN GOTO 295
107 PRINT "S = "; S; " ";
110 FOR I = 1 TO NE: IF RA(I) = 0 THEN GOTO 125
115 RA(I) = RA(I) + (S1 - S) * G(I): REM + for min, - for max
125 NEXT
130 cflag = 3: GOTO 135
132 S1 = S: F1 = TC: IF FLAG = 1 THEN GOTO 65
133 GOTO 105
135 FOR I = 1 TO NP: V(I) = 0: FOR J = 1 TO NP: C(I, J) = 0
NEXT: NEXT
140 FOR K = 1 TO NE
145 R = RA(K): I = NN(K, 1): J = NN(K, 2)
150 IF R = 0 THEN GOTO 175
152 R = R / 1: REM r/1 for primal
155 C(I, I) = C(I, I) + 1 / R: C(I, J) = C(I, J) - 1 / R
165 C(J, I) = C(J, I) - 1 / R: C(J, J) = C(J, J) + 1 / R
175 NEXT
180 FOR K = 1 TO NP: IF IB(K) <> 1 THEN GOTO 215
185 F = SPEC(K)
190 FOR I = 1 TO NP
195 IF IB(I) = 1 THEN GOTO 205
200 V(I) = V(I) - F * C(I, N)
205 NEXT I
210 V(N) = F
215 NEXT
220 FOR I = 1 TO NP: V(I) = V(I) + Q(I): NEXT
225 FOR I = 1 TO NP
230 IF IB(I) = 1 THEN GOTO 285
235 X = C(I, I): IF X = 0 THEN X = 10 ^ -6
237 V(I) = V(I) / X
240 FOR J = I + 1 TO NP
245 C(I, J) = C(I, J) / X: NEXT
250 FOR K = 1 TO NP
```

15. Optimal Networks

```
255 IF IB(K) = 1 THEN GOTO 280
260 IF K = I THEN GOTO 280
265 X = C(K, I): V(K) = V(K) - X * V(I)
270 FOR J = I + 1 TO NP
275 C(K, J) = C(K, J) - X * C(I, J): NEXT J
280 NEXT K
285 NEXT I
290 GOTO 345
295 PRINT "Node   Potential"
300 FOR I = 1 TO NP
305 PRINT I, V(I): NEXT I
310 PRINT "Flows"
315 FOR I = 1 TO NP
320 IF IB(I) <> 1 THEN GOTO 340
325 F = 0: FOR K = 1 TO NP
330 F = F + C(I, K) * V(K): NEXT
335 PRINT I, F
340 NEXT I
345 TC = 0: TQ = 0
350 FOR K = 1TO NE: R = RC(K): F = 0: A = RA(K)
IF A=0 THEN GOTO 370
352 A = A / 1: REM A/1 for primal
355 I = NN(K, 1): J = NN(K, 2): F = (V(I) - V(J)) / A
360 IF GF = 1 THEN GOTO 370
365 IF F >= 0 THEN GOTO 370
367 RA(K) = 0: RC(K) = 0: FLAG = 1
370 IF S <> 99 THEN GOTO 374
372 PRINT NN(K, 1), NN(K, 2), " Route flow = ", F: GOTO 375
374 IF S <> 0 THEN PRINT CINT(F * 100) / 100;
375 TC = TC + F * R: TQ = TQ + F: NEXT
380 IF S = 0 THEN GOTO 385
382 PRINT " TC = "; TC; " TQ = "; TQ
385 IF FLAG = 1 THEN GOTO 65
386 IF S = 99 THEN GOTO 400
387 IF cflag = 1 THEN GOTO 72
388 IF cflag = 2 THEN GOTO 82
399 IF cflag = 3 THEN GOTO 132
400 END
500 DATA 6,9,1
505 DATA 1,4,5, 1,5,10, 1,6,10
520 DATA 2,4,20, 2,5,30, 2,6,20
535 DATA 3,4,10, 3,5,20, 3,6,30
550 DATA 6,0
555 DATA 1,110, 2,160, 3,150
570 DATA 4,-140, 5,-200, 0,0
```

15. OPTIMAL NETWORKS

```
1000 DATA 9,20,1
DATA 1,6,50, 1,7,51, 1,8,62, 1,9,80
DATA 2,6,55, 2,7,50, 2,8,51, 2,9,62
DATA 3,6,59, 3,7,55, 3,8,50, 3,9,51
DATA 4,6,63, 4,7,59, 4,8,55, 4,9,50
DATA 5,6,70, 5,7,69, 5,8,68, 5,9,67
DATA 9,0
DATA 1,51, 2,80, 3,119, 4,100, 5,20
DATA 6,-60, 7,-97, 8,-118, 0,0
```

The data in lines 500 - 570 is for the problem of Table 15.1, for which the solutions shown in Table 15.3 can be obtained with the searches used in Table 15.3. Note that these S^* were determined by trial with a gradually increasing S until a member is eliminated. Use of excessively large S will abort the process so a certain amount of trial is required.

When a very small initial search length of circa 0.0001 produces little change in the objective function, and any larger search length produces an unchanged solution, then the solution has converged. Then the program is terminated by input of a search length of 99, when the final results for the route flows and other data is output.

The sign is changed in line 115 for maximization and in lines 152 and 352 the statements are 'inverted' for the dual problem.

INVENTORY PROBLEMS MODELLED AS DISTRIBUTION PROBLEMS

In these the supply (S) and demand (D) points are periods of time. As an example (Battersby, 1966), ACME Co. makes a chemical for which demand is seasonal and production follows this approximately. The sales forecast is: 1st quarter 60,000 mg; 2nd quarter 97,000 mg; 3rd quarter 118,000 mg; 4th quarter 95,000 mg [total = 370,000].

Production scheduled is: 51,000, 80,000, 119,000 and 100,000 for the respective quarters [total = 350,000 so that 20,000 mg must be bought from outside at $70 per 1000 mg, but this price is falling at an estimated $1 per quarter].

15. Optimal Networks

Internal production cost is $50 per 1000 mg. To this is added $1 for storage for a quarter if kept for later sale and $2 for two quarters storage, when $10 is also needed for filtering and re-testing of the material. If kept for three quarters some reprocessing is required and cost, including storage, is $30 per 1000 mg.

If orders are held over for one quarter cost in administration and loss of customers is $5 (per 1000 mg), for two quarters this is $9 and $13 for three. Thus the S & D tableau is, with costs as $/1000 mg and sales/production in units of 1,000 mg:

Costs /1,000 mg	1st quarter	2nd quarter	3rd quarter	4th quarter	Production capacity (S)
1st quarter	50 [51]	51	62	80	51 (S1)
2nd quarter	55	50 [80]	51	62	80 (S2)
3rd quarter	59	55	50 [1] [118]	51	119 (S3)
4th quarter	63	59	55 [5]	50 [95]	100 (S4)
Buy outside	70 [9]	69 [11]	68	67	20 (S5)
Sales forecast	60 (D1)	97 (D2)	118 (D3)	95 (D4)	Total: 370

Note that we would expect to buy outside in the fourth quarter when that is cheapest but this is not the optimum solution. Interpretation of the solution is also a little confusing. Essentially flows above the diagonal in the table are 'holds' and those below are 'delay in filling order.'

The route flows for the exact solution to the problem are shown in [ ] brackets in the tableau and these give total revenue of $18,939 (x 1000).

15. OPTIMAL NETWORKS

The data for this problem is appended to the foregoing program (in and after line 1000). Using searches
$S^* = $ 8, 9, 16, 21, 13, 23, 28, 36, 42, 0.2, 0.2
the route flows obtained are
16 =40, 17 =11, 27 =80, 37 =1, 38 =118, 47 =5, 49 =95, 56 =20
and the total revenue with these flows is \$18,961 (x 1000), whereas the exact solution is 18,939 (obtained using the Direct LP program given in Chapter 12 with its third set of data), an excellent result considering that our search method is approximate.

FRD FOR FEM DISTRIBUTION MODELS

For distribution problems the element constitutive parameters are their unit costs and for minimization using Flow Ratio Design (FRD) these are adjusted at each iteration using

$$c_{ij} = R c_{ij} \text{ where } R = q_m / |q_{ij}|, \quad q_m \approx q_{av}/2, \quad q_{av} = \Sigma Q/N \qquad (15.6)$$

where ΣQ is the total flow in the network of N routes and q_m is the 'median' flow. For maximization $c_{ij} = c_{ij}/R$ is used to adjust the element unit costs (iteratively).

Then to obtain the minimum solution lower and upper route cost limits

$$c_L = c_{av}/40 \text{ to } c_{av}/10, \quad c_U = 10^6 \qquad (15.7)$$

where $c_{av} = \Sigma c_{ij}/N$ are used.

For maximization the lower limit is chosen from 10 to 100% of the value used for minimization and the upper limit is chosen in the range $5*c_{av}$ to $100*c_{av}$, using the value 100 in the examples studied in the present work.

For the dual problem c_{ij} is replaced by its inverse.

Observing these limits iteration proceeds and some routes vanish as their c_{ij} values approach c_U, flows $q_{ij} < 0.001$ being set to zero prior to calculating the total distribution cost

$$T_0 = \Sigma |q_{ij}| (c_{ij})_0$$

where $(c_{ij})_0$ are the initial unit costs for each route.

15. OPTIMAL NETWORKS

Note that the lower limit 0.001 for q_{ij} was used with 8 d.p. computation and a value of 0.01 gave the same results and might be needed with less accurate computation.

Table 15.4 shows the route flows obtained using $q_m = 25$ compared to the exact LP solutions (columns 3 and 4) for the problem of Figure 13.2 and Table 15.1.

Table 15.4. Results for the distribution problem of Table 15.1.

Route	c_0	Min	Max	P_{min}	D_{max}	P_{max}	D_{min}
14	5	0	110	0	0.09	32.50	32.50
15	10	110	0	110	109.8	52.50	52.50
16	10	0	0	0	0.1	25.01	25.00
24	20	80/0	0/30	80	69.8	55.42	55.42
25	30	0/80	160/130	0	90.1	75.42	75.42
26	20	80	0	80	0.08	29.16	29.17
34	10	60/140	30/0	60	70.1	52.09	52.08
35	20	90/10	40/70	90	0.09	72.09	72.08
36	30	0	80	0	79.8	25.83	25.83
T_0		6700	8850	6700	8297.9	7629.2	7629.2
I (iterations)				12	21	80	150

For minimization we have $c_{av} = 155/9 \approx 17$ and take $c_L = 1 \approx c_{av}/20$, so that c_L is in the middle of the range suggested in Equation 15.7. Then after I = 12 iterations (of the primal FEM model) the exact minimum solution (P_{min} in Table 15.4) is obtained, the final element costs being $c_{ij} = c_L = 1$ for routes with non-zero flows and for the vanishing routes

c_{14}, c_{25}, c_{16} and c_{36} are close to or $= 10^6$

so that, indeed, in these $q_{ij} \simeq 0$.

For the dual minimum, D_{min}, all the final $c_{ij} = c_L = 1$ except that $c_{16} \gg 1$ initially but $c_{16} \to c_L$ slowly with iteration. Here an 'intermediate' solution with no zero flows is found, this being the saddle point between the primal and dual solutions.

15. OPTIMAL NETWORKS

For maximization the same q_m value is used and the cost limits are

$c_L = 0.1$ (10% the value for MIN), $c_U = 100$

The dual maximum solution (D_{max} in Table 15.4) is only a lower bound to the exact solution (column 4) and the final element costs are $c_{ij} = c_L$ for routes with $q_{ij} = 0$ and $c_{ij} = c_U$ for routes with 'non-zero' flows.

For the primal maximum (P_{max}) the saddle point solution is obtained again, here with all final element costs $c_{ij} = c_U$ except that $c_{16} \simeq 0$ initially but $c_{16} \to c_U$ slowly with iteration.

Note that for this saddle point solution $T_0 =$ is here close to the average of the initial primal and dual solutions after one iteration, that is $(P_1 + D_1)/2 = (7313.5 + 7929.6)/2 = 7621.6$.

Note also that a large number of iterations was needed to obtain $P_{max} = D_{min}$, but with only a few iterations the total cost is close to the saddle point value, e.g. 5 iterations gives $P_{max} = 7697.1$ and $D_{min} = 7597.0$.

Note also that use of a median value for q_m here was found by trial to provide satisfactory results, particularly in the case of the primal minimum problem which is that of usual interest. Doubtless improved results for the dual maximum can be obtained with alternative values for q_m (and perhaps c_U). Doubtless too the 'dual' appearance of the saddle point solution is the result of use of this median value q_m, an intriguing result.

DISTRIBUTION NETWORK WITH DUMMY ROUTES

Table 15.5 shows the route flows obtained using $q_m = 5$ for a 4 × 5 problem with supply flows (i = 1,2,3,4) of 90, 75, 35, 25 and demand flows (j = 5,6,7,8,9) of -40, -35, -70, -30, -50. Here demand exceeds supply by 25 units and a dummy supply point 4 with route costs of 50 is introduced to model this situation.

Here $q_m = 5 \simeq q_{av}/2$ is used and for minimization $c_L = 0.1 \simeq c_{av}/40$ (set in the third line of code as RL) and the result (column 5) is close to the exact solution.

15. OPTIMAL NETWORKS

Table 15.5. Results for 4 x 5 problem (Mohr, 2000).

Route	c_0	Min	Max	P_{min}	D_{max}	P_{max}	D_{min}
15	1.5	0	0	30.5	0.00	16.50	16.49
16	6.4	0	35	0	34.99	14.31	14.31
17	1.8	70	25	45.5	21.68	24.94	24.94
18	4.0	0	30	0	11.67	14.31	14.31
19	3.5	20	0	14.0	21.67	19.94	19.94
25	1.6	40	0	9.5	0.00	13.50	13.49
26	2.6	35	0	35.0	0.00	11.31	11.31
27	1.9	0	25	24.5	28.34	21.94	21.94
28	3.1	0	0	6.0	18.33	11.31	11.31
29	5.8	0	50	0	28.33	16.94	16.94
35	5.3	0	35	0	34.98	5.00	5.01
36	3.5	0	0	0	0.01	5.00	5.02
37	2.4	0	0	0	0.01	12.50	12.48
38	1.3	30	0	24	0.00	5.00	5.02
39	2.2	5	0	11.0	0.01	7.50	7.46
45	50.0	0	5	0	5.02	5.00	5.00
46	50.0	0	0	0	0.00	4.38	4.36
47	50.0	0	20	0	19.98	10.62	10.64
48	50.0	0	0	0	0.00	-0.62	-0.64
49	50.0	25	0	25.0	0.00	5.62	5.64
T_0		1651	2162	1653.4	2095.8	1923.5	1925.0
I (iterations)				10	12	70	40

For maximization c_L = 10% of the value for minimization is again used (set in the sixth line of code), and also for the other three problems in Table 15.6. The dual maximum is a lower bound and P_{max} and D_{min} are almost identical and their T_0 values are close to the average of the exact extremal solutions.

For P_{max} and D_{min} there is a small negative flow for route 48 and in this route flow cycles between values of 0 and 1 during iteration to obtain the saddle point solution.

15. OPTIMAL NETWORKS

Note too that the initial solution for the dual minimum results in a few negative flows (and consequently $D_1 = 4630.4$) and that generally in other problems negative route flows may be introduced, sometimes temporarily, by flow ratio iteration, particularly if q_m is not close to $q_{av}/2$ when alternative solutions to those found here may be obtained.

Here for D_{min}, therefore, double precision must be used by inserting DEFDBL A-Z as the first program line.

Table 15.6. Summary of results for four distribution problems

Problem:	1 (3x3)	2 (3x4)	3 (3x4)	4 (4x5)
Exact:				
Min	6700	330	743	1651
Max	8850	760	1548	2162
Steepest descent:				
Min	6700	340	779	1651
Max	8850	760	1548	2160.5
FRD:				
Min	6700	340	798	1653.4
Max:	8298	680	1530	2095.8

Table 15.6 compares extremal total cost (T_0) solutions for the 3x3 and 4x5 problems of Tables 15.1 and 15.5 and two other problems obtained using the present flow ratio design procedure with the exact solutions and those obtained using the steepest descent procedure with 'element access' parameters introduced at the beginning of this chapter (Mohr, 2004b).

Note that maximum solutions are here for the dual problem.

Overall the simple FRD approach gives good results. Generally, we will require only the minimum (primal) solutions in practice and, as the FRD method used here shows, this occurs when all (non-zero) route flows have equal cost.

15. OPTIMAL NETWORKS

This result, Mohr's third (equality principle) law of distribution, corresponds to the 'constant strain' character of (optimal) Michell structures (Michell, 1904), an important result.

PROGRAM FOR FRD OF DISTRIBUTION PROBLEMS

The following working listing is for flow ratio optimization of FEM distribution models. Note that upper/lower case are mixed somewhat as the program was converted to QBASIC from MegaBasic, the latter using automatic assignation of upper and lower case according to context. Key variables are

NP,NE,NS,NQ number of nodes, elements, boundary nodes, nodal loads
QM   the mean element flow parameter q_m of Equation 15.6
RL, RU   the lower and upper route cost limits of Equation 15.7
NN( )   the element node numbers
RI( )   the initial element unit costs
ER( )   the element unit costs as they vary during iteration
C( )   the system matrix
Q( )   the nodal 'loads'
V( )   the nodal 'potentials' obtained after solution
IB( )   boundary condition flags=1 for boundary condition nodes
SP( )   specified values at boundary condition nodes
F   element/route flow
TQ, TCI system total flows and costs

Lines 8-117 define and input data. Iterative solution commences at line 120, the system matrix being assembled in lines 122-170 and specified boundary condition values and loads are introduced in lines 172-238. Then solution for the nodal potentials V( ) is obtained in lines 240-340.

In lines 375-386 the boundary 'reaction' flows are calculated (here only that at the last node at which zero potential is always specified). In lines 391-398 the route flows F are calculated and for significant flows (> 0.001) their unit costs are adjusted according to Equation 15.6 in line 394.

15. OPTIMAL NETWORKS

In lines 394 and 395 route costs outside the limit values are set to these. In line 399 any number is input to continue iteration and 99 is input to terminate iteration. For the first set of data the solution will have converged after 12 iterations.

Note that the listing is for minimization of the primal problem. For maximization set MINM = 2 in line 9 so that the element costs are factored in inverse fashion in line 394. For the dual problem set FPD = 2 in line 9 so that the element parameter is inverted in the statements following lines 125 and 392.

```
5 REM FEM model of distribution networks
7 RESTORE 600
8 QM = 25: RL = 1: RU = 1000000
MINM = 1: FPD = 1
REM MINM =1/2 for Min/Max: FPD = 1/2 for primal/dual
IF MINM = 2 THEN RU = 100
IF MINM = 2 THEN RL = RL / 10
10 DIM C(20, 20), V(20), IB(20), NN(20, 2), ER(20), SP(20), Q(20), RI(20)
20 READ NP, NE, NS, NQ: ITN = 0
100 FOR K = 1 TO NE: READ I, J, R
110 NN(K, 1) = I: NN(K, 2) = J: ER(K) = R: RI(K) = R: NEXT
115 FOR K = 1 TO NS: READ N, S: IB(N) = 1: SP(N) = S: NEXT
117 FOR K = 1 TO NQ: READ Z, Q(Z): NEXT
120 FOR I=1 TO NP: FOR J=1 TO NP: C(I, J) =0: NEXT: NEXT
ITN = ITN + 1
122 FOR K = 1 TO NE: I = NN(K, 1): J = NN(K, 2): R = ER(K)
125 IF R = 0 THEN 170
IF FPD = 2 THEN R = 1 / R
130 C(I, I) = C(I, I) + 1 / R
140 C(I, J) = C(I, J) - 1 / R
150 C(J, I) = C(J, I) - 1 / R
160 C(J, J) = C(J, J) + 1 / R
170 NEXT
172 FOR I = 1 TO NP: V(I) = 0: NEXT
180 FOR K = 1 TO NP
190 IF IB(K) <> 1 THEN 230: S = SP(K)
200 FOR I = 1 TO NP
205 IF IB(I) = 1 THEN 220
210 V(I) = V(I) - S * C(I, K)
220 NEXT I
225 V(K) = S
230 NEXT
```

15. Optimal Networks

```
232 FOR K = 1 TO NP
235 IF IB(K) = 1 THEN 238
236 V(K) = V(K) + Q(K)
238 NEXT
240 FOR I = 1 TO NP
245 IF IB(I) = 1 THEN 340
250 X = C(I, I): V(I) = V(I) / X
260 FOR J = I + 1 TO NP
270 C(I, J) = C(I, J) / X: NEXT
280 FOR K = 1 TO NP
285 IF IB(K) = 1 THEN 330
290 IF K = I THEN GOTO 330
300 X = C(K, I): V(K) = V(K) - X * V(I)
310 FOR J = I + 1 TO NP
320 C(K, J) = C(K, J) - X * C(I, J): NEXT J
330 NEXT K
340 NEXT I
350 PRINT "Node   Potential"
360 FOR I = 1 TO NP
370 PRINT I, V(I): NEXT I
375 PRINT "Flows"
380 FOR I = 1 TO NP
381 IF IB(I) <> 1 THEN 386
382 Z = 0: FOR K = 1 TO NP
383 Z = Z + C(I, K) * V(K): NEXT
385 PRINT I, Z
386 NEXT I
391 TC = 0: TQ = 0: TCI = 0
392 FOR K = 1 TO NE: I = NN(K, 1): J = NN(K, 2): R = ER(K)
IF FPD = 2 THEN R = 1 / R
393 IF R = 0 THEN 396:
F = (V(J) - V(I)) / R: IF ABS(F) < .001 THEN F = 0
IF ABS(F) < .001 THEN GOTO 396
FRF = QM / ABS(F): IF MINM = 2 THEN FRF = 1 / FRF
394 ER(K) = ER(K) * FRF: IF ER(K) > RU THEN ER(K) = RU
395 IF ER(K) < RL THEN ER(K) = RL
396 PRINT I; J; " route flow = "; F, " r = "; ER(K)
397 TCI =TCI +ABS(F) * RI(K): TC =TC +ABS(F)*R: TQ=TQ + ABS(F)
NEXT
398 PRINT "tc = "; TC; " tq = "; TQ; " tci ="; TCI; " itn ="; ITN
399 INPUT Z: IF Z = 99 THEN END
GOTO 120
```

15. OPTIMAL NETWORKS

```
600 DATA 6,9,1,5
610 DATA 1,4,5, 1,5,10, 1,6,10
640 DATA 2,4,20, 2,5,30, 2,6,20
670 DATA 3,4,10, 3,5,20, 3,6,30
700 DATA 6,0
710 DATA 1,110, 2,160, 3,150
740 DATA 4,-140, 5,-200, 0,0

800 DATA 9,20,1,8
805 DATA 1,5,1.5, 1,6,6.4, 1,7,1.8, 1,8,4, 1,9,3.5
830 DATA 2,5,1.6, 2,6,2.6, 2,7,1.9, 2,8,3.1, 2,9,5.8
855 DATA 3,5,5.3, 3,6,3.5, 3,7,2.4, 3,8,1.3, 3,9,2.2
880 DATA 4,5,50, 4,6,50, 4,7,50, 4,8,50, 4,9,50
905 DATA 9,0
910 DATA 1,90, 2,75, 3,35, 4,25
930 DATA 5,-40, 6,-35, 7,-70, 8,-30, 0,0
```

The data of lines 600 - 740 is for the problem of Table 15.1. The data in the remaining lines is for the problem of Table 15.5 (note that for this problem put QM=5 and RL=0.1 in line 8 of code).

The program is run by keying F5. Results for the first iteration are printed and an 'Input ?'. Enter a 1 (or any other number) to continue iteration. When convergence has been obtained a 99 is input to terminate computation.

OPTIMIZATION OF TRAFFIC FLOW NETWORKS

As shown in Equation 13.9, for traffic flow optimization the element constitutive parameter is $K_{ij}V_f/L_{ij}$ rather than $1/c_{ij}$ for distribution problems. Then the 'element access' parameter A_{ij} used at the start of each steepest descent search is the initial value this, that is $A_{ij}^0 = (K_{ij}V_f/L_{ij})^0$ and here the free flow velocity is assumed to be the same for all elements.

Solution then proceeds as for distribution problems, that is using perturbation of each A_{ij}^0 in turn to calculate the gradient vector for search in the direction of steepest descent.

During search element values of A_{ij} are then adjusted according to Equation 15.3.

15. OPTIMAL NETWORKS

If, during search, the magnitude of a route flow is less than a small value q_{min} then we set $A_{ij} = 0$ for that route and omit it from the model, also setting a flag which returns to calculation of a new gradient vector once the other route flows and thence T have been calculated.

Note that such element omission is disallowed during calculation of the gradient vector.

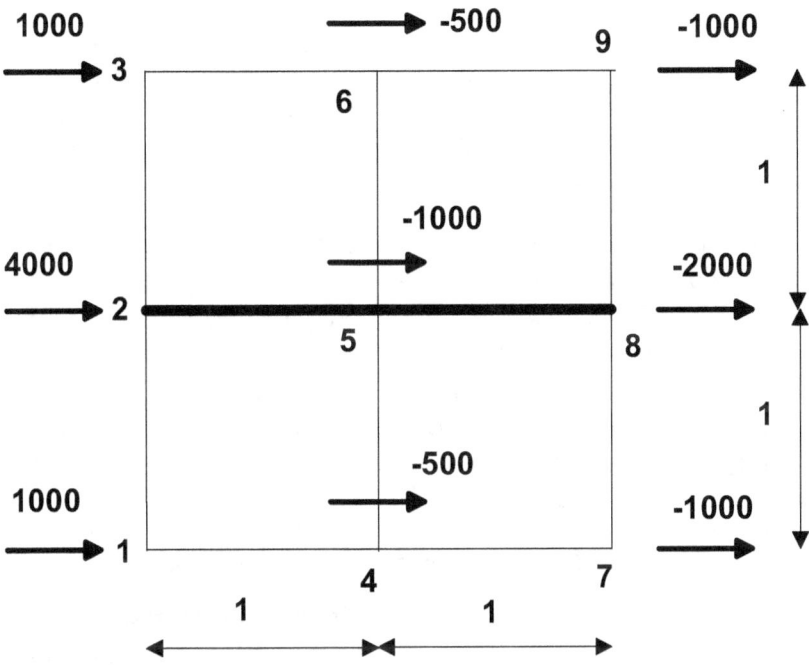

Figure 15.2. Traffic flow network: $v_f = 60$ for all routes, $k_j = 600$ for routes 25, 58 and $= 100$ for the others.

For the example problem of case (b) in Table 13.3 and shown in Figure 15.2, using $V_f = 60$ for all routes, $q_{min} = 10$, and successive searches $S = 0.9$, 200 and 0.00001, the resulting solution which gives minimum total travel time has only eight routes and is given in Table 15.7 (Mohr, 2005).

15. OPTIMAL NETWORKS

Table 15.7. Steepest descent solution for optimum network in Figure 15.2.

Route	q_{ij}	K_{ij}	k_b	v_b
14	1000	100	21.132	47.321
36	1000	100	21.132	47.321
25	4000	600	76.393	52.36
58	3000	600	55.051	54.495
47	500	100	9.175	54.495
69	500	100	9.175	54.495
78	-500	100	9.175	-54.495
89	500	100	9.175	54.495

The initial value of the total travel time was $T = 213.44$, and the final value is $T = 210.41$, a significant saving considering that four routes have also been omitted. This result is identical to the exact solution obtained by linear programming. The exact LP solution was obtained using a 'direct' LP method (Mohr, 2000) but only after some improvisation because the variables in LP must always be positive whereas in Table 15.7, for example, one flow is negative.

APPLICATION OF FRD TO TRAFFIC FLOW PROBLEMS

For traffic flow networks the constitutive parameter is $R_{ij} = K_{ij}V_{ij}/L_{ij}$. Returning to the example problem of Figure 15.2, only K_{ij} is variable and this is updated at each iteration using

$$K_{ij}^* = K_{ij} (|q_{ij}|/q_m) \qquad (15.8)$$

For this network the total flow is 6000 with 12 routes, giving $q_{av} = 500$ and this value is used for q_m.

Using lower and upper limits $(K_{ij})_L = 100$, $(K_{ij})_U = 10000$ and omitting routes with $|q_{ij}| < q_{min} = 100$, the solution of Table 15.8 for the route flows which give the minimum total travel time is obtained after seven iterations, four routes having been eliminated (Mohr, 2005).

15. OPTIMAL NETWORKS

Table 15.8.
FRD solution for the optimum network in Figure 15.2.

Route	q_{ij}	K_{ij}	k_b	v_b
14	1000	10000	16.595	59.900
36	1000	10000	16.595	59.900
25	4000	10000	67.117	59.597
58	3000	10000	50.253	59.698
47	500	143.72	8.882	56.292
69	500	143.72	8.882	56.292
78	-500	100	9.175	-54.495
89	500	100	9.175	54.495

The route flows are the same as obtained using steepest descent in Table 15.7, but the densities and velocities differ so that the total travel time $T = 186.87$ is less than obtained using steepest descent.

This is because FRD allows the element jam densities to vary (as the only variable part of the element parameter R_{ij}). As a result the values are close to or equal to the limiting values, an interesting but somewhat impractical solution.

To obtain the correct results for the element densities and velocities they must be calculated using the original values of the route parameters R_{ij}, the flow values shown in Table 15.8, and Equation 13.11, when the results are identical with those in Table 15.7.

CONCLUSIONS

A steepest descent method yields good results for a distribution problem with 9 nodes and another with 20 nodes, the latter an inventory problem in which the 'S & D' points are replaced by intervals in time.

15. Optimal Networks

The new FRD method is applied to the 'introductory' 9 node distribution problem of Figure 13.2 and then to a problem with 20 nodes with good results (Table 15.5). In the latter problem the primal MAX and dual MIN solutions turn out to be the saddle point solution approximately midway between the initial primal and dual solutions before optimization.

Overall both methods are seen to give good results for the primal and dual MIN and MAX solutions of four problems in Table 15.6

Finally, the optimal solution for a traffic network is obtained using both steepest descent and FRD. The programs used for this were basically the same as those given here for distribution problems except that the element constitutive parameter is $K_{ij} V_f / L_{ij}$ rather than $1/c_{ij}$ for distribution problems, and Equation 13.11 is needed to calculate the element flow velocities and densities once the element flow volume q_{ij} is known.

Chapter 16

ECONOMIC MODELLING

INPUT-OUTPUT ANALYSIS

Input-Output Analysis (IOA) was developed by Wassily Leontief at Harvard in 1931 and his study of the US economy with it gained a Nobel Prize. Later Laurence Klein applied IOA to the world economy, also receiving a Nobel Prize.

At a basic level IOA analyses the interdependence of companies. Consider, for example, three companies X, Y and Z that sell/buy products/materials to/from each other, the value of these transactions over some regular period being shown in Table 16.1.

Table 16.1. Input-output analysis data

	Purchases				Total
	X	Y	Z	External	Output ($)
Sales					
X	-	60	40	100	200
Y	40	-	100	260	400
Z	50	100	-	50	200
Labour	110	240	60	-	410
Total input	200	400	200	410	1,210

This table also includes labour costs for the period, as well as external sales (other than to the other two companies). Then company Y, for example, sells $40 of goods to X and $100 to Z, the remaining $260 of its total output ($400) being sold externally.

16. ECONOMIC MODELLING

To produce this output Y purchases $60 in goods from X and $100 from Z, also spending $240 on labour costs.

Table 16.2. Input coefficients.

	X	Y	Z
X	-	0.15	0.2
Y	0.2	-	0.5
Z	0.25	0.25	-
Labour	0.55	0.6	0.3

Then from Table 16.1 we can easily calculate *input coefficients* by dividing the three X, Y, Z columns by their totals, giving the results shown in Table 16.2.

Then for company Y, for example, Table 16.2 shows that for each $1 of output produced 15 cents is spent on purchases from X, 25 cents on purchases from Z, and 60 cents is spent on labour costs.

Then using the coefficients of Table 16.2 we can write the outputs x, y, z for companies X, Y, Z as

$$x = 0.15y + 0.20z + 100$$
$$y = 0.20x + 0.50z + 260$$
$$z = 0.25x + 0.25y + 50$$

Now suppose we wish to determine the effect of increasing the external sales of X to $120 (from $100). Then we change this number in these equations and rearrange them to give:

$$\begin{bmatrix} 1 & -0.15 & -0.20 \\ -0.20 & 1 & -0.50 \\ -0.25 & -0.25 & 1 \end{bmatrix} \begin{Bmatrix} x \\ y \\ x \end{Bmatrix} = \begin{Bmatrix} 120 \\ 260 \\ 50 \end{Bmatrix}$$

and solving this matrix equation we obtain

$$x = \$223, \; y = \$408, \; z = \$208$$

16. Economic Modelling

From these results we are then able to calculate the increased labour costs resulting for each company as:

X: 223 x 0.55 = 122.7   (increase of $12.7)
Y: 408 x 0.60 = 244.8   (increase of $4.8)
Z: 208 x 0.30 = 62.4   (increase of $2.4)

Here a 'flow through' effect to other companies is immediately apparent, whereas a more superficial approach would predict the increase in labour cost for X as increase in external output (20) multiplied by 0.55 = $11, and effects on other companies would be neglected.

The following QBASIC program solves these equations using the Gauss-Mohr reduction method detailed in Chapter 10. Here line 2 sets the problem size and lines 6 and 8 read the data from the last DATA statements to fill the matrix SM and the RHS matrix Q( ).

```
REM GMR routine
2 N = 3
4 DIM SM(N, N), Q(N)
6 FOR I = 1 TO N: FOR J = 1 TO N: READ SM(I, J): NEXT: NEXT
8 FOR I = 1 TO N: READ Q(I): NEXT
10 FOR I = 1 TO N
20 X = SM(I, I): Q(I) = Q(I) / X
30 FOR J = I + 1 TO N
40 SM(I, J) = SM(I, J) / X: NEXT
50 FOR K = 1 TO N
60 IF K = I THEN 100
70 X = SM(K, I): Q(K) = Q(K) - X * Q(I)
80 FOR J = I + 1 TO N
90 SM(K, J) = SM(K, J) - X * SM(I, J): NEXT J
100 NEXT K: NEXT I
110 FOR I = 1 TO N: PRINT Q(I): NEXT
120 END
DATA 1, -0.15, -0.2
DATA -0.2,1,-0.5
DATA -0.25,-0.25,1
DATA 120, 260, 50
```

Then lines 10 to 100 carry out Gauss-Mohr reduction. Line 20 selects the *pivot* for each row and lines 20 and 40 divide this row by it in both the matrix and in the RHS vector Q( ). Line 70 selects the *row multiplier* needed to 'zero out' this column above and below the pivot and lines 70 and 90 perform this reduction operation in both SM( ) and Q( ) using this, thus directly solving the problem (without inverting matrix A).

Finally the solution to the input-output analysis problem:

$x = \$223, \ y = \$408, \ z = \$208$

is printed in line 110.

ECONOMIC MODELLING

Lawrence Klein modelled the performance of the US economy in the years 1921 - 1941 using three *structural equations* (in $B US)

$$C = 16.8 + 0.02P + 0.23P_L + 0.8(W + S) \qquad (1)$$

$$I = 17.8 + 0.23P + 0.55P_L - 0.15K_L \qquad (2)$$

$$W = 1.6 + 0.42X + 0.16X_L + 0.131|t - 1931| \qquad (3)$$

where $|t - 1931|$ is a heavy side step function $= 0$ if $t <= 1931$ and $= (t - 1931)$ if $t > 1931$.

Three *definitive equations* are added:

$$X = C + I + G \qquad (4)$$

$$P = X - W - T \qquad (5)$$

$$K = K_L + I \qquad (6)$$

where C = total consumption, I = total investment, W, S are the private/public sector wages, X is the private sector production, P is the private sector profits (non wage income), K = stocks (capital goods at end of year), G = government spending, T = business taxes, and subscript L denotes value for previous year.

We can make the model more 'self contained' by assuming

$$S = 0.3G \text{ and } T = 0.2(W_L + P) \qquad (7)$$

and including these equations in the analysis.

16. Economic Modelling

Then the equations can be rearranged and written in the matrix form

$$A\{V\} = \begin{bmatrix} 1 & 0 & -0.8 & 0 & -0.02 & 0 \\ 0 & 1 & 0 & 0 & -0.23 & 0 \\ 0 & 0 & 1 & -0.42 & 0 & 0 \\ -1 & -1 & 0 & 1 & 0 & 0 \\ 0 & 0 & 1.2 & -1 & 1.2 & 0 \\ 0 & -1 & 0 & 0 & 0 & 1 \end{bmatrix} \begin{Bmatrix} C \\ I \\ W \\ X \\ P \\ K \end{Bmatrix} = \begin{Bmatrix} Q_1 \\ Q_2 \\ Q_3 \\ G \\ 0 \\ K_L \end{Bmatrix} \quad (8)$$

where $Q_1 = 16.8 + 0.23 P_L + 0.8 S$ (and $S = 0.3 G$)

$Q_2 = 17.8 + 0.55 P_L - 0.15 K_L$

$Q_3 = 1.6 + 0.16 X_L + 0.131 t - t_0 I$

Now they can be coded and Gauss-Jordan reduction used to invert the matrix A of constant coefficients. Then *time stepping is used* to determine the values of the variables $\{V\}$ after each of a succession of one year steps

This is done in the following QBASIC program and the Gauss-Jordan reduction routine in lines 100 - 120 is similar to the Gauss-Mohr routine used in the preceding section except that reduction operations are carried out on the entire matrix A and not upon a RHS vector.

```
5 DIM A(6, 6), Q(6), R(6), V(6), S(6), F(6), PR(100, 2), FR(6)
10 FOR J = 1 TO 6: S(J) = 0: F(J) = 1: L(J) = 0: NEXT J: SCREEN 1
COLOR 4, 1
15 F(6) = 2
20 N = 6: Z = 0: D = 0: K1 = 100: X1 = 100: P1 = 10: W1 = 25
25 FOR I = 1 TO N: FOR J = 1 TO N: READ A(I, J): NEXT J: NEXT I
GOSUB 100
30 T = .2: G = .3: Z = Z + 1: IF Z > 30 GOTO 85
32 REM IF Z >= 20 THEN G = .5 AND T = .5
35 R(2) = 17.8 + .55 * P1 - .15 * K1: R(3) = 1.6 + .16 * X1 + .13 * D
R(6) = K1
40 R(5) = -T * (W1 + P1): R(4) = G * R(5): S = .8 * R(4)
R(1) = 16.8 + .23 * P1 + .8 * S
```

16. Economic Modelling

```
45 FOR I = 1 TO N: Q(I) = 0: FOR K = 1 TO N
50 Q(I) = Q(I) + A(I, K) * R(K): NEXT K: NEXT I
55 FOR J = 1 TO N: V(J) = (2 * Q(J) + S(J)) / F(J)
60 A = 10 * (Z - 2): B = 150 - L(J)
65 X = 10 * (Z - 1): Y = 150 - V(J): LINE (A, B)-(X, Y)
V = INT(Y / 8.5) + 2
66 IF Z < 30 GOTO 68
67 LOCATE V, 38: PRINT J
68 NEXT J
70 P1 = Q(5): X1 = Q(4): K1 = Q(6): W1 = Q(3)
75 FOR J = 1 TO N: L(J) = V(J): NEXT J: IF Z > 10 THEN D = D + 1
80 PR(Z, 1) = P1: PR(Z, 2) = K1
82 GOTO 30
85 FOR I = 1 TO N: FR(I) = Q(I): NEXT I
PRINT "PP = ", Q(4), "Profit = ", Q(5)
86 DRAW "bm0,150 m300,150 bm0,0 m0,200"
LOCATE 21, 2
PRINT "1=C 2=I 3 = WP 4 = priv. prod 5 = profit 6 = stocks"
90 END
100 FOR I = 1 TO N: X = A(I, I): A(I, I) = 1
105 FOR J = 1 TO N: A(I, J) = A(I, J) / X: NEXT J
110 FOR K = 1 TO N: IF K = I GOTO 120
112 X = A(K, I): A(K, I) = 0
115 FOR J = 1 TO N: A(K, J) = A(K, J) - X * A(I, J): NEXT J
120 NEXT K: NEXT I
125 RETURN
130 DATA 1,0,-.8,0,-.02,0
135 DATA 0,1,0,0,-.23,0
140 DATA 0,0,1,-.42,0,0
145 DATA -1,-1,0,1,0,0
150 DATA 0,0,1,-1,1,0
155 DATA 0,-1,0,0,0,1
```

Here the initial values of *K, X, P, W* required by Equations (1), (2), (3), (7) are set in line 20 and the values chosen in Equations (7) are set in line 30. R( ) are the RHS values in equation (8) and Q( ) are the solutions for the values of *C, I, W, X, P, K* and these are plotted after each of 30 iterations and S( ) and F( ) are scale factors for this plotting.

16. Economic Modelling

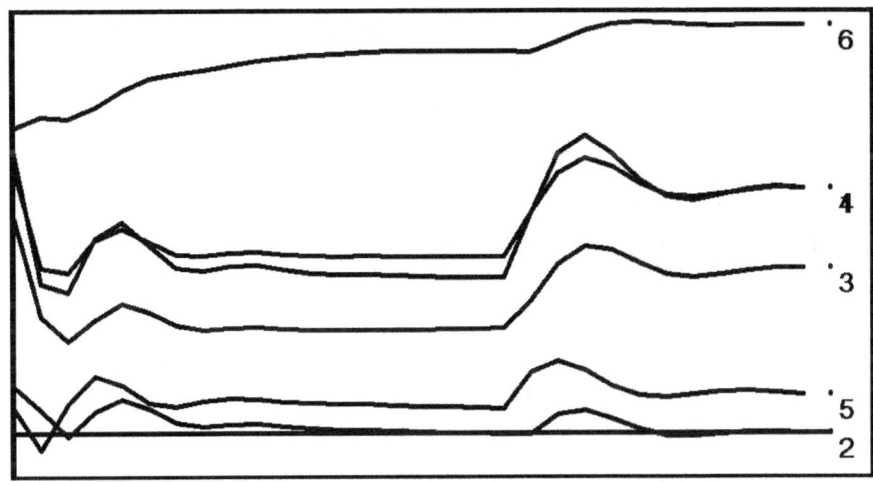

Figure 16.1. Output from program using Klein's equations.

If the REM is removed from line 32 then values T = 0.5 and G = 0.5 apply at and after year 20, increasing private production, Q(4), and profit, Q(5), from 33.49 & 4.45 to 39.74 & 5.96 at year 30, demonstrating the 'Keynes effect' of an increase in taxes and government spending boosting the economy.

Figure 16.1 shows the program output, clearly showing the boost in values circa year 20 (i.e., two-thirds across from the left side).

Macroeconomic modelling

Many economists still mistakenly believe that increasing interest rates reduces inflation. Intuition suggests otherwise, as does Australia's economic history of the last 60 years, there having only been one instance of interest rates and inflation going in opposite directions, this being some time after the OPEC oil shocks of 1979/80 and the floating of the Australian dollar in 1983.

The proof is found using the equations of Jack Vernon's *liquid money supply* (LMS) and *interest sensitive expenditure* curves (ISE) given in his book *Macroeconomics* (Vernon, 1980).

16. Economic Modelling

Very concisely, with the modification transfer payments $D = f(r)$, the proof is as follows:

Real money supply = MS = M/P
   = money demand = MD = $L + kQ - qr$

where P = price inflation = 1
M is non-inflation deflated money supply = 200
L is money demand constant = 50
Q is total output
r is the official interest rate
k is income responsiveness of money demand = 0.2
q is interest responsiveness of money demand = 1,000
giving

$$qr - kQ = L - M/P \qquad (16.1)$$

and this is the LMS curve, an 'up' supply curve with r the up/rate axis and Q the across/quantity axis.

For demand, we have expenditure $E = C + I + G$

with C the consumption expenditure function = $a + bQ^* - sr$
where $a = 50$, $b = 0.8$, s = interest responsiveness of C = 1,000
so that $C = 50 + 0.8Q^* - 1,000r$
with $Q^* = Q(1 - t) - T + D$
where T is the tax constant, t is the tax rate, D is the transfer payments, and I is the investment expenditure function

$$= I^* - ir = 200 - 1,000r$$

where i is interest responsiveness of I and $i = 1,000$
(early versions of the Fed-MIT model take s approx. = i)
and G is equal to 230 (government spending)
so that $E = E^* + b(1 - t)Q - (i + s)r$
with $E^* = a - bT + bD + I^* + G$
where $a = 50$, $b = 0.8$, $t = 0.25$, $T = 50$, $I^* = 200$, $G = 230$

Now let D = transfer payments = $D^* + yU$
with $D^* = 25$, $y = 1,000$
where U = unemployment rate = $U^* + r/2$ with $U^* = 0.025$
so that $E^* = a - bT + bD^* + byU^* + byr/2 + I^* + G$

16. ECONOMIC MODELLING

Then $E = Q$ for equilibrium gives

$Q = a - bT + bD^* + byU^* + byr/2 + I^* + G + b(1 - t)Q - (i + s)r$

or

$(i + s - by/2)r + [1 - b(1 - t)]Q = a - bT + bD^* + byU^* + I^* + G$ \hfill (16.2)

and this is the ISE curve, a 'down' demand curve.

Solving Equations (16.1) and (16.2) gives the equilibrium values of r and Q (and thence U).
With the values of constants stated above, we obtain

$$1{,}000r - 0.2Q = -150 \qquad (16.3a)$$
$$1{,}600r + 0.4Q = 480 \qquad (16.3b)$$

Adding twice the first to the second gives $r = 0.05$ and thence $Q = 1{,}000$ and $U = 0.05$.

With inflation $P = 1.1$, however, the solution is
$r = 0.0601$, $\qquad Q = 959.6$, $\qquad$ and $U = 0.0551$.

Looking in reverse, this shows that increasing interest rates to 6% will cause 10% inflation, increase unemployment by 0.5%, and reduce total output by 4%.

To prove this beyond doubt, put $r = 0.0601$ in Equation 16.3b [not Equation 16.3a as this originally involved P which is now taken unknown], giving $Q = 959.6$ and put these values of r and Q (and $L = 50$, $M = 200$, $q = 1{,}000$, $k = 0.2$) in Equation 16.1, giving $P = 1.10$.

The bottom line is that increasing official interest rates increases inflation. This is because greater interest rates increase company debt repayments, leading to higher costs which are passed on to the consumer and the economy at large.

16. Economic Modelling

INVERSE LAW OF SUPPLY AND DEMAND

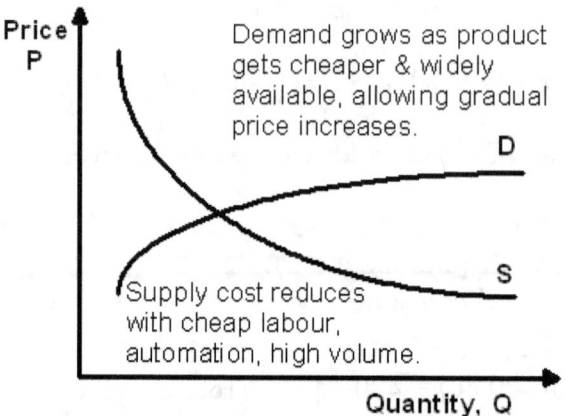

Figure 16.2. Inverse law of supply and demand.

The cornerstone of modern economics is the law of supply and demand. In this the supply curve goes up as price increases, motivating greater production, and the demand curve goes down with increasing production, greater availability of goods decreasing their price. The two curves intersect at the equilibrium point at which supply equals demand.

The original 'D down' form applied OK in Adam Smith's day (1723 – 1790) but for today's global market S & D curves should often be the reverse, as shown in Figure 16.2, because:

(a) Economies of scale, use of casual labour, cheap labour in developing countries, etc. reduce cost.

(b) Mass marketing tends to sell as much as is produced.

The original 'D down' form still applies sometimes, for example in the case of food and commodities such as oil:

> *The first law of economics is that when the price goes up, consumption goes down. This is a divine law.*
> *You cannot change it.*
> Sheikh Ahmed Yamani, Saudi Arabian Politician referring to OPEC's raising of oil prices in the early 1970s.

16. Economic Modelling

In modern global markets in which products are mass produced and heavily marketed my 'reversed' S&D model is that which applies and the massive growth in China's economy in recent decades is testament to this.

Some years ago the PC might have been a good example. The first microcomputers were tiny affairs suitable only for hobbyists but Clive Sinclair brought their price down to the point that they were affordable as toys for children. Then the first PCs suitable for business purposes, however, were quite expensive at first. Along came the IBM 'clone' from ASIA, however, and that brought the price of PCs down to the affordable levels we still see today for 'bottom of the range' but extremely powerful PCs with dazzling clock speeds compared to those of yore.

EXTRAPOLATION TECHNIQUES

In the world of business forecasting techniques are, of course, important, and there are many of these, some of them somewhat rule of thumb methods (Hewat, 1988).

Linear regression is one important method and spreadsheet programs perform this operation efficiently, finding the line of best fit (on a least squares basis) to a set of points, that line then being able to be used to predict the next few points (Cissell et al., 1990; Lotus, 1996).

One extrapolation technique not found in any textbook as yet is that of the Mohr Plot. This applies when a set of figures appear to have a hyperbolic form and thus be converging towards some limiting asymptotic value.

Figure 16.3(a) shows a hyperbolic curve approaching a horizontal asymptote at $p = a$, its equation being:

$$p = an/(b + n) = a/(b/n + 1)$$

As we are only interested in values of p approaching the horizontal asymptote, the vertical asymptote at $x = -b$ is not of interest.

16. Economic Modelling

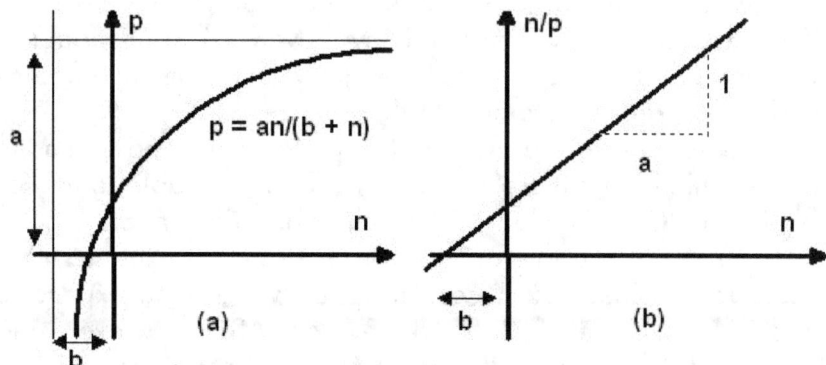

Figure 16.3. The Mohr Plot.

These values at the right side of the curve can be used to determine the limiting value $p = a$ if we rearrange the equation for the curve to

$$n/p = n/a + b/a$$

showing that plotting n/p against n, as shown in Figure 16.3(b), should give a straight line, the inverse slope of which is the value of the asymptote a. In practice, of course, this plot will not yield a straight line but linear regression of the figures in a spreadsheet program will indicate the required asymptote.

The Mohr Plot was used in Chapter 3 as a learning curve, illustrating that there is a 'diminishing return' situation with each further learning repetition, and also that 'large subjects' cannot be learnt perfectly.

The author has also used the Mohr Plot to extrapolate FEM solutions for slowly converging elements (Mohr, 1992), and no doubt it could also be applied to economic and financial market data.

The Mohr Plot also finds application in Mohr's Law of Heating which is discussed briefly in Appendix C, as well as in extrapolation of blood pressure readings over a few weeks during a 'get fit quick' routine (Mohr 2012d; 2013a) and this application is also discussed briefly in Appendix C.

16. Economic Modelling

Finally, the hyperbolic form of the Mohr Plot is also used for the assumed declining rate of expansion of the Universe, and also the declining rate of star formation in the Universe, in the recent books *The Evolving Universe* (Mohr et al., 2014) and *New Theories of the Universe, Evolution, and Relativity* (Mohr et al. 2018).

CONCLUSIONS

Input-Output Analysis is an essential tool in economic analysis and is used to model national economies, as well as the global economy.

The coefficients in Klein's simple model of the US economy in the years 1921 – 1941 can easily be adjusted to model other economies, providing a very useful way of modelling the 'flow on' effects inherent in modern economies.

Vernon's simple LMS and ISE equations provide a useful way of showing that, as intuition would suggest, and in contrast to the views of nearly all economists, increasing interest rates increases inflation.

Finally, extrapolation techniques are, of course, widely used in business and economics. Here Richardson extrapolation, which is widely used in the Finite Element method in generalized form, is used to good effect to perform a two-way extrapolation.

The Mohr Plot for estimating limiting (asymptotic) values of a series of converging figures is based on the Southwell plot for buckling failure of structural columns, and has proved useful in a variety of other situations.

For most economic applications, for example analysing current trends in a real estate market, curves based on moving averages are useful and easily obtained using spreadsheet programs. A further refinement is exponential smoothing, whilst in the economic context autoregressive moving average (ARIMA) models are much used (Newbold & Bos, 1990).

16. Economic Modelling

Finally, an interesting example of the use of spreadsheet calculations involving time dependent terms is that of forecasting the effect of future war, famine and disease upon the world's population, an exercise which the author undertook in his book *The Doomsday Calculation* (Mohr, 2012a), a further edition of which was entitled *The Population Explosion* (Mohr et al. 2018).

Chapter 17

CONCLUSIONS

THINKING AND COMMUNICATION

As noted in Chapter 1, Homo sapiens sapiens, or modern man, is simply an evolved hominid. What makes us different, however, is the enlarged cerebral cortex needed to store the semantic memory needed for our advanced languages. In addition, our delicate fingers play an important role in our ability to use tools, and in particular to write. So it is that Neanderthals produced wall paintings that were a precursor to the hieroglyphic writing of ancient peoples.

In primitive societies, a few of which survive at least in part today, tribal customs and folklore were passed on by elders to succeeding generations verbally. With the development of writing if became possible to disseminate information more efficiently and enduringly.

More important, being able to write down ideas, one was then able to review them and communicate them to others, adding to and improving them over time much more effectively.

The early polytheistic religions of primitive man give a record of much of man's earliest thinking, postulating spirits and Gods to explain the myriad of puzzling phenomena in our complex world.

With the invention of printing religious and other documents were able to be distributed widely, helping spread the major religions of the world to many millions of people around the world.

17. Conclusions

Printing also played a major role in the development of science, allowing each new scientific discovery to quickly become widely known so that other scientists could then make further advances.

Communication, therefore, plays a major role in thinking. Even when we talk to ourselves, most of us find that this helps us think and make decisions, or add to and improve earlier ideas. Writing also plays a part in this process, of course, allowing us to record our thoughts and ideas and later review and perhaps improve them.

Communication, both verbal, pictorial, and written, is also the means by which we learn from others, infants progressing from learning some of their first words from pictures to eventually developing a large vocabulary and learning to read and write.

MODERN TOOLS FOR THINKING

Earlier chapters having discussed learning, memory and basic thinking processes, later chapters (chapter numbers indicated as [5] etc.) discussed many useful tools for modern thinking, including:

- Decision matrices, tables and trees [5].
- Probability trees [5].
- Benefit-cost analysis [5].
- Meetings and printed agendas therefore [6].
- Group brainstorming [6].
- Mind maps [6].
- Fixed and controllable element analysis [7].
- Corporate structure [7].
- Effect of leadership on loyalty and performance [7].
- Market research and measurement of attitudes [8].
- Person scaling and Likert scaling [8].
- Mathematical logic and propositional calculus [9].
- Computer programming and flow diagrams [10].
- Dynamic programming [10].
- Input-output analysis [10].

17. CONCLUSIONS

- Flow-line production [11].
- Group technology and line-of-balance systems [11].
- The Critical Path Method for project scheduling (CPM) [11].
- Linear programming: solution of primal and dual problems [12].
- Finite element models of distribution and traffic flow [13].
- Non-linear optimization techniques: steepest descent and conjugate gradient methods [14].
- Optimality criterion techniques: fully stressed design (FSD) and flow ratio design (FRD) [14].
- Optimal FEM distribution networks [15].
- Inventory problems modelled as distribution problems [15].
- FRD of distribution problems [15].
- Optimization of FEM traffic flow models [15].

KEY APPLICATIONS OF THE PRESENT WORK

Novel applications of the work of the present text might include:

- Use of FEM to model distribution networks.
- Use of FEM to model traffic flow networks.
- Application of steepest descent to these models to optimize them.
- Application of flow ratio design (FRD) to these models to obtain approximate optimum solutions.
- Inclusion of time interpolations in scheduling networks and thence optimization of them.
- Inclusion of penalty constraints and optimization in input-output analysis.
- Modelling of traffic flows with 2D elements for the background flow and 1D elements for the major routes, including sources, sinks, infinite boundaries and other refinements (Mohr & Power, 2003).

17. CONCLUSIONS

In addition, many of the numerical methods discussed might find application in many areas of management science, for example:
- The iterative, search and predictor-corrector methods.
- The matrix inversion and solution methods.
- Interpolation and numerical integration methods.
- The LP programs for MIN and MAX.
- The direct LP program for distribution.
- The steepest descent and conjugate gradient methods.
- The CPM and shortest route programs.
- Time stepping of macroeconomic models.

To take a couple of simple examples:

(a) The idea of perturbing a system to determine *gradients,* as in the steepest descent method, might be applied to any large accounting system, treating it as a black box and simply altering one variable at a time to determine the *sensitivity* of the system to them.

(b) The idea of iterating a system according to some *optimality criterion*, as in the FRD method, might be applied to any numerical model of a business system.

APPLICATIONS EXAMPLES

The many thinking tools discussed in foregoing chapters have a wide range of usage from board and committee meetings to planning, building and operation of major construction and industrial projects.

The Finite Element Method (FEM) is an extension of the Matrix Structural Analysis techniques developed in Germany in the 1940s for the analysis and design of aircraft using 'skeletal' or line elements. Strictly speaking, FEM is an extension of this which subdivides continuous parts of structures such as suspended concrete floor slabs into a number of two-dimensional elements (Argyris, 1965, 1968; Mohr 1992).

17. CONCLUSIONS

The present author pioneered the use of FEM techniques to analyze distribution, input-output analysis and traffic flow networks. Though these largely involve naturally 'discrete' elements, and not arbitrary subdivision of a 2D or 3D structure into an arbitrary number of discrete elements for the purposes of approximate analysis, the term FEM is still used as the solution techniques used are still those of FEM.

Distribution problems, however, can be approximately modelled as 2D flow problems (Mohr, 2002). Indeed, traffic flow network problems can be appropriately modelled as a two dimensional continuum (to represent a 'background' of minor roads and streets) with major roads and arterial roads being represented by 1D line elements as in the present book.

The author has researched many of the techniques discussed in the present book extensively, including:

[1] Use of fully stressed design to optimize structures (Mohr 1976, 1979).
[2] Use of steepest descent techniques to optimize structural and fluid flow problems (Mohr 1992, 1994(2)).
[3] Use of FEM techniques for the Critical Path Method (Mohr, 1994).
[4] Inclusion of constraints in the matrix solution of Input-Output Analysis (Mohr, 1999a).
[5] A modification of Laurence Klein's matrix model of the US economy 1921 – 1941 (Mohr, 1999b).
[6] Use of FEM to model and optimize distribution problems (Mohr, 1999c, 2000).
[7] Development of the flow ratio design method (FRD) to optimize flow problems (Mohr, 2004b, 2005).

The author hopes, therefore, that many others will find useful application for some of the techniques discussed in this book.

Near the end of Appendix C the 10 laws of my new religion Mohronism are given. In the following three sections three more of my many laws are given.

17. Conclusions

Mohr's Metrology

This requires a little elaboration. It asserts that all human traits can be measured. Madness, for example, is not a black and white thing, and we should be given a score, though this may vary a little according to such factors as the weather and countless others that hardly need mention.

For this law we use the **Mohr Scale**, noting that a score of 10 is not possible as perfect madness, for example, would surely be rapidly terminal. Furthermore a score of zero is not possible as perfect sanity would surely constitute insanity.

Hence the Mohr Scale is 0 - 9, and the median score is the sum of the possible scores divided by the number of possible scores, that is 45/9 = 5. This is the median score with four possible scores above and below it. With this score you don't pass or fail but are borderline.

The Mohr scale is also useful in the study of *ethics* where the questions of what is 'right' or 'good' are put, quickly followed by the question: "how good?" For this purpose the Mohr scale provides a set of ordinal numbers where, for example, 9 is the maximum goodness (10 would be too good to be true).

A couple of final laws are needed.

Mohr's Universal Law

Junk fills the time and space available.

At last this is it, the meaning of life. All other laws are clearly subsets of this as clearly this new law encompasses both Parkinson's law, where the junk is work, and the Peter Principle, where the junk is the workers!

Consider, for just a moment, the myriad of examples that immediately come to mind, just for example:
- Advertising
- Cars
- Clothes: irrational jeans, shoes, ties etc.
- Chemicals (cleaning compounds, cosmetics)
- Education: new courses are invented every minute and MBAs are sold on almost every street corner (Mohr, 2017).

17. CONCLUSIONS

- Drugs, including cigarettes, booze and tranquilizers
- Fads and gadgets
- Food fads: from exotic to health diets
- New games and sports
- Graffiti
- Health fads: exercise machines, plastic surgery etc.
- Junk food (burgers and Coke etc.)
- Music: endless reiteration of the old and the new pushing the limits
- Movies
- Magazines and newspapers
- Plastic supermarket bags are filling parts of the world
- Pornography
- PCs & video games
- Phones: mobile phones need no further comment
- Radio: it wasn't always 24 hours of music, news or talk
- Radios/CD players: they weren't always next to the bed, in the car or carried around with you
- Roads and road furniture (signs, speed humps etc.)
- Shares (with everything being privatized etc.)
- Toys: from cradle to grave we have rattles, skateboards, roller blades and yachts for executives
- TV: endless new 'soaps' and lots of cable channels to show all the old junk too

Now, last but not least, I will mention the people who make and peddle all the junk.

Mohr's Law of Money is derived in Appendix C. Like that for population growth, it is an exponential result, explaining how in capitalism the rich get richer, and richer than ever before.

The pigs in Orwell's *Animal Farm* are the fat capitalists. You don't matter except when some capitalist, imperialist, religious, racist or other unjustified excuse is used to start yet another war (Cowie et al., 1994). Then you or yours may be required to die for a lie.

17. Conclusions

Mohr's Law of Politics

This is that, if you build a fence of any kind, there will usually be substantial numbers of people on both sides – this applies in *The War of The Sexes* (Mohr, 2012c, 2018c), where the numbers are fairly equal, but also to the farcical and outdated Westminster system of government where these days the two main parties are relatively similar in policies, incompetence etcetera, so many a voter makes up their mind on which side of the political fence to place their vote only at the last minute.

We do not have democracy in the increasingly capitalist West, and the situation is far worse that when Aristotle complained that Greece had oligarchy way back then:

*A democracy exists whenever those who are free
and are not well-off, being in the majority,
are in sovereign control of government,
an oligarchy when control lies with the rich and better born.*
Aristotle, *The Politics* (343 BC).

As for the ongoing battle of the US-British war machine against the pink peril, as I have said elsewhere, China still has a central committee socialist government that now the US must kow tow to, being so much in debt to China. Russia has not forgotten the USSR by any means, India is perhaps a little pink, as are a few counties in Africa and South America. So it may be that Engels was right when he said:

*Just as Darwin discovered the law of evolution
of organic matter, so Marx discovered
the law of evolution of human history.*
Friedrich Engels, said at the funeral of Karl Marx (1883).

I'm not taking any bets on this, however, in view of my predictions of a great deal of trouble for the human kind in my recent book *The Doomsday Calculation* (Mohr, 2012a).

17. Conclusions

Conclusions

I have had many more ideas than those discussed in this book and its appendices, sometimes thinking that I had at least one good idea every day. That is not, in fact, true - but I'm sure I have an idea that is quite good every week or so, and sometimes (perhaps every month) I have a really good idea. Indeed, if you pay me enough, I might dream up one for you!

So now some ideas to improve the degenerating situation for mankind that I discuss in the recent books *The Doomsday Calculation* and *The Population Explosion* (Mohr, 2012a; Mohr et al., 2018b).

In approximate order of importance:

[1] I believe we should have a unilateral ban on nuclear and biochemical weapons, if not all weapons (full stop).

[2] I believe we need to set about halving the world's population.

[3] I believe we need to reduce consumption of such things as oil in the high GNP per capita countries such as the USA by about 50%.

[4] I believe children born in Australia should be *given* a block of land in some regional city as a birthright and should not spend their lives paying off a mortgage for their own cave.

[5] I believe we should have a 4 day week as a general rule, not people working like slaves for multinational companies that sell needless junk to *consumer zombies* (Mohr, 2013b).

[6] I believe we need to build up regional towns and cities in Australia and like countries to good self-sufficient size rather than cram ourselves into megacities in which people live and work in multistory buildings that are, as one Scottish union leader called them, *"architectural representations of filing cabinets."*

These megacities have increasingly complex networks jammed with cars, many of which take an hour or two to get people who live in outer suburbs to work, causing considerable atmospheric pollution as they do so.

In the suburbs too, of course, increasingly high apartment buildings are being constructed, despite objections by residents.

17. Conclusions

[7] I believe we need to look at alternative power sources and alternative materials for products and buildings to make them last.

[8] In dry and arid areas such as much of Australia or the Middle East it might be worthwhile building only a few nuclear desalination plants to help establish new towns and cities to take the pressure of capital cities.

Note, however, that as the Club of Rome report pointed out over three decades ago (Meadows et al., 1972) the stacks of nuclear power plants give off substantial amounts of radioactive isotopes such as those of Krypton with a half-life of many years.

In other words nuclear power will not save us and can only be used safely to a limited extent and, perhaps, for a limited time.

[9] I believe an education system which has children in long-day-care almost from birth and then in school for an absurdly long 12 years, this to be followed by absurd University courses such as in Puppetry (Macquarie U) and Sexology (Curtin U), is all quite ridiculous. For starters 10 years at a school is more than ample, e.g., Francis Bacon *left* Cambridge at 14.

[10] We need to start working towards *Real Democracy* and this I make a few suggestions about in Chapter 20 of my book *The Doomsday Calculation,* and also in Chapter 28 of my recent book *The History and Psychology of Human Conflicts.*

We also need to decide what the purpose of human life is. We are animals and ideas about God are bullshit invented for profit and power by charlatans, crooks and paedophiles, e.g., the monasteries in Europe under which the bones of countless children were found.

I believe the purpose of human life is to advance our standard of living and our non-animal part as far as possible. To create a better, fairer, 'nicer' world in which our children can live in peace to explore their potential for those things in which humans are superior to other animals, that is, experimentation, discovery, learning and so forth.

17. CONCLUSIONS

In a fair society, at the risk of repeating myself:

(a) One's own cave should be a birthright, not something you spend your life working to pay off.

(b) Decent products such as small fibreglass electric cars which run on only a few kW should have been around for ages and could probably be recharged by just one of a couple of solar power cell banks on the roof of a house.

(c) The major industries in the world should not be arms, drugs, booze, cigarettes and junk food filled with fat and sugar. Modern man eats more refined sugar in day than his ancestors ate in a lifetime (Somer, 2001) with disastrous results such as heart disease.

I should not need to point out that unused sugar is converted and stored as fat but, before that, as lipids in the blood of which the VLDL and LDL do quite a bit of damage.

I should not need to point out that carbohydrates, alcohol etc. are converted to sugar. But it won't do to cut down only on the carbs. You need to eliminate all the bad things in the diet and, indeed, in your life such as stress (Mohr 2012d, 2013a).

With 'real democracy' it could be hoped that quality of life would improve for all, and in my recent book *2045* I describe how a remote town establishes new, more democratic and egalitarian codes for living after the world's major cities have been destroyed by a global nuclear and biochemical warfare (Mohr, 2014b). In the books *The Doomsday Calculation* (Mohr, 2012) and *The Population Explosion* (Mohr et al., 2018b) I conclude that real democracy may help reduce the growing number of problems such as overpopulation, pollution, and resource depletion threatening mankind, and I describe what real democracy should entail in more detail in two books on the psychology of human conflict (Mohr, 2014; Mohr et al. 2018c).

The End

17. Conclusions

Appendix A

Introduction to BASIC

A brief history of BASIC

A feature of the book is many short programs in BASIC. BASIC was developed by Kemeny and Kurtz at Dartmouth College (New Hampshire) in the early 1960s and was much used on minicomputers (which typically had 16 terminals, each being allowed 16 kb of RAM, the amount required by the then versions of BASIC) in the 1970s.

In 1975 the first microcomputer was sold, a clumsy box + switches affair with storage of only 256 bytes. In the same year Tiny BASIC, consisting of just 20 pages of code, was written and many versions of this quickly appeared and, also in 1975, Gates and Allen launched Microsoft Corporation with their version, this being marketed with the Altair microcomputer.

A flood of microcomputers with as little as 16 kb of RAM then appeared, the Apple, the Commodore 64, the Spectravideo, the HP85 and many others, all having their own version of BASIC.

In the early 1980s IBM quit their near monopoly of the electric ('golfball') typewriter market, switching to production of *PCs* with about a MB of RAM. Now there was a flood of PCs, Apple, IBM, ICL, NEC, Olivetti etc., as well as many IBM 'clones.'

On the IBM BASICJ, BASICA and GW ('Gee Whiz") BASIC appeared. All used about 64 kb and the latter is quite powerful. With the advent of a MB of RAM or more on PCs Chris Cochran and American Planning Corp's MegaBasic appeared to make full use of it.

Appendix A: Introduction to BASIC

From Microsoft QBASIC, using a rudimentary GUI (graphic user interface), followed and this was shipped with DOS 5. QuickBASIC, which was largely the same but included a compiler soon followed. Then came Visual Basic (VB) for Windows, VB4 being somewhat clumsy to use, but VB5 and later versions are very user friendly though somewhat complicated.

VB5 was quite quick, but not as quick as the original computer language, FORTRAN, or the later C++. There are still reminders of its predecessors, for example the QBColor( ) function. VB6 and VB7 or VB.NET, however, are about as quick as C++ when compiled so that BASIC was finally competitive speedwise.

The great attraction of BASIC is having a command interpreter which allows programs to run on an almost 'line by line' basis without full compilation, that is, you don't type the whole program in, compile and receive a long list of cryptic error messages which don't even tell you where the program stopped. Instead, mistyped lines produce an immediate error as you type the program in.

When you do run the program, therefore, there will be only one error message at a time, telling you where the program stopped and you go to that line and correct the usually obvious error, and thus work your way through what should be only a few errors.

The many programs in this book use QBASIC**, which takes only about 500 kb, half of this being its HELP file which gives a fairly good, concise introduction to BASIC (c.f. VB takes about 100 MB and the Pro version is very expensive). QBASIC programs read directly into a VB 'module' (i.e. subroutine) or can be attached as the code for a 'Form.'

In this appendix some introductory BASIC exercises are given. For additional help the reader might track down books such as those listed at the end of this Appendix.

**Finally, note that QBASIC and its extension QuickBASIC, which includes a compiler, can easily be downloaded free from the internet.

Appendix A: Introduction to BASIC

Introduction to BASIC programming

BASIC commands
The most elementary BASIC commands are:
RUN - to run a program
SAVE - to store a program
ENTER - to add lines
REN - renumber program lines (with default 'gaps' of 10)
LIST - to list the program (on screen)
BYE - to leave BASIC

Arithmetic operations
The following program determines the square toot of a number using Newton's method (see also Chapter 10) in which the root is given by iterating the recursion relation
$$x_{new} = (x_{old} + num/x_{old})/2$$
where num = number for which the square root is required
x_{old} = initial estimate of the square root

Then, using a tolerance number TOL as a termination criterion the program is:

```
10 Rem SQRT using Newton's method
20 INPUT "Input, xold, num, tol", XOLD, NUM, TOL
30 XNEW = 0.5*(XOLD+NUM/XOLD)
40 DIFF = ABS(XNEW-XOLD)
50 IF DIFF<TOL THEN GOTO 80
60 XOLD = XNEW: PRINT XNEW
70 GOTO 30
80 PRINT "SQRT =", XNEW
```

and to test the program input 1,4,0.001 to obtain $\sqrt{4} = 2$.

Note that ABS( ) is a library function for the absolute value and that in some versions of BASIC a final line, 90 END is required (and in VB a first line Sub MYPROG( ) is needed to declare a subroutine).

In early versions of BASIC line numbers were necessary and in very early versions of BASIC variable names were restricted to a single alphabetic character plus a single optional digit.

Appendix A: Introduction to BASIC

In QBASIC (and VB) line numbers are not necessary and variable names can be many characters but statements are upper case (converted thus if typed otherwise). Then when computation is redirected by a GOTO (or THEN GOTO, for which only THEN is actually required) statement the target line must have a *label* (e.g. LAB1:) which is given in the GOTO statement. Thus the foregoing example can be written more briefly as

```
INPUT xold, num, tol
LAB1: xnew = (xold + num/xold)/2 : diff = ABS(xnew-xold)
IF diff<tol GOTO LAB2
xold = xnew: GOTO LAB1
LAB2:PRINT xnew
```

where a semicolon is used as a *statement separator*. The author, however, generally uses line numbers throughout his programs, one reason being that, having put many BASIC programs in books, they are very handy in this situation to help describe the program (i.e. "lines 110 - 160 do - - - ').

Strings

Ease of string handling is one of the advantages of BASIC. The following program reads three names (given in the DATA statement at the end) and prints them (on screen) with three spaces between. It then prints an integer and a real number using PRINT USING to format these.

```
10 READ a$, b$, c$
20 x$ = SPACES$(3)
30 PRINT A$;x$;b$;x$;c$
40 P$="#####" : Q$ = "#####.##"
50 n = 2 : c = 14/3
60 PRINT USING P$ ; n ; : PRINT USING Q$;c
70 DATA 'Bob", "Jim", "Ted"
```

Note that a ; follows the 'n' of the first PRINT USING statement to print both numbers on the same line, otherwise the second number will appear on a second line.

APPENDIX A: INTRODUCTION TO BASIC

Arrays and Loops

The following *database* program dimensions (i.e declares their size) *arrays* and then uses a *loop* (on i) to read some names and ages and print them out, indenting the names using the LEN function.
```
DIM names$(10),num(10)
FOR i = 1 to 3
READ names$(i), num(i)
j = LEN(names(i)) : x$ = SPACE$( j )
PRINT x$; names$(i), num(i) : NEXT
DATA Jane, 25
DATA June, 35
DATA Caroline, 15
```

Functions

The following coding gives a simple example of a user defined function to calculate the square of a number. Note the way the variable Z is passed to the function as an *argument* and the function result is returned as Z.
```
10 DECLARE FUNCTION SQ(Z)
20 Z=2
30 Y = SQ(Z)
40 PRINT Z
100 FUNCTION SQ(Z)
110 Z=Z*Z
END FUNCTION
```

Note that QBASIC automatically stores the function as a *subroutine* in a separate *workspace* accessed via the VIEW menu from the menu bar (at the top of the screen).

Standard functions

Standard arithmetic, mathematical and string functions used in BASIC include
INT( ) - gives the integer (truncated) value of a number
ABS( ) - gives absolute value of a number (unsigned)

Appendix A: Introduction to BASIC

RND(x) - gives a random number [x <0 gives same number, x> 0 (or x not given) gives the next number in the sequence, = 0 gives the last number]
SQR( ) - gives square root
SIN( ) - gives SIN( ) of an angle in radians
LEN(A$) - see example program in "Arrays and loops" earlier in this section
CHR$(n) - gives the ASCII character corresponding to integer n (e.g. n = 65 gives A)

Subroutines

The simplest way of forming subroutines is using the GOSUB command to move to program segments appended after the END statement

```
10 PRINT "main"
20 GOSUB 50
30 PRINT "main"
40 END
50 PRINT "sub"
60 RETURN
```

Alternatively subroutines are stored as separate programs and called by a main program. The following program has a subroutine 'datin' which is called and variables N, M passed to it, another variable array Y( ) being declared SHARED.

```
DECLARE SUB datin (N, M)
REM MAIN
DIM X(10), Y(10)
COMMON SHARED Y()
X(1) = 5: Y(2) = 3: N = 10: M = 10
datin N, M
PRINT "main", X(1), Y(2), N, M
END
SUB datin (N, M)
DIM X(10)
PRINT "sub", X(1), Y(2), N, M
END SUB
```

Appendix A: Introduction to BASIC

Here the argument list passes N, M to the subroutine and the COMMON SHARED statement allows listed variables to be accessed by all other subroutines. As the array X() is not included in the shared statement, X(1) will print from the subroutine as zero.

Data files

The following code creates and accesses data files (as distinct from program files):

```
OPEN "c:\ET\tempdat" FOR OUTPUT AS #7
OPEN "c:\ET\gmdata" FOR RANDOM AS #8 LEN = 100
x = 2: y = 3
PUT #8, 1, x :PUT #8, 2, y
WRITE #7, x, y
CLOSE #7
OPEN "c:\ET\tempdat" FOR INPUT AS #7
GET #8, 2, z : PRINT z
INPUT #7, z : PRINT z
```

Here two files are used for *sequential* access and *direct* or *random* access, in the second case overestimating the *record* length and reading back only the second number written to it.

Searching and comparing data

The following code is a very simple example of comparing data, in this case string data. In conjunction with search, therefore, such comparisons can be used to locate specific data.

```
10 a$ = "jim" : b$ = "jim"
30 IF a$ = b$ THEN PRINT "OK"
40 b$="ted"
50 IF a$ = b$ THEN PRINT "OK" ELSE PRINT "NO"
```

Such comparisons might be used to extract negative numbers (perhaps corresponding to negative account balances) and the associated personal details from a file.

APPENDIX A: INTRODUCTION TO BASIC

VISUAL BASIC (VB)

The following VB5/6 program is for the steepest descent problem: Minimize $f(x_1,x_2) = (x_1 - 2)^2 + (x_2 - 1)^2$ subject to the constraints:

$1 - x_1^2/4 - x_2 \geq 0$
$x_1 - 2x_2 + 1 = 0$

Then the sequence of unconstrained minima technique (SUMT – see Chapter 14) problem is stated as

Min: $F = f(x_1,x_2) + \beta|1-x_1^2/4-x_2|^2 + \beta(x_1-2x_2+1)^2 \quad \beta \to \infty$

And steepest descent proceeds with search lengths S as

$\{x\}_n = \{x\}_{n-1} - S\{\delta F/\delta x_1, \delta F/\delta x_2\}$

These gradients are obtained by using perturbations of each *design variable* in turn (by about 5 or 10%) and calculating approximate gradients from the *finite difference* approximations $g_i = (F_2 - F_1)/\delta x_i$ for each variable *i*.

This is done in following program and the simple coding can be generalized to deal with many variables and problems in any context.

Starting from $x_1 = x_2 = 2$ (set in the program) and using only two searches with $\beta = 1$ (with searches $S = 0.082$ and $S = 0.14$) and also two searches with $\beta = 100$ ($S = 0.0047$ and $S = 0.00035$) a reasonably good solution can be obtained as:

$x_1 = 0.7326$ and $x_2 = 0.8662$ with $F = 1.6242$.

whereas the exact solution is $x_1 = \sqrt{3} - 1 = 0.7321$, $x_2 = \sqrt{3}/2 = 0.8660$ and $F = 13.75 - 7\sqrt{3} = 1.6256$.

If exact gradients are used for $\beta = 1, 10, 100, 1000, 10^4, 10^5, 10^6$ six or so searches can be used with each β to obtain a no more accurate result.

This is because using exact gradients is like following tangents on a curve looking for a turning point. The results can be 'miles off'. The approximate steepest descent gradients, however, act like a 'chord approximation' and give much better results, the chord (at reasonable intervals) giving a much better idea where a curve is going than the slope.

Appendix A: Introduction to BASIC

```
Private Sub Command1_Click()
Call main
End Sub
Rem The latter code is attached to the form Form1

DefSng A-H, M, O-Z: DefInt I-L, N
Private op As Object: Public X1, X2, B, F
Sub main()
Rem searches: B=1, 0.082 & 0.14; B=100, 0.0047 & 0.00035
Set op = Form1: op.DrawWidth = 3: op.FontItalic = True
Dim C(10, 10): I = 0: M = 1.05: S = 0: op.FontSize = 14: op.FontBold = True
op.PSet (2400, 1400), RGB(255, 255, 255): op.Print "Optimum"
op.PSet (1100, 2100), RGB(255, 255, 255)
op.Print ">= constraint"
op.PSet (700, 500), RGB(255, 255, 255): op.Print "= constraint"
op.PSet (3200, 1000), RGB(255, 255, 255)
op.Print "Solution path"
X = 0: Y = 1000: op.Line (X, Y)-(X, Y)
For Z = 0 To 2 Step 0.01
X = Z: Y = 1 - X * X / 4: X = 2000 * X: Y = 3000 - 2000 * Y
op.Line -(X, Y): Next Z
op.Line (0, 2000)-(4000, 0): op.Line (0, 3000)-(6000, 3000)
op.Line (0, 3000)-(0, 0)
X1 = 2: X2 = 2: C(1, 1) = X1: C(1, 2) = X2
X = 2000 * X1: Y = 3000 - 2000 * X2: op.Line (X, Y)-(X, Y)
NEWB: a$ = InputBox("B", , , 5000, 4000): B = CSng(a$)
I = I + 1: C(I, 1) = X1: C(I, 2) = X2: S1 = 0
If B = 0 Then GoTo PEND
Call Subb: Debug.Print "IF =", F
F1 = F: X1 = X1 * M: Call Subb: F2 = F: X1 = X1 / M
G1 = (F2 - F1) / (X1 * (M - 1))
X2 = X2 * M: Call Subb: F2 = F: X2 = X2 / M
G2 = (F2 - F1) / (X2 * (M - 1))
NEWS: a$ = InputBox("S", , , 5000, 4000): S = CSng(a$)
If S = 0 Then GoTo NEWB
X1 = X1 + (S1 - S) * G1: X2 = X2 + (S1 - S) * G2
Call Subb: Debug.Print X1; " "; X2; "F= "; F
S1 = S
X = 2000 * X1: Y = 3000 - 2000 * X2: op.Line -(X, Y)
GoTo NEWS
PEND: End Sub
```

Appendix A: Introduction to BASIC

```
Sub Subb()
G = 1 - X1 * X1 / 4 - X2: E = X1 - 2 * X2 + 1
If G > 0 Then G = 0
FU = (X1 - 2) ^ 2 + (X2 - 1) ^ 2
F = FU + B * G * G + B * E * E
End Sub
```

The program has a form *Form1* to which is attached a command button and the first three lines of code and a Command Button must be attached to this. This button is clicked to call the program module *Module1* (which contains the rest of the coding) and an input box appears asking for the value of the penalty factor B. Input this value and the box asks for the search step length S. Input trial values and when this search is complete use S = 0 to terminate the search, when a B value for the next search (and then S) is requested.

Progress results are printed in the immediate window using Debug.Print and plotted on Form1.

To terminate execution use S = 0 followed by B = 0.

BIBLIOGRAPHY

Brown S, *Visual Basic in Record Time,* Sybex, Alameda CA, 1998.
Cochran C, *MegaBasic Users Manual*, American Planning Corp., Alexandria VA, 1984.
Fox D, *Pure Visual Basic*, Sams 1999.
Lien DA, *The BASIC Handbook*, 3rd edn, Microtech, Dubai, UAE, 1989.
Perry G, *Introduction to Computer Programming*, SAMS, New York, 2001.
Price WT, *Fundamentals of Computers and Data Processing with Basic*, Holt Rinehard and Winston, New York NY, 1983.
Time-Life (eds), *Computer Languages*, Time-Life Inc., 1986.
MS GW-BASIC User's Guide and User's Reference, MS Corp., 1987.

Appendix B

Two-Dimensional Finite Elements

Triangular and Rectangular Finite Elements

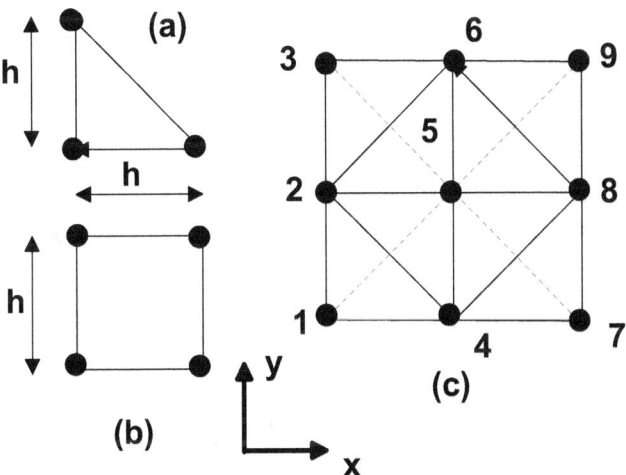

Figure B.1. Use of triangular and rectangular elements.

Using right angled isosceles triangular elements of the form shown in Figure B.1(a) the appropriate finite element matrix when the governing differential equation is LaPlace's equation ($\nabla^2 \phi = 0$) is given by (Mohr, 2001):

$$(t/2h)\begin{bmatrix} 2 & -1 & -1 \\ -1 & 1 & 0 \\ -1 & 0 & 1 \end{bmatrix} \begin{Bmatrix} \phi_1 \\ \phi_4 \\ \phi_2 \end{Bmatrix} = \begin{Bmatrix} q_1 \\ q_2 \\ q_2 \end{Bmatrix} \quad \text{(B.1)}$$

APPENDIX B: TWO-DIMENSIONAL FINITE ELEMENTS

where $\{q\}$ are the nodal loads or fluxes, $\{\phi\}$ are the nodal potentials for the bottom left hand corner element in Figure B.1(c), and t is the (uniform) transverse thickness. The element matrices are deployed in the system matrix according to its node numbers in the same fashion as for line elements in earlier chapters.

For a square element with one freedom (such as a *potential* function) at each corner the element matrix takes the form (Mohr, 2001):

$$k = (t/12h) \begin{bmatrix} 8 & -2 & -4 & -2 \\ -2 & 8 & -2 & -4 \\ -4 & -2 & 8 & -2 \\ -2 & -4 & -2 & 8 \end{bmatrix} \quad (B.2)$$

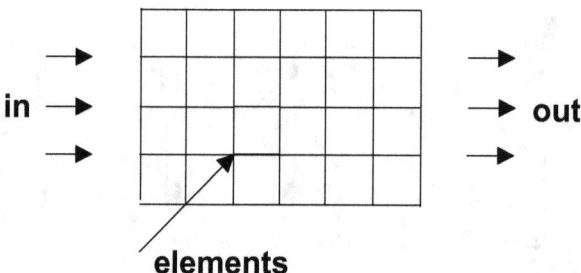

Figure B.2. Two dimensional flow problem.

Such simple matrices can be used to model a wide range of problems in physical science, for example that of *rectilinear flow* (e.g. of fluid, traffic) in a two dimensional field, as illustrated in Figure B.2.

Here there are input and output fluxes, as shown, and the problem might be one in which the *permeabilities* differ in the x and y directions.

The procedure for deriving finite elements to model *potential flow* is detailed in the following section, a further section then giving a simple program for finite element analysis of two dimensional potential flow.

APPENDIX B: TWO-DIMENSIONAL FINITE ELEMENTS

POTENTIAL FLOW

Two dimensional potential flow is governed by the partial differential equation (LaPlace's equation),

$$\nabla^2 \phi = \partial^2\phi/\partial x^2 + \partial^2\phi/\partial y^2 = 0 \quad \phi = \phi(x,y) \quad (B.3)$$

where ϕ is a two dimensional potential function and $\nabla^2(\;)$ is called the *Laplacian function* or *operator*.

The equations for a finite element are formed using the following procedure:

[1] In each element an interpolation function of the nodal values is formed: $\phi = \{f\}^t \{\phi\}$ (B.4)

[2] This interpolation is substituted into the governing partial differential equation, giving, if this is Equation B.3,

$$\int [\{f_{xx}\}^t + \{f_{yy}\}^t] \{\phi\} \, dV = R \; (\approx 0) \quad (B.5)$$

where f_{xx} and f_{yy} are the second partial derivatives of the interpolation functions and the PDE is approximately satisfied (leaving a small *residual* R) over the volume V of the element.

[3] Then the *method of weighted residuals (MWR)* is used, multiplying the residuals for each element by a weighting factor. In the *Galerkin method* the interpolation functions themselves are used as weights so that we obtain

$$\iint \{f\} [\{f_{xx}\}^t + \{f_{yy}\}^t] \, dxdy \, \{\phi\} \approx 0 \quad (B.6)$$

[4] Applying *integration by parts* to this result (writing $f = \{f\}$ to simplify the resulting expressions) we obtain

$$\iint \{f\}[\{f_{xx}\}^t dxdy = \int f f_x^t \, dy \; | \; - \iint f_x \, f_x^t \, dxdy \quad (B.7)$$

$$\iint \{f\}[\{f_{yy}\}^t dxdy = \int f f_y^t \, dy \; | \; - \iint f_y \, f_y^t \, dxdy \quad (B.8)$$

where the first terms on the right sides are boundary forcing terms for the problem. Then combining Equations B.7 and B.8 we obtain element equations of the form

$$k\{\phi\} = \{q\} \quad (B.9)$$

APPENDIX B: TWO-DIMENSIONAL FINITE ELEMENTS

[5] These element equations are summed to give system equations of the form

$$K\{\phi\}=\{Q\} \quad (B.10)$$

Then, first setting the boundary conditions or known values of ϕ, these equations are solved to determine the unknown ϕ values at the nodes.

We have already worked through this procedure for a line element in Chapter 13 and in the following section it is used to formulate a very useful 2D element.

Note that using the *Galerkin method*, and thence using the interpolation functions as a multiplying weighting factor, yields element matrices involving 'squaring' terms on the RHSs of Equations B.7 and B.8. This gives the solutions a maximal 'least squares' type of accuracy so that the weighting by $\{f\}$ is the natural and most accurate option in FEM.

THE QUADRATIC TRIANGLE ELEMENT

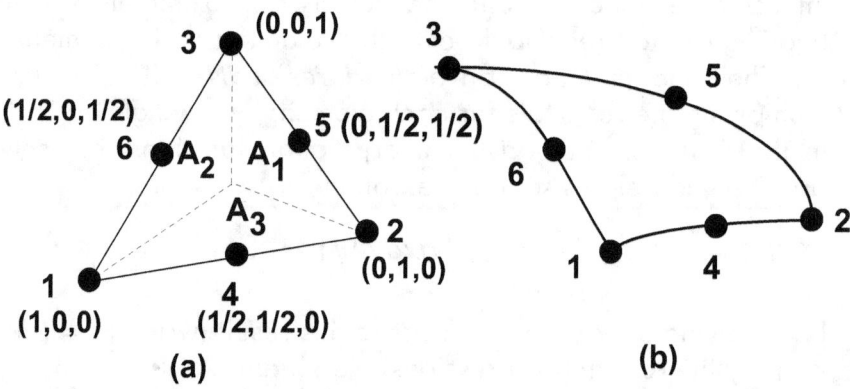

Figure B.3. (a) Quadratic triangle element showing area coordinates of nodes; (b) mapped isoparametrically.

Figure 12.3 shows one of the most useful finite elements, a triangular element with six nodes, three of these at the mid points of the sides. Using a process called *isoparametric mapping* the element can have the curved sides shown in Figure B.3(b), making it particularly useful.

APPENDIX B: TWO-DIMENSIONAL FINITE ELEMENTS

Area coordinates

For triangular elements it is useful to define *area coordinates* for any point in the element using the ratios of the interior areas shown in Figure B.3(a) to the total area A of the element. After a little algebraic manipulation it can be shown that the area coordinates L_1, L_2, L_3 are given by

$$L_1 = A_1/A = (a - y_{32}x + x_{32}y)/2A \qquad \text{(B.11a)}$$
$$L_2 = A_2/A = (a - y_{13}x + x_{13}y)/2A \qquad \text{(B.11b)}$$
$$L_3 = A_3/A = (a - y_{21}x + x_{21}y)/2A \qquad \text{(B.11c)}$$

where $a = 2A/3$ and $2A = x_{21}y_{32} - x_{32}y_{21}$ with

$$x_{32} = x_3 - x_2, \quad x_{13} = x_1 - x_3, \quad x_{21} = x_2 - x_1$$
$$y_{32} = y_3 - y_2, \quad y_{13} = y_1 - y_3, \quad y_{21} = y_2 - y_1$$

and the reader can verify that Equations B.11 give the nodal coordinates shown in Figure B.3a.

From the nature of the definition of the area coordinates the identity $L_1 + L_2 + L_3 = 1$ \qquad (B.12)
also follows and note that the coordinates of the centroid are $L_1 = L_2 = L_3 = 1/3$.

Interpolation

To develop an interpolation for the element we begin by writing an interpolation polynomial in terms of a vector of modes $\{M\}$ and modal amplitudes $\{c\}$

$$\phi = \{c\}^t\{M\} = c_1 L_1^2 + c_2 L_2^2 + c_3 L_3^2 + c_4 L_1 L_2 + c_5 L_2 L_3 + c_6 L_3 L_1 \quad \text{(B.13)}$$

and substituting the area coordinates of the nodes we obtain

$$\{\phi\} = \begin{Bmatrix} \phi_1 \\ \phi_2 \\ \phi_3 \\ \phi_4 \\ \phi_5 \\ \phi_6 \end{Bmatrix} = \begin{bmatrix} 1 & 0 & 0 & 0 & 0 & 0 \\ 0 & 1 & 0 & 0 & 0 & 0 \\ 0 & 0 & 1 & 0 & 0 & 0 \\ 1/2 & 1/2 & 0 & 1/2 & 0 & 0 \\ 0 & 1/2 & 1/2 & 0 & 1/2 & 0 \\ 1/2 & 0 & 1/2 & 0 & 0 & 1/2 \end{bmatrix} \begin{Bmatrix} c_1 \\ c_2 \\ c_3 \\ c_4 \\ c_5 \\ c_6 \end{Bmatrix} = C\{c\}$$

(B.14)

APPENDIX B: TWO-DIMENSIONAL FINITE ELEMENTS

Inverting the matrix C (alternatively Equations B.14 are easily solved by elimination) the interpolation functions $\{f\}$ for the interpolation

$$\phi = \{f\}^t\{\phi\} \tag{B.15}$$

are given by

$$\{f\}^t = \{M\}^t C^{-1} = \{M\}^t \begin{bmatrix} 1 & 0 & 0 & 0 & 0 & 0 \\ 0 & 1 & 0 & 0 & 0 & 0 \\ 0 & 0 & 1 & 0 & 0 & 0 \\ -1 & -1 & 0 & 4 & 0 & 0 \\ 0 & -1 & -1 & 0 & 4 & 0 \\ -1 & 0 & -1 & 0 & 0 & 4 \end{bmatrix} \tag{B.16}$$

yielding the results

$$f_1 = L_1^2 - L_1L_2 - L_3L_1 = L_1(2L_1 - 1)$$
$$f_2 = L_2(2L_2 - 1), \quad f_3 = L_3(2L_3 - 1) \tag{B.17}$$
$$f_4 = 4L_1L_2, \quad f_5 = 4L_2L_3, \quad f_6 = 4L_3L_1$$

using the identity of Equation B.12 to simplify the results for f_1, f_2 and f_3. These area coordinate functions are much simpler than the Cartesian formulas obtained by substituting Equations B.11 into Equations B.17.

Isoparametric mapping

Using the area coordinate interpolation functions we can now calculate the derivatives using the interpolation matrix

$$S = \begin{Bmatrix} \partial(\ )/\partial L_1 \\ \partial(\ )/\partial L_2 \end{Bmatrix} = \begin{bmatrix} 4L_1 - 1 & 0 & 4L_1 + 4L_2 - 3 & 4L_2 & -4L_2 & 4 - 8L_1 - 4L_2 \\ 0 & 4L_2 - 1 & 4L_1 + 4L_2 - 3 & 4L_1 & 4 - 4L_1 - 8L_2 & -4L_1 \end{bmatrix} \tag{B.18}$$

using the identity of Equation B.12 to eliminate L_3.

Then the Cartesian derivatives are related to these local derivatives by

$$\begin{Bmatrix} \partial\phi/\partial L_1 \\ \partial\phi/\partial L_2 \end{Bmatrix} = \begin{bmatrix} \partial x/\partial L_1 & \partial y/\partial L_1 \\ \partial x/\partial L_2 & \partial y/\partial L_2 \end{bmatrix} \begin{Bmatrix} \partial\phi/\partial x \\ \partial\phi/\partial y \end{Bmatrix} \tag{B.19}$$

APPENDIX B: TWO-DIMENSIONAL FINITE ELEMENTS

and the connecting matrix is the *Jacobian matrix J*. This can be calculated numerically at each integration point (using numerical integration to form the element equations) using the matrix of Equation B.18:

$$J = S [\ \{x\}\ \{y\}\ ] \quad (B.20)$$

so that the interpolation for the Cartesian derivatives is given by

$$\begin{Bmatrix} \partial\phi/\partial x \\ \partial\phi/\partial y \end{Bmatrix} = J^{-1} S\{\phi\} = T\{\phi\} \quad (B.21)$$

and this process is easily coded in the program given later in this chapter. Now the reason for eliminating L_3 in Equation B.18 is clear, namely in order to obtain an invertible 2 × 2 Jacobian matrix.

Numerical integration

The appropriate numerical integration when first derivatives of the interpolation functions are used to form the element equations is simply at the three midside nodes. This exactly integrates terms of the form $\int L_1^2$, as required, so that we calculate contributions to the element matrix which take the form

$$\iint \{f_x\}^t \{f_x\}\ dxdy \quad (B.22)$$

as $\quad \sum_{i=1}^{3} T_1 T_1^t\ |J_{abs}|\ \omega_i/2 \qquad \omega_i = 1/3 \quad (B.23)$

where T_1 denotes row 1 of the matrix T obtained in Equation B.21 and $|J|_{abs}$ gives approximately twice the element area as Equation B.19 suggests.

Then to calculate finite element matrices for the quadratic triangle element an integration loop is required by Equation B.23 and in this loop Equation B.18 is coded literally and this result used to calculate the Jacobian matrix using Equation B.20. The matrix T is formed numerically using Equation B.21 and the result used in Equation B.23 to calculate the terms required for the element matrices by equations like Equations B.7 and B.8 derived in the following section.

APPENDIX B: TWO-DIMENSIONAL FINITE ELEMENTS

Conclusion

Using area coordinates, the interpolation functions for the quadratic triangle are much simplified. Then use of the numerically calculated Jacobian matrix at each integration point allows the element to have curved (quadratic) sides, greatly simplifying element formulation as well.

FEM ANALYSIS OF POTENTIAL FLOW

In the following section we develop the equations required to form mathematical models of potential flow problems. Using the results of the previous section we are then able to formulate finite elements to analyze potential flow problems.

Potential flow

In potential flow the flow pattern is represented by *orthogonal* sets of curves (that is, intersecting at right angles) for the values of a *potential function* ϕ and a *stream function* ψ. In terms of these functions the flow velocities are given by

$$u = -\partial\phi/\partial x, \quad v = -\partial\phi/\partial y \quad (B.24)$$
$$u = \partial\psi/\partial y, \quad v = -\partial\psi/\partial x \quad (B.25)$$

and the contours of the stream function are the *streamlines* of flow whilst the orgthogonal contours of the potential function are those of the *potential* of the flow. We will use the potential function approach as it is more appropriate for our present purposes (e.g. we have already defined a 'potential' in FEM distribution models).

Equations B.24 already satisfy the *irrotationality condition*

$$\omega_z = (\partial v/\partial x - \partial u/\partial y)\hat{k} = 0 \quad (B.26)$$

where ω_z = is the vorticity, being a vector with the direction of k, the unit vector perpendicular to the plane.

We must also satisfy the *continuity condition*

$$\partial u/\partial x + \partial v/\partial y = 0 \quad (B.27)$$

Appendix B: Two-Dimensional Finite Elements

this ensuring conservation of matter as it states that for a control volume $dxdy$ 'flow in = flow out'.

Then substituting Equations B.24 into Equation B.27 we obtain the governing equation for the problem

$$\nabla^2 \phi = \partial^2\phi/\partial^2 x^2 + \partial^2\phi/\partial y^2 = 0 \qquad (B.28)$$

namely LaPlace's equation.

Finite element interpolation

Substituting the interpolation $\phi = \{f\}^t\{\phi\}$ into Equation B.28 we obtain

$$\iint \{f\}[\{f_{xx}\}^t + \{f_{yy}\}^t]\,dxdy\,\{\phi\} = \{0\} \qquad (B.29)$$

using Galerkin weighting with the interpolation functions and integrating over the element volume (assuming the element has constant thickness = 1).

Then applying integration by parts to both terms on the left of Equation B.29 the results of Equations B.7 and B.8 are obtained so that the element equations are given by

$$k\{\phi\} = \{q\} \qquad (B.30)$$

where

$$k = \int[\{f_x\}\{f_x\}^t + \{f_y\}\{f_y\}^t]\,dxdy \qquad (B.31)$$

$$\{q\} = \int\{f\}\{f_x\}^t\{\phi\}\,dy + \int\{f\}\{f_y\}^t\{\phi\}\,dx \qquad (B.32)$$

The forcing terms of Equation B.32 can be simplified by transforming to the normal and tangential axes at the boundary shown in Figure B.4.

Denoting the angle of the normal to the boundary from the x axis as α the direction cosines at the boundary are

$$c_x = \cos\alpha \text{ and } c_y = \sin\alpha$$

APPENDIX B: TWO-DIMENSIONAL FINITE ELEMENTS

we can write, assuming all direction cosines positive (to ensure that $\int ds$ around the boundary yields a positive result)

$$dx/dn = c_x, \quad dy/dn = c_y \qquad (B.33a)$$
$$dx/ds = c_y, \quad dy/ds = c_x \qquad (B.33b)$$

Using Equations B.33b in Equation B.32 we obtain

$$\{q\} = \int \{f\}[c_x \phi_x + c_y \phi_y] ds$$
$$= - \int \{f\}[c_x u + c_y v] ds \quad (B.34a)$$

including the definitions of Equations B.24 to obtain the final result. Then, for example, for a side of an element parallel to the y axis we have $\alpha = 0$, $c_x = 1$, $c_y = 0$ and the flux loads on it are given by

$$\{q\} = \int \{f\} u \, dy = \int \{f\}\{f\}'\{u\} dy = (\int \{f\} dy)\{u\} \quad (B.34b)$$

Then the element matrices are obtained by using Equations B.22 and B.23 to evaluate Equation B.31 by numerical integration and a short program which does this is given in the following section.

Rectilinear flow

Figure B.4 shows an element mesh of quadratic triangular elements for the rectilinear flow problem. To force the flow the loads shown are specified at inlet and $\phi = 0$ is set as a datum at outlet.

Here the *consistent* (with a quadratic interpolation) loads corresponding to a uniformly distributed load q normal to the side of an element are $qh/6, 4qh/6, qh/6$ if h is the length of this side. This follows from Equation B.34b and thus integrating the 1D quadratic Lagrangian interpolation

$$u = (s^2 - s)u_1/2 + (1 - s^2)u_2 + (s^2 + s)u_3/2$$

between the limits $s = -1$ and $s = 1$, noting that the element length here $= 2$.

APPENDIX B: TWO-DIMENSIONAL FINITE ELEMENTS

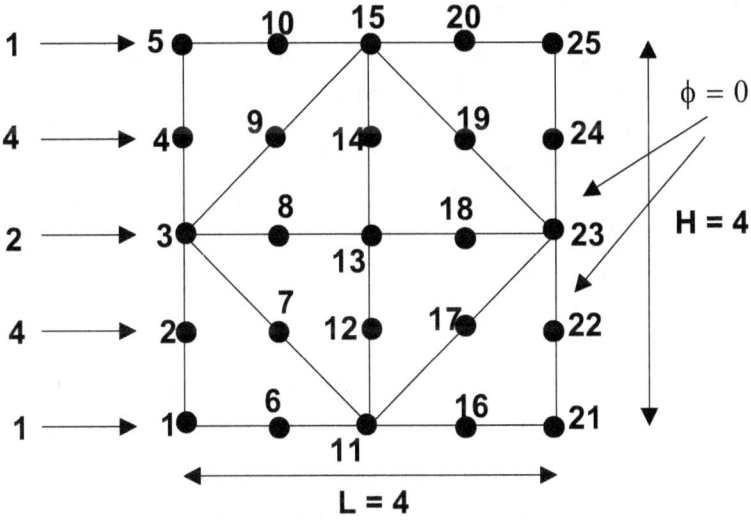

Figure B.4. Rectilinear flow.

For this simple problem the exact solutions are

$$\phi_{in} = QL/H, \quad u = \phi_{in}/L \tag{B.34}$$

where $Q = \Sigma\, q_\phi$ at inlet.

A program for such potential flow problems is given in the following section. This uses the quadratic triangle element described earlier and for best results the *consistent loads* shown must be used.

The problem is simple but with the use of FEM irregular domains, sources and sinks etc. can be dealt with simply by the addition of a line or two of data and a program for this purpose is given in the following section.

Appendix B: Two-Dimensional Finite Elements

Program for Potential Flow

The following program is for potential flow problems and uses the quadratic triangle element described earlier. It automatically generates the nodal coordinates for a regular rectangular array, reading the data for this in line 45 of the program. The node number sets for each element are then read in line 70 of the program.

After obtaining the solution for the nodal potentials these are used to calculate the velocities (= the gradients of the potentials) at the nodes, then calculating average nodal velocities = sum of velocities calculated in the N elements impinging at the node (the *nodal valency*) divided by N.

Data is read as

Line 1: # nodes = NP, # elements = NE, # boundary condition nodes = NB, half band width = BW = max value of (max node # - min node # + 1) for an element.
With specification of a band width, reduction of the system matrix sweeps to the right of the pivot only to the extent of the band width. This decreases computation considerably in larger problems.

Line 2: # grid lines in X direction = NX, # grid lines in Y direction, domain size in X direction = XLIM, domain size in Y direction = YLIM.

NB lines: number of set values for potential function

Loads: nodal loads - terminate with a data 0,0 line.

The program output is the nodal potentials, then a ? prompt from an input statement. Input any number and the final output of the boundary node reactions and the average nodal horizontal and vertical velocities will be given.

Appendix B: Two-Dimensional Finite Elements

```
5   REM Potential Flow Program
10  UDL = 0: REM Distributed load - deployed in line 155
15  DIM CORD(90, 2), EM(6, 6), S(90, 90), Q(90), XY(6, 2), NOP(40, 6), SI(90, 90)
20  DIM CI(6, 2), DL(2, 6), TJ(2, 2), T(2, 6), IB(90), EV(6), NCN(90), U(90), V(90)
25  REM ***** Data for integration at midside nodes
30  CI(1, 1) = 1: CI(1, 2) = 0: CI(2, 1) = 0: CI(2, 2) = 1: CI(3, 1) = 0: CI(3, 2) = 0
35  CI(4, 1) = .5: CI(4, 2) = .5: CI(5, 1) = 0: CI(5, 2) = .5: CI(6, 1) = .5: CI(6, 2) = 0
40  READ NP, NE, NB, BW
45  READ NX, NY, XLIM, YLIM
50  NEX = NX - 1: NEY = NY - 1: DX = XLIM / NEX: DY = YLIM / NEY
55  FOR I = 1 TO NX: FOR J = 1 TO NY: NN = NY * (I - 1) + J
60  CORD(NN, 1) = DX * (I - 1): CORD(NN, 2) = DY * (J - 1): NEXT: NEXT
70  FOR NEL = 1 TO NE: FOR J = 1 TO 6: READ NOP(NEL, J): NEXT
80  NEXT
90  FOR L = 1 TO NE: REM ############### LOOP ON ELEMENTS
100 FOR I = 1 TO 6: K = NOP(L, I)
110 XY(I, 1) = CORD(K, 1): XY(I, 2) = CORD(K, 2)
130 FOR J = 1 TO 6: EM(I, J) = 0: NEXT: NEXT
135 FOR IP = 4 TO 6: REM ************* START NUMERICAL INTEG LOOP
140 F1 = 4 * CI(IP, 1): F2 = 4 * CI(IP, 2)
145 GOSUB 510
150 F = ABS(DJ) / 6
155 FOR K = 1 TO 3: NK = NOP(L, K + 3): Q(NK) = Q(NK) + F * UDL / 3: NEXT
160 FOR I = 1 TO 6: FOR J = 1 TO 6
165 EM(I, J) = EM(I, J) + F * (T(1, I) * T(1, J) + T(2, I) * T(2, J)): REM EQN B.31
170 NEXT: NEXT
175 NEXT IP: REM END NUMERICAL INTEGRATION LOOP ****************
180 FOR I = 1 TO 6: NR = NOP(L, I)
185 FOR J = 1 TO 6: NC = NOP(L, J)
190 S(NR, NC) = S(NR, NC) + EM(I, J): NEXT: NEXT
REM ADD k TO SYSTEM MATRIX
195 NEXT L: REM END LOOP ON ELEMENTS #################
200 FOR I = 1 TO NP: FOR J = 1 TO NP
205 SI(I, J) = S(I, J): NEXT: NEXT
210 FOR L = 1 TO NB: REM LOOP BOUNDARY CONDITION NODES
215 READ N, F: IB(N) = 1: Q(N) = F
220 FOR I = 1 TO NP
225 IF IB(I) = 1 THEN 235
230 Q(I) = Q(I) - F * S(I, N)
235 NEXT I
240 Q(N) = F: NEXT L
270 READ NQ, F
275 IF NQ = 0 THEN 290
280 IF IB(NQ) = 1 THEN 270
285 Q(NQ) = Q(NQ) + F: GOTO 270
```

Appendix B: Two-Dimensional Finite Elements

```
290 REM SOLVE THE MATRIX EQUATION FOR THE SYSTEM
295 FOR I = 1 TO NP
300 IF IB(I) = 1 THEN 360
305 X = S(I, I): Q(I) = Q(I) / X: REM X=PIVOT
310 J2 = I + BW: IF J2 > NP THEN J2 = NP
315 FOR J = I + 1 TO J2
320 S(I, J) = S(I, J) / X: NEXT J: REM ROW/PIVOT
325 FOR K = 1 TO J2: IF K = I THEN GOTO 355
330 IF IB(K) = 1 THEN 355
335 X = S(K, I): IF X = 0 THEN 355
340 Q(K) = Q(K) - X * Q(I)
345 FOR J = I + 1 TO J2
350 S(K, J) = S(K, J) - X * S(I, J): NEXT J
REM ROW SUBTRACTION OPERATION
355 NEXT K
360 NEXT I
365 PRINT : PRINT "Nodal Stream Function Values"
370 FOR I = 1 TO NP
375 PRINT USING "#####"; I; : PRINT USING "########.#####"; Q(I);
380 NEXT
383 INPUT "I/P a # to continue O/P", ZZ
385 PRINT "Boundary Flows"
390 FOR I = 1 TO NP
395 IF IB(I) <> 1 THEN 420
400 F = 0: FOR K = 1 TO NP
405 F = F + S(I, K) * Q(K)
410 NEXT
415 PRINT USING "#####"; I; : PRINT USING "########.#####"; F
420 NEXT I
425 REM
430 FOR I = 1 TO NP: NCN(I) = 0: U(I) = 0: V(I) = 0: NEXT
435 FOR I = 1 TO NE: FOR J = 1 TO 6
440 NN = NOP(I, J): NCN(NN) = NCN(NN) + 1: NEXT: NEXT
445 FOR EN = 1 TO NE
450 FOR I = 1 TO 6: K = NOP(EN, I)
455 XY(I, 1) = CORD(K, 1): XY(I, 2) = CORD(K, 2): EV(I) = Q(K): NEXT
460 FOR NL = 1 TO 6: N = NOP(EN, NL)
465 F1 = 4 * CI(NL, 1): F2 = 4 * CI(NL, 2): GOSUB 510
470 FOR J = 1 TO 6
475 U(N) = U(N) - T(1, J) * EV(J) / NCN(N)
480 V(N) = V(N) - T(2, J) * EV(J) / NCN(N): NEXT
485 NEXT NL: NEXT EN
490 PRINT "Nodal average velocities u,v"
495 FOR I = 1 TO NP
500 PRINT USING "#####"; I; : PRINT USING "#####.###"; U(I); V(I); : NEXT
505 END
```

APPENDIX B: TWO-DIMENSIONAL FINITE ELEMENTS

```
510 DL(1, 1) = F1 - 1: DL(1, 2) = 0: DL(1, 3) = F1 + F2 - 3
515 DL(1, 4) = F2: DL(1, 5) = -F2: DL(1, 6) = 4 - 2 * F1 - F2: REM EQN B.18
520 DL(2, 1) = 0: DL(2, 2) = F2 - 1: DL(2, 3) = F1 + F2 - 3
525 DL(2, 4) = F1: DL(2, 5) = 4 - F1 - 2 * F2: DL(2, 6) = -F1
530 FOR I = 1 TO 2: FOR J = 1 TO 2: TJ(I, J) = 0: FOR K = 1 TO 6
535 TJ(I, J) = TJ(I, J) + DL(I, K) * XY(K, J): NEXT: NEXT: NEXT: REM Det(J)
540 DJ = TJ(1, 1) * TJ(2, 2) - TJ(1, 2) * TJ(2, 1): DD = TJ(1, 1)
545 TJ(1, 1) = TJ(2, 2) / DJ: TJ(2, 2) = DD / DJ: REM INVERT JACOBIAN
550 TJ(1, 2) = -TJ(1, 2) / DJ: TJ(2, 1) = -TJ(2, 1) / DJ
555 FOR I = 1 TO 2: FOR J = 1 TO 6: T(I, J) = 0: FOR K = 1 TO 2
560 T(I, J) = T(I, J) + TJ(I, K) * DL(K, J): NEXT: NEXT: NEXT: REM EQN 12.21
565 RETURN

900 DATA 25,8,5,11
910 DATA 5,5,4,4
912 DATA 1,11,3,6,7,2, 3,11,13,7,12,8
914 DATA 3,13,15,8,14,9, 3,15,5,9,10,4
916 DATA 11,21,23,16,22,17, 11,23,13,17,18,12
918 DATA 13,23,15,18,19,14, 15,23,25,19,24,20
920 DATA 21,0, 22,0, 23,0, 24,0, 25,0
925 DATA 1,1
930 DATA 2,4
940 DATA 3,2
950 DATA 4,4
960 DATA 5,1
970 DATA 0,0
```

The data is for the potential flow problem of Figure B.4 and the solution will be potentials = 12 at inlet, decreasing in steps of 3 to zero at the RHS. The nodal average velocities will be 3 horizontally and zero vertically, corresponding to the exact solution given by Equation B.34.

INCLUSION OF LINE ELEMENTS

Figure B.5 shows a source and sink problem modelled using Mohr's Patch Method (Mohr, 2001), a hybrid finite difference/FEM method. As shown there are two line or link elements and these have conductances = 10/12, compared to values of 4/12 for half a grid division width for the continuum.

APPENDIX B: TWO-DIMENSIONAL FINITE ELEMENTS

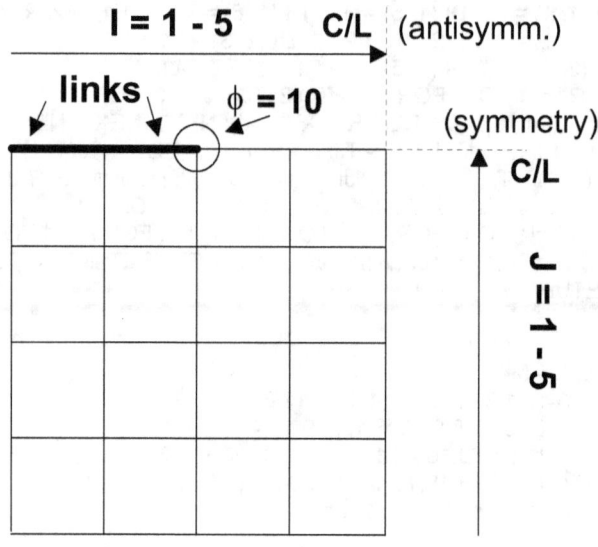

Fig. B.5. Problem including line elements.

The result for $\phi(I=1,J=5)$ is 6.36 whereas with no links it was 4.98. This indicates a flow between grid points (3,5) and (1,5) of approximately

$$\delta\phi(k + \delta k)/k = (10 - 6.4)(10 + 4)/4 \approx 12 \qquad (B.35)$$

whereas without the links the flow is

$$\delta\phi k/k = \delta\phi = 10 - 4.98 \approx 5 \qquad (B.36)$$

so that the links have indeed increased the flow, as expected. In the structural context we would be speaking of increased stiffness absorbing more load and reducing deformations.

Inclusion of such line elements requires just a few lines of coding to read in their node numbers and conductances and deploy these in the same way as for the simple two freedom DC network elements discussed in earlier chapters.

APPENDIX B: TWO-DIMENSIONAL FINITE ELEMENTS

INFINITE BOUNDARY MODELLING

Figure B.6 shows a quadrant of a circular domain (of radius 4) with a point source at its centre modelled using (a) 6 node isoparametric elements, and (b) cubic Hermitian elements with nine freedoms (Mohr & Power, 2003).

Then to simulate an infinite domain no boundary conditions other than $\phi = 1000$ at the centre are imposed but 'stiffnesses' equal to the angle (in radians) subtended by each node's 'share' of the boundary are added to the pivot for each boundary node's ϕ freedom before final solution of the problem. In Figure B.6(a), for example, the added values (in degrees) are 11.25 for the two nodes at x = 0 and y = 0 and 22.5 at the other three nodes of the circular boundary.

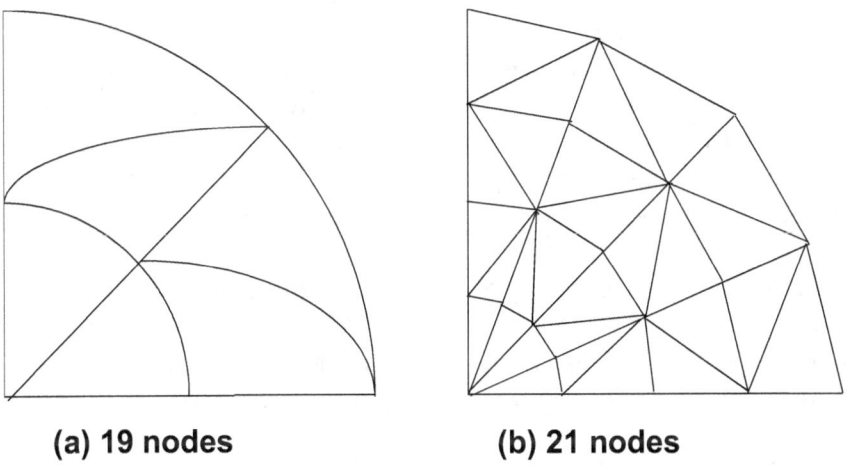

(a) 19 nodes   (b) 21 nodes

Figure B.6. Meshes for a quadrant of an infinite domain with point source at centre.

Table B.1 shows the results obtained. The expected results are obtained by fitting the appropriate decay function which is

$$\phi = - (1/2\pi)\phi_0 \ln(r) + C \qquad (B.37)$$

and this is that much used in the boundary element method.

APPENDIX B: TWO-DIMENSIONAL FINITE ELEMENTS

Table B.1. Results for the problem of Figure B.5

Case	r = 1	r = 2	r = 3	r = 4
6 node FE (1a)	525	367	276	210
6 node FE (1b)	520	365	275	209
Cubic FE (2a)	620	447	341	261
Cubic FE (2b)	520	374	284	218
Expected (3)	520	410	345	299
Expected (4)	480	370	305	259

In case (3) the constant C is calculated by substituting $\phi = 520$ at $r = 1$ in Equation B.37 and using the result to calculate ϕ for the other radii. Then for case (4) $\phi = 370$ and $r = 2$ is used to obtain the final row of Table B.1.

Cases (1a) and (2a) are the FEM results with only 'elastic' boundary conditions. Here a 'natural' decay rate occurs in the meshes used but in general the desired rate of decay should be modelled by choosing an appropriate C value and setting a corresponding ϕ value as a boundary condition at an inner radius.

This is done for cases (1b) and (2b), setting $\phi = 520$ for the nodes at $r = 1$. Agreement of the two FEM results is now good and agreement with the expected (logarithmic) decay results is reasonable with such coarse meshes and such a rapid decay rate.

Finally, note that from Equation B.37 it follows that

$$\partial\phi/\partial r = -\phi_0/2\pi r$$

and this can be set as a boundary condition in Fig. B.6 (at $r = 4$) but this gives little change in the results of Table B.1.

Appendix B: Two-Dimensional Finite Elements

Conclusion

The simple element matrices given in the first section of this appendix are for elements with very restricted geometries, but are reminiscent of those for DC and distribution networks given in Chapter 13.

The 6 node isoparametric element detailed in a later section, however, is very versatile, being able to have curved sides when required. The use of area coordinates makes derivation of the interpolation functions for triangular elements far easier and isoparametric mapping, which simply involves numerical calculation of a small Jacobian matrix, allows the element to have curved sides.

Formulation of finite elements for the analysis of potential flow requires the introduction of simple partial differential equations and the use of the Galerkin method, a weighted residual method in which the PDE's are weighted by the element interpolation functions and integrated over the element area to satisfy the PDE at the (numerical) integration points used for this purpose.

A useful program is given, and this gives the correct solutions for the simple rectilinear flow problem of Figure B.4.

Other refinements such as the inclusion of line elements and 'elastic' boundary conditions are then discussed, illustrating how the Finite Element Method can solve highly complex two dimensional problems.

Appendix B: Two-Dimensional Finite Elements

Appendix C

Mohr Ideas

Corrosion

One of my first important ideas was around the age of 26 when I began studying several compounds to determine which might be useful as 'admixtures' in concrete to inhibit corrosion of its steel reinforcement, still ignorantly referred to as "concrete cancer" and the cause of countless buildings of only 30+ years in age being demolished at a great cost.

I came up with a compound (sodium orthophosphate) which was quite effective and also acted as a WRDA (water reducing dispersion agent) for the concrete so that its use was virtually cost free. I sent the paper to the USA in 1973 and they asked: "How long does it work for." A year or so later I went to Cambridge and got buried in other work.

I sent the paper to a man in the industry about a decade ago and he said: "If it worked it would have been done before."

I rewrote the paper in 2004 and sent it to the Australian Journal of Chemistry (run by CSIRO) who replied 'too busy.'

The paper remains unpublished except in a very limited distribution form without the original photos of the original early 1970s paper (Mohr, Dec. 2001).

In this work I found that potassium chromate and sodium nitrite did a better job of inhibiting corrosion, but did not have the additional plasticizing effect of the sodium orthophosphate.

I did not consider recommending the chromate because of the toxicity of chromium, and do not recall why I did not recommend the nitrite compound, but now assume I recommended the orthophosphate because of its side benefit of being a WRDA.

APPENDIX C: MOHR IDEAS

Since that time I have noticed in reading the 1973 Club of Rome report that chromium is one of the metals becoming much scarcer as we plunder the world's resources to satisfy the demands of our excessive and unsustainable population – hence the chromate compound might be quite expensive now.

Recently I found that one company does now market calcium nitrite as a concrete admixture, showing that my original work in the area in the early 1970s was on the right track. Thinking about people in the industry and in CSIRO declining interest, I gave a few people an opportunity to perhaps patent my corrosion inhibiting concrete admixture ideas and make quite a lot of money out of it. Indeed, I had given a good deal of thought to patenting my original 1970s work somehow, but never got around to doing so.

Calcium nitrite has the drawback that it hastens setting of the concrete so that the admixture should have a set retarder added to it. Thus my sodium orthophosphate idea was not too bad since it had perhaps 8 or 9/10 on the main 'CI' + the benefit of being a WRDA (water reducing dispersing agent).

THE LARGE CURVATURE CORRECTION (LCC)

My PhD work in Cambridge in 1975 and 1976 was 50% spent on useless stuff my supervisor was interested in, and 50% on FEM. One 'neat' thing I came up with was a 3-D coordinate transformation for flat triangular finite elements of shell structures that was not to be found in the scientific literature, another was the shell shape optimization technique is demonstrate well for an arch in my OUP tome (Mohr, 1992).

I did learn a bit and kept up the work and in 1979 came up with the LCC for correcting the calculations in structures with large curvatures of deformation. Previously no correction for this existed. My original 1979 paper had a slight error in the LCC. I corrected it in 1998 and curvatures are calculated in the usual way as $= \partial^2 v/\partial x^2 / F^3$ where $F = [1 + (\partial v/\partial x)^2]^{1/2}$

but *increments* in curvature are calculated as

$$\delta v_{xx}/F^{-3} - v_{xx}\delta(F^{-3}) = \delta v_{xx} F^{-3} - 3 v_{xx} v_x F^{-5} \delta(v_x) = (\delta v_{xx}/F^3)[1 - 3 v_x^2/F^2]$$

APPENDIX C: MOHR IDEAS

Further results were obtained circa 2005 that further proved the validity of the LCC and some of those results are given in an appendix of a recent book (Mohr et al., 2014) whilst some of the many results obtained during my work on the LCC are used to demonstrate 2-way extrapolation in the following section.

TWO-WAY EXTRAPOLATION

In the Finite Element Method h^N extrapolation is often used, h being the dimension or size of the elements into which a problem is divided to model it. Then if the solution for a displacement d with an element size h_a is $d_a = d^* - (\text{const.}) h_a^N$ where d^* is the exact solution, then the solution with a smaller element size h_b is $d_b = d^* - (\text{const.}) h_b^N$

Eliminating the constant from these equations yields the extrapolation formula
$$d^* = d_b + (d_b - d_a)/[(h_a/h_b)^N - 1]$$
which in the case of $N = 2$ is known as Richardson's extrapolation formula. As an example of the application of this, consider the results shown in Table C.1.

Table C.1. Tip deflection v (cm) using 3 iterations/load step

Load steps, s	e = 25	e = 50	e = 100
10	45.88721	45.88530	45.88483
20	45.95118	45.94906	45.94853
40	45.96736	45.96514	45.96436
50	45.96931	45.96708	45.96652
100	45.97193	45.96967	45.96910
Extrapolated	45.97270	45.97046	45.96984
Exact		45.96977	
(Linear solution		50.0)	

These are the solutions for large displacement of a 100 cm beam with moment loading 10^5 Ncm at its end, the beam having a cross sectional area $A = 10 \text{ cm}^2$, the moment of inertia of its cross section being $I = 5 \text{ cm}^4$, and the material of the beam having Young's modulus of elasticity $E = 2 \times 10^6 \text{ N/cm}^2$.

Appendix C: Mohr Ideas

Table C.1 shows the results obtained using e = 25, 50, and 100 elements and an increasing number of load steps.

Such a large deflection in proportion to the length of the beam requires that the problem be analyzed with the load being built up in steps, using a few iterations of the non-linear solution technique at each step. In addition, more complex equations for the extensional strain are used, Mohr also including a new 'large curvature correction' in calculations to obtain the results of Table C.1 (Mohr et al., 2014).

Here extrapolation can be applied with increasing numbers of load steps (s), or with increasing numbers of elements (e), and in Table C.1 the results for increasing numbers of load steps are extrapolated assuming h^2 convergence (where h is proportional to $1/s$) so that the ordinal intercept of the regression line for the plot of v vs. $1/s^2$ is the extrapolation result. For all three columns of data R^2 = 1 to 5 decimal places is obtained. Accurate regression lines for increasing e can be obtained in the same way.

Better still, 2-way extrapolation can be used for the results with s = 50, 100 and e = 50, 100 (with h proportional to $1/e$), the extrapolations for increasing s being:

45.96967 + (45.96967 − 45.96708)/3 = 45.97053
45.96910 + (45.96910 − 45.96652)/3 = 45.96996

Extrapolation these last two results gives:

45.96996 + (45.96996 − 45.97053)/3 = 45.96977

which is the exact solution, an excellent result.

Note too that extrapolating in reverse order with these four results, that is 'across then down', yields the same result, and it is a simple algebraic exercise to prove that this will always be the case.

The Patch Method

This sums explicit matrices for simple finite elements to model 'patches' of a domain, the problem being solved iteratively by very short programs (Mohr, 2001), and Figure B.5 gives an example of a problem studied in this way.

Appendix C: Mohr Ideas

Natural Strains & Nested Interpolations

My main interest in FEM was in the 'elements' themselves and good new elements are easier said than done. I found the late John Argyris' *natural strains* (which are derived using the equations of Mohr's circle – not a relative) helpful and studied some of his work circa 1978 and 1979.

One day in 1981 I tried using an interpolation of 'natural slopes' (as distinct from slopes referred to Cartesian axes *x* and *y*) parallel to the sides of triangular thin plate elements to define *freedoms* at the midpoints of the sides, then using a well-known interpolation of these and some of the original freedoms at the vertices of the element. I called my method *the method of nested interpolations* and it proved useful on other problems later.

Using this method I obtained perhaps the best solution for one of the two most important and difficult finite elements, the 9 freedom thin plate element, having been interested in and worked on the problem occasionally since 1972 (Mohr, 1981).

The Drilling Freedom

The 9 degree of freedom (d.f.) thin plate triangle is one of two classic FEM problems, another the 9 d.f. plane stress triangle, these combining to produce the smallest sensible and somewhat accurate thin shell element. This is what matrix structural analysis and FEM was really invented for, that is, to analyze aircraft fuselages, Argyris having been a pioneer in such work in the 1940s in Germany.

In 1980 I formulated a rectangular plane stress element including the drilling freedom, but this has limited application (Mohr, 1981c). In a paper on the 9 d.f. plane stress triangle with the drilling freedom I found very nice natural strain equations for the three drilling freedoms at the vertices (Mohr, 1982, 1992), these being:

$4\Delta\phi_1/L_{12}L_{31} = \partial\alpha/\partial c - \partial\gamma/\partial a$

$4\Delta\phi_2/L_{23}L_{12} = \partial\beta/\partial a - \partial\alpha/\partial b$

$4\Delta\phi_3/L_{31}L_{23} = \partial\gamma/\partial b - \partial\beta/\partial c$

Appendix C: Mohr Ideas

Unfortunately, I was not able to utilize these nicely 'rounded' equations successfully in developing the final element formulation because they resulted in a singularity, requiring a relatively complex set of assumptions and equations to derive the 9 d.f. plane stress triangle (DFT1, Mohr, 1982) which, coupled with an accurate 9 d.f. thin plate triangle (Mohr, 1981), formed a useful facet element for thin shells (Mohr, 1992).

Many years later I obtained a simpler and slightly more accurate 9 d.f. plane stress triangle (DFT2) by assigning half the value of each vertex drilling freedom to the 'natural slopes' parallel to the two sides meeting at each vertex. Combined with my accurate 1981 9 d.f. thin plate triangle, DFT2 gave an improved facet element for thin shells (Mohr, Dec. 2001), some details and results for which are given in the following section, and were also included in a 2003 book which had extremely limited circulation (Mohr, 2003).

A Facet Element for 3-D Analysis

Extracts from paper on a new facet shell element (the best yet?).

Such elements are what FEM was originally aimed at, i.e. stress analysis of aircraft shells etc. Here Mohr's *method of nested interpolations*, a *basis transformation* technique, is used to formulate an accurate 9 *freedom* thin plate element (historically a difficult problem) and a unique 9 freedom plane stress element including the in-plane *drilling freedom* (very rarely attempted and never before so successfully). The two component elements are then combined to obtain an accurate *facet* element for stress analysis of 'shell' structures. An important feature is that the two 9 df component elements have the same *kernel stiffness matrix*, that of the classical *linear strain triangle LST)* element, the interpolation functions for which were derived in the section that began with Figure B.3.

APPENDIX C: MOHR IDEAS

FORMULATION OF THE ELEMENT

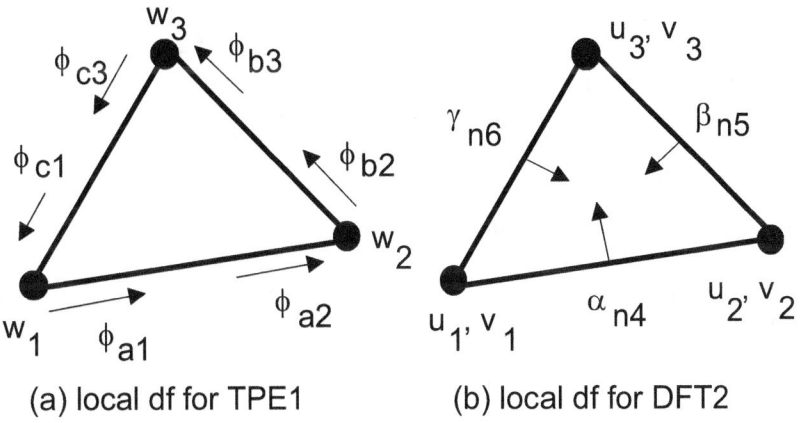

Figure 1. Local freedoms for the component elements

In the present work the accurate 9 d.f. thin plate element (TPE1)[3,6] and the new 'drilling freedom triangle' (DFT2) of Mohr are combined and 14 d.p. computation used. The plate element is derived by transforming the global slopes $\phi_x = \partial w/\partial x$, $\phi_y = \partial w/\partial y$ to the natural slopes parallel to the sides shown in Fig. 1(a). Then using cubic interpolation on each side and assuming linear variation of the normal slopes the basis transformation

$$\{\phi_x, \phi_y\}_{i+3} = T_f \{w, \phi_x, \phi_y\}_i \qquad i = 1, 2, 3 \qquad (1)$$

yields the slopes at the midsides.

Now a kernel stiffness matrix k^* can be obtained for the freedoms ϕ_x, ϕ_y at the vertices *(i = 1,2,3)* and midsides *(i = 4,5,6)* and this is exactly that for the classical linear strain triangle (LST),[4] the final stiffness matrix for flexure being given by the congruent transformation:

$$k_f = T_f^t \, k^* \, T_f \qquad (2)$$

The new DFT2 element is derived by assuming that, on each side, the natural derivatives of the transverse natural displacements at its ends are equal to the vertex drilling freedom, that is:

$$(\partial a_n / \partial s_a)_1 = \phi_1, \quad (\partial a_n / \partial s_a)_2 = \phi_2 \qquad (3)$$

on side 12.

APPENDIX C: MOHR IDEAS

Then applying quadratic interpolation to the transverse natural displacement the value at the middle of this side (a fictitious node designated 'local' node 4) is expressed in terms of the vertex freedoms. Repeating on the other two sides and assuming a linear variation of the parallel displacements (α, β, γ) the basis transformation:

$$\{u, v\}_{i+3} = T_e\{u, v, \phi\}_i \quad i = 1, 2, 3 \tag{4}$$

yields the displacements at the midside nodes.

Again the kernel stiffness matrix is that for the LST (obtained here using three point numerical integration) so that the final extensional stiffness matrix is given by:

$$k_e = T_e^t k^* T_e \tag{5}$$

The final 18 x 18 element stiffness matrix is given by:

$$k = T_s^t \begin{bmatrix} k_e & O_9 \\ O_9 & k_f \end{bmatrix} T_s \tag{6}$$

where O_9 is a 9 x 9 null matrix and

$$T_s = \begin{bmatrix} T_n & O_6 & O_6 \\ O_6 & T_n & O_6 \\ O_6 & O_6 & T_n \end{bmatrix}, \quad T_n = \begin{bmatrix} T_c & O_3 \\ O_3 & T_c^* \end{bmatrix} \tag{7}$$

in which T_c is the 3-D coordinate transformation matrix of Mohr,[4,9] that is

$$\begin{Bmatrix} x^* \\ y^* \\ z^* \end{Bmatrix} = \begin{bmatrix} c_x & -s_x t_y & s_x \\ -s_y t_x & c_y & s_y \\ -c_y s_x & -c_x s_y & c_x c_y \end{bmatrix} \begin{Bmatrix} x \\ y \\ z \end{Bmatrix} = T_c\{x\} \tag{8}$$

in which

$t_x = -(y_{32}z_1 + y_{13}z_2 + y_{21}z_3)/2\Delta$, $t_y = (x_{32}z_1 + x_{13}z_2 + x_{21}z_3)/2\Delta$

$s_x = \sin(\tan^{-1}(t_x))$ etc., $x_{21} = x_2 - x_1$ etc., $2\Delta = |x_{21}y_{32} - x_{32}y_{21}|$

and

$$T_c^* = \begin{bmatrix} 0 & 1 & 0 \\ -1 & 0 & 0 \\ 0 & 0 & 1 \end{bmatrix} T_c \tag{9}$$

is a Boolean transformation required because globally the rotational freedoms are the right handed system

$$\phi_x = -\partial w/\partial y, \quad \phi_y = \partial w/\partial x, \quad \phi_z = \partial u/\partial y - \partial v/\partial x \tag{10a}$$

whereas matrix k_f is derived using local freedoms

$$\phi_x^* = \partial w/\partial wx \text{ and } \phi_y^* = \partial w/\partial y \tag{10b}$$

SPHERICAL SHELLS

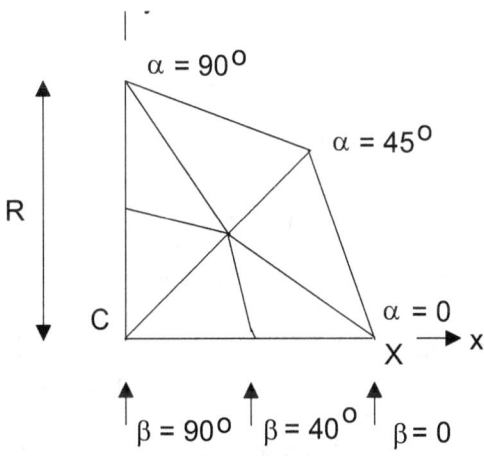

Figure 2. Spherical coordinates for coarse mesh for octant of a sphere

Figure 2 is a plan view of the seven node mesh used for an octant of a spherical shell. The nodal coordinate data is spherical in α and β from which the Cartesian coordinates are easily calculated as:

$$(11) \quad z = R\sin\beta, \quad R_p = R\cos\beta, \quad x = R_p\cos\alpha, \quad y = R_p\sin\alpha$$

APPENDIX C: MOHR IDEAS

The meshes used had 10, 13, 16, 25 and 34 nodes, $\delta\alpha = 22.5$ deg. (after the first $\delta\beta$), the increments in β, beginning from the crown C, being

10 nodes: $\delta\beta = 2 \times 22.5 + 45$; 13 nodes: $\delta\beta = 3 \times 18 + 36$;
16 nodes: $\delta\beta = 4 \times 15 + 30$; 25 nodes: $\delta\beta = 6 \times 10 + 2 \times 15$
34 nodes: $\delta\beta = 10 \times 7.5 + 15$

here using large elements near the 'waist' of the sphere to reduce the tendency for comparatively steep elements which tend to reduce solution accuracy.

The problem of a pinched sphere is considered with data and boundary conditions:

$E = 1$, $v = 0$, $R = 4$, $t = 0.5$ and 0.05, $P = 1$ at C
$u, v, \phi_x, \phi_y, \phi_z = 0$ at C, $v, \phi_x = 0$ along CX (curved)
$u, \phi_y = 0$ along CY (curved), $w, \phi_z = 0$ along XY (curved)

combining these 'line' boundary conditions at points X and Y.

The results are given in Table 3 compared to the exact solutions which are given by[11]

$$(12) \quad w = \sqrt{3}\,(1 - v^2)PR/4Et^2$$

and note that $P = 4$ (or unity in the FEM analysis for an octant of the sphere).

The numerical results are excellent with no more than 34 nodes and variations of the normal displacements close to the crown (for $\beta = 65 - 90$ deg.) is also close to the analytical solution.[11]

The stress solutions are generally reasonable but a much finer mesh is needed near the crown where the problem may be treated as that of a shallow spherical cap to obtain solutions of greater accuracy (and in line with the manner in which the classical analytical solution is obtained.[11]

APPENDIX C: MOHR IDEAS

Table 3
Deflections under load on a pinched sphere

Nodes (mesh)	t = 0.5		t = 0.05	
	DFT1	DFT2	DFT1	DFT2
10 (2 x 3)	20.392	28.512	1166.3	1101.8
13 (2 x 4)	23.827	28.160	1632.9	1475.7
16 (2 x 5)	25.782	28.098	1945.6	1827.2
25 (2 x 8)	27.006	27.517	2549.7	2554.7
34 (2 x 11)	27.663	27.703	2766.3	2770.3
Theory		27.713		2771.3

As does the DFT1 formulation, the new DFT2 formulation (+ TPE1) also gives satisfactory solutions to the problem of a pressurized sphere,[6] but here the main accuracy problem is that of calculation of nodal loads. Overall, however, both elements perform satisfactorily over a range of shell problems but the DFT1 element does poorly on constant stress patch tests.[1] The new DFT2 element, however, passes these exactly,[1] also performing slightly better on shell problems than the original element. As derivation of both the TPE1 and DFT2 elements is remarkably simple, it is expected that their combined used as a facet shell element will be popular.

INFINITE DOMAIN MODELLING

My first paper on this issue was published in 1978, my having had the original idea in some form during my days of PhD torture amongst the Cambridge clods (1975-76). Here I used 'elastic boundary conditions' to model infinite and semi-infinite solid media (Mohr & Power, 1978). Somewhat related to this work I developed a "contact stiffness matrix" a couple of years later (Mohr, 1980), and many years later I extended this work to model potential fields in infinite domains (Mohr & Power, 2003), work perhaps applicable to modelling the Universe (Mohr et al., 2014).

APPENDIX C: MOHR IDEAS

MOHR'S LAW OF MONEY

The fundamental principle of capitalism is the exponential growth law of money (S) with time t:

$$d(\$)/d(t) = c_1 \, a \, (=\text{activity}), \text{ where } a = c_2 \, \$$$

where c_1 and c_2 are constants.

Here the rate at which money is made is proportional to the rate of business activity, this in turn proportional to the amount of money available to fund this activity.

Combining the two constants above as $k = c_1 c_2$ we have

$$d(\$)/d(t) = k \, \$ \text{ where } k \text{ is the } \textit{growth factor}.$$

This is *separable* which means that it can be integrated in the form

$$\text{Integral}[\, d(\$)/\$ \,] = \text{Integral}[\, k \, d(t) \,]$$

giving, with the inclusion of the initial values, the exponential growth law

$$\log_e \$ - \log_e \$_0 = k \, (t - t_0), \text{ or } \$/\$_0 = \exp[k \, (t - t_0)]$$

where $\log_e(\,)$ are natural logarithms and $\exp[\,]$ denotes the exponential function $e^{(\,)}$.

If, for example, the growth rate is 10% per year, that is $k = 0.1$, then over 10 years we obtain the growth ratio $\$/\$_0 = 2.7$, so that we have nearly *tripled* our money. Not bad at all!

The same law governs population growth (using a symbol such as x for population in place of $). For example, if every 25 years 0.5 more children are born than people die we have $k = 0.02$, and this will give a 22% increase in population every 10 years, or 2.7 times in 50 years.

Noting that old adage about suckers attributed to PT Barnum:

There's one born every minute.

this population growth could also be factored into Mohr's Law of Money, further increasing the profits.

APPENDIX C: MOHR IDEAS

Finally, note that the foregoing calculation considers business *growth*, not interest rates. In most cases the business is financed by both debt (bank loans) and equity (share issues) and interest and dividend payments need to be subtracted from the growth ratio result. If the cost of capital, that is the weighted average of the interest rate and the dividend rate is 10%, the same as the growth rate, then we will have had to pay out this 10% ten times so the profit = (growth ratio - 1) = (2.7 - 1) = 1.7. Still quite good as we have here borrowed *all* the money for the business and repaid none of it. If we now repay all the debt we are still left with a tidy 0.7 profit.

OTHER INNOVATIONS IN ECONOMICS

Other innovations in economics I claim to have originated include:
- My inverse law of supply and demand which was briefly discussed in Chapter 16.
- Application of Jack Vernon's simple algebraic equations (Vernon, 1980) for his Liquid Money Supply and Interest Sensitive Expenditure curves to show that, as intuition would suggest to most people, increasing interest rates does indeed increase price inflation. Extension of Vernon's equations and application of them to prove this point was undertaken in Chapter 16.
- Application of FEM to Input-Output Analysis problems (Mohr, 1999a).
- Time-stepping of macroeconomic models using Gauss-Mohr reduction, the latter having been discussed in Chapter 10 and used in the first section of Chapter 16 (Mohr 1999b).

Appendix C: Mohr Ideas

FEM DISTRIBUTION MODELS

Around 1996 I stumbled across an HP85 computer, complete with several spare thermal paper rolls, in an opportunity shop. One of the early microcomputers these have 16 kb of RAM and an inbuilt 5" screen (with 'type over' memory) and thermal printer (about 4" width).

Though I didn't have a cartridge for it and had to type programs in again each time I used it, this small machine amused me and I used it for some research in which I developed the Patch Method by using Finite Differences (Mohr, 2001).

Around that time I was working on some LP programs and using them to solve distribution problems. One day I got the idea of typing the data for a distribution program into a small program for FEM models of DC networks.

I put in the data for the problem of Figure 13.2, but only for the five routes of the optimum (MIN) network with a boundary condition of zero potential at node 6. The little program didn't even calculate the route flows but the version I was using calculated a *boundary reaction* which came out as 80, the correct flow at node 6.

I added route flow calculations and they were correct so I knew I could model distribution problems using FEM, a major advance. The HP85 computer that helped make this discovery cost me $10 and I published a paper on this work in 1999 (Mohr, 1999c).

FLOW RATIO DESIGN (FRD)

Not long after the latter discovery I decided to try looking for an iterative optimality criterion approach to distribution problems. Familiar with the well known iterative Fully Stressed Design (FSD) method I came up with the *Flow Ratio Design* (FRD) method described and used in Chapters 14 and 15 almost immediately.

The idea was that, unlike solid structures where we specify a stress limit for the material, flow problems generally don't have some flow velocity or quantity limit.

Appendix C: Mohr Ideas

I hit on the idea of updating the element unit costs using Eqn 14.16, that is $c_{ij}^* = c_{ij}(q_m/|q_{ij}|)$ immediately and believe this criterion, because it leads to all elements remaining in the system having equal unit cost (c_L), is comparable to the 'constant strain' for optimality idea of AGM Michelle's famous 1904 paper on optimum building structures.

Not for the first time, one can come up with great ideas overnight! Indeed, I had come up with the idea of using the 'element access' parameters A_{ij} in using steepest descent to optimize FEM models of distribution just days earlier!

The Lambda-Beta Transformation

Almost at the outset of my work on applying FEM to fluid flow problems I came up with one of my nicest ideas, one I call (to myself) the lambda-beta transformation. In studying Lagrange multiplier and penalty factor formulations of FEM for the analysis of viscous flow I found that I could convert Lagrange multiplier formulations into more compact penalty factor ones. Indeed I had shown an equivalence between penalty factors and inverted Lagrange multipliers and those interested in this matter may find some illumination of it in a couple of papers and my 1992 OUP tome (Mohr, 1984; Mohr & Caffin, 1985; Mohr, 1992).

XF Effect

One of Newton's finest moments was the morning he "took me a prism" and discovered refraction of white light into different colour beams. Having moved house in 2001 I was chilling out one night with some beers and playing old CDs and I noticed that an energy saving looped Neon bulb in a standard light near the CD player was blocking reception of the infrared remote control unit.

Recalling that Neon tubes produce some (invisible) UV radiation I concluded that the IR signal was on the (outside) edge of the visible spectrum and had about double the wavelength and half the amplitude (or strength) of the interfering UV radiation, as shown in Figure C.2.

Appendix C: Mohr Ideas

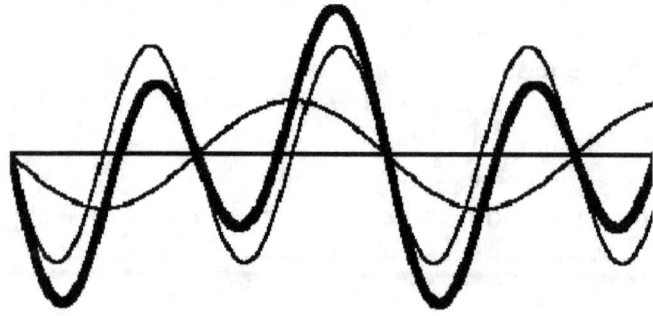

Figure C.2. The IR radiation has half the amplitude of the UV, resulting in a combined wave with wavelength similar to that of the interfering UV.

Not quite like Newton's prism but then great minds do not think alike whereas the *consumer zombies* of today's consumer society do (Mohr, 2013b). I have reproduced this effect a couple of times over the years, doing so repeatedly a couple of weeks ago with a certain type of long life bulb and also 100W incandescent bulbs. Here the light acts like 'noise' in blocking the IR signal and such effects have military applications, of course, signal strength depending far more upon bandwidth than signal power (Abelson et al. (2008).

The Mohr Plan

One day in 2003 I walked into the closing down sale of a book shop nearby. I stumbled across Mary McGowan's *Heart Fitness for Life* (1998) which reminded me of a book I had had lying around for years, Robert Kowalski's *The 8-Week Cholesterol Cure* (1987).

Kowalski had had a quadruple bypass and been swimming many miles a week but still could not normalize his cholesterol levels. He fixed the problem with 4 gm of Niacin daily and a high fibre diet.

Appendix C: Mohr Ideas

In the shop I saw that McGowan's book mentioned Niacin. It also gave several case studies, one or two of which made me realize that a sore neck that had taken 18 months to improve somewhat had been a thrombosis of my left carotid artery, my also having had chest pains for 30 years and a couple of mild strokes (TIA's) many years earlier.

I also realized that a good sized spot on my right ankle was stasis dermatitis, another symptom of venous clogging.

So I embarked on what I called *The Mohr Plan* of a very low fat diet (Kurzweil, 1993) and exercise to tackle the atherosclerosis that had bugged me for three decades (Mohr, 2012d, 2013a).

The battle continued for years and my book on heart disease, cancer etc. went through many editions from 1993 to 2012 when the first of several health books was published (Mohr, 2012, 2013a, 2015, 2018a, 2018b).

I have a look-alike elder brother (6 years older) who had major heart surgery about 10 years ago, having been on BP medication for a decade (a one-way trip to the undertaker in whom the American pharmaceutical company probably has shares). This included an artificial heart valve (no doubt American) and a couple of arterial grafts. I don't know whether he had the umpteen bypass now as popular in the USA as Coke but no doubt that will be scheduled sooner or later to help line the surgeon's pockets and pay for his wife's next Rolls Royce.

I'm sticking to my *natural* approach of *reversing* the damage as far as possible and my plan only goes out the window when I have a few too many beers which only happens every few months, but then for more than just one night, probably recovering from a PDQ book effort of which there have been many over the years.

In my books *Curing Cancer & Heart Disease* (2012d) and *Heart Disease, Cancer & Aging* (2013a) I tackle the problem of curing cancer with a lot of background from a book on the 'theory' of cancer (Weinberg, 1999), and a book on the Dutch government approved Moerman Therapy (Jochems, 1990) and Kurzweil's *The 10% Solution for a Healthy Life, How to Eliminate Virtually All Risk of Heart Disease and Cancer* (1993).

APPENDIX C: MOHR IDEAS

Besides a few dietary supplements and exercise, I also recommend controversial vitamin B17 for cancer prevention and treatment (Day, 2001). I do this because a couple of hospitals in Mexico have twice as good (or better) 5-year survival rates than the best the USA can do at present – you can google 'vitamin B17' on this (or Oasis of Hope Hospital).

Myself, prior to doing two health books (Mohr, 2012d, 2013a), I correctly diagnosed myself as having Prinzmetal's variant angina and thus began taking magnesium supplements (which worked) from that time in early 2011. Other health books followed to extend such work (Mohr, 2015, 2018a, 2018b)

THE MOHR PLOT FOR BLOOD PRESSURE

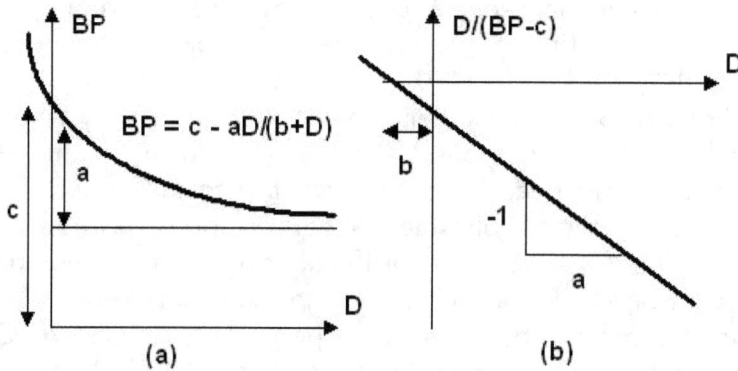

Figure C.3. Inverted Mohr Plot.

In my book on heart disease, cancer and aging I used the Mohr Plot introduced in Chapter 16 to check convergence of blood pressure reading during a 40 day get fitter routine (Mohr, 2012d; 2013a). Here blood pressure is being reduced day by day so BP follows an 'inverted' rectangular hyperbola of the form $BP = c - aD/(b + D)$

so that its vertical asymptote is at day $D = -b$ and its horizontal asymptote is at $BP = c - a$, and for practical purposes the vertical asymptote at $-b$ can be ignored.

Appendix C: Mohr Ideas

We can easily rearrange the foregoing equation to give

$D/(BP - c) = -(b + D)/a$

so that a plot of $D/(BP - c)$ against D yields a straight line in the same fashion as shown in Figure 16.3(b). Then the inverse slope of this line = $-a$ where $c - a$ is the horizontal asymptote of the original hyperbola of Figure C.3(a).

The author's BP readings during the get fitter routine fell gradually and Mohr Plots of these were obtained by choosing a value for the vertical intercept c of Figure C.3 based on the trend of the earliest BP readings. For systolic BP $c = 180$ was chosen $D/(BP-180)$ was plotted for the vertical axis of the Mohr Plot and the inverse slope of the linear regression line thus plotted gave the asymptote as

$c - a = c + 1/\text{slope} = 180 + 1/(-0.0157) = 116.3$ with $R^2 = 0.91$.

For the diastolic readings choosing $c = 100$ gave the asymptote value $c - a$ as 68.2 with $R^2 = 0.86$.

Choosing the intercept c is a subjective exercise, however, and this can be avoided by shifting the vertical axis by 1 day and using the first BP value/point as the intercept, thus plotting $(D - 1)/(BP - BP_1)$, where BP_1 is the first BP reading, the slope of this regression line giving the asymptote as $BP_1 + 1/\text{slope}$.

Using this procedure the asymptotes for the systolic and diastolic BP readings were obtained as 117.6 ($R^2 = 0.82$) and 68.9 ($R^2 = 0.81$), close to the values obtained using estimated intercepts c.

The average readings for the last week of the 40 day get fitter routine were 114 and 68.6, the similarity of these averages to the Mohr Plot asymptotes indicating that the BP readings had almost converged and could be expected to remain fairly steady at or below this level unless circumstances changed.

Appendix C: Mohr Ideas

Mohr's Law of Heating

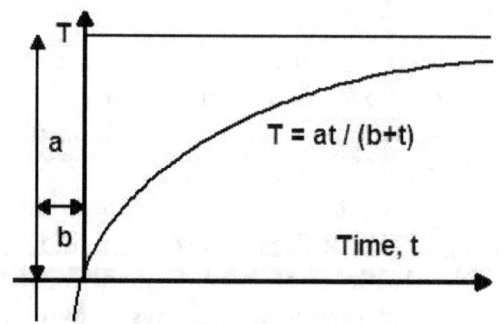

Figure C.4. Mohr's Law of Heating.

Newton's law of cooling is well known and assumes that the time rate of cooling is proportional to the difference between the temperature of the cooling object, T, and the ambient temperature T_A, resulting in an exponential curve of temperature decline. Mohr's Law of Heating assumes that the temperature of the heated object relative to the ambient temperature (hereafter denoted simply as T) follows the hyperbolic path shown in Figure C.4 with the temperature asymptote a being the maximum temperature achievable under the circumstances

Figure C.4 shows this hyperbolic curve approaching a horizontal asymptote at $T = a$, its equation being:

$$T = at/(b + t) = a/(b/t + 1)$$

As we are only interested in values of T approaching the horizontal asymptote, the vertical asymptote at $t = -b$ is not of interest.

These values at the right side of the curve can be used to determine the limiting value $T = a$ if we rearrange the equation for the curve to

$$t/T = t/a + b/a$$

showing that plotting t/T against t, as shown in Figure 16.3(b) (with different symbols), should give a straight line, the inverse slope of which is the value of the asymptote a.

APPENDIX C: MOHR IDEAS

I claim that it is possible that this is the better law than Newton's Law of cooling as exponential rates of heating or cooling seem too extreme an (implicit) assumption, whereas hyperbolic rates with an asymptotic limit seem more rational.

The hyperbolic form assumed in the Mohr Plot was also used for learning curves in Chapter 3, and was also used in the recent book *The Evolving Universe* to extrapolate the assumed declining rate of expansion of the Universe, and the declining rate of star formation (Mohr et al., 2014).

SURVIVAL OF THE HUMAN RACE

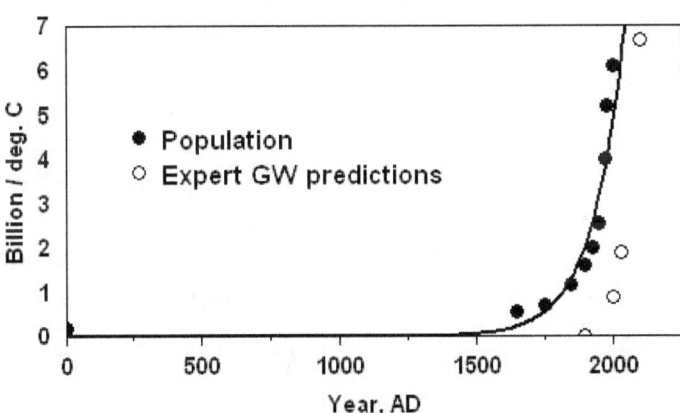

Figure C.5. Global warming and population growth.

In 2005 I wrote the book *The Doomsday Calculation, The End of The Human Race* (Mohr, 2012a). In this I discuss the many issues that now threaten the planet and, indeed, our very survival as a species, these including:
  ➢ Overpopulation (I feel our population should be half, or even a quarter of that at present if we all are to have a nice, house, car or two, TV, PC etc. etc.).
  ➢ Excessive consumption by the consumer zombies (the term I coin in my book *The Pretentious Persuaders*) in our modern consumer society.
  ➢ Resource depletion.

Appendix C: Mohr Ideas

- The impending energy crisis.
- Pollution.
- Global warming: as shown in Figure C.5 this has resulted from the industrial revolution and its associated population increase, latter day IR's taking place, of course, in China and India.
- Environmental destruction.
- Evolution of new diseases: Ebola, the first filovirus to hit us, interested me from day 1, and now we see a fairly large epidemic of it in Africa right now.
- Economic collapse, e.g. the US is in a quagmire of debt that it will never escape from. China, because it holds most of that debt, can sink the US any time but is not likely to do so any time soon because, of course, it wants to sell its many cheaper (in part because they don't spend a fortune on mindless ads to addict fools to junk like Coke) products into that market via its government-fixed exchange rate.
- War: there are usually a few wars going on at any one time (Sampson, 1977) and, of course, the American war machine is not set to stop any time soon in its quest to keep down the 'pink peril' and make money for those filthy rich capitalist pigs that run it, and the US government indirectly (Scott, 2003).
- Terrorism: the Muslims will be at it for decades to come yet, if not a century or two, just as the Protestants and Catholics fought it out for a couple of centuries a few centuries ago (Mohr, 2014; Mohr & Fear, 2014).

I concluded *The Doomsday Calculation* with a couple of full page spreadsheets including in various ways many of the foregoing factors, showing that we might become extinct by the year 3000, or at least that our population might peak somewhere about the middle of this millennium, and then decline a great deal.

Appendix C: Mohr Ideas

Mohronism

In a book on religion I point out how all religions were invented, often by nutters, for political and/or financial gain, power etc., later in the book proposing a new religion Mohronism (Mohr & Fear, 2014). That is, if you are a moron, you should follow my new religion which has the laws shown in Table C.2.

Table C.2. Table of Mohr's Laws

Law #	Law name	Subject	Principle
1	Mohr's morphology	human personality	three basic personality types
2	Mohr's mentation	education etc.	brainwashing
3	Mohr's metamorphosis	home, pub & coffin	life in three boxes
4	Mohr's mirage	sex	myth of love
5	Mohr's malady	hierarchy & power	law of the 'rat race'
6	Mohr's mechanism	achievement	madness required
7	Mohr's motto	power	power corrupts
8	Mohr's misery	crime & war	human condition
9	Mohr's mantra	man's history	the prophet Murphy
10	Mohr's metrology	final judgment	?/9

I shan't explain these laws again here, and those interested should buy the book *World Religions* (Mohr & Fear, 2015; Mohr et al., 2018d). I will, however, elaborate briefly on the 9th law. This is that the prophet of my new religion is Murphy of Murphy's Law:

"Anything that can go wrong, will go wrong."

Appendix C: Mohr Ideas

The bottom line, of course, is that in mankind's ongoing history of one disaster after another, everything does indeed go wrong usually. Occasionally, something good happens, for example the discovery of penicillin, but that too was an accident resulting from 'bugs' from a lab whose door had been mistakenly left open overnight invading a Petri dish in another lab. The next morning it was discovered that a mould in that dish had prevented multiplication of bacteria.

Murphy's God (MG), indeed, must have been the person who so many writers of religious fables and creeds had visions of, and who commanded them to write such drivel as is found in almost all religious texts.

They should be converted from insanity to Mohronism, and to believing that, indeed, Murphy was God's prophet. I can even give you his phone number but have forgotten it right now, just when I need it. Even when I do remember it, however, I only get his answering machine on the line with the message:

I can't get to the phone right now because I've lost it.

Therefore, anyone offended by anything I have said should not blame me because Murphy's God is to blame for anything that goes wrong, including anything that I've said that might be deemed by some to be wrong and, of course, I was only trying show the true path to righteousness and salvation.

Furthermore, anyone so inclined should beware of having a fatwa issued about me, or placing a curse on me. Even if you do, you see, in all probability Murphy's God will make sure it backfires and comes back to haunt you.

The first corollary to Murphy's Law is: *If anything can go wrong, it will, and at the worst possible time.*

There are countless other Murphy's Law, for example:

- *The first 90% of the job takes 90% of the time, the last 10% takes the other 90%.*
- *When you throw out the instructions and warranty for an appliance, it is then that it will break down.*
- The law of selective gravity: *An object will fall so as to do the most damage.*

Appendix C: Mohr Ideas

Bearing in mind that Christianity was not accepted as the official religion in Rome until 380 AD, I will not guess how long the new religion that Murphy was God's prophet (Mohronism) will take to be accepted by more than a handful of people.

When disciples of the prophet Murphy do get around to writing the Bible of Mohronism I hope it is filled with outlandish claims, dire predictions, and repetition and mistakes, just as other religious texts are, and in accordance with Murphy's Law which, of course, governs all religions.

The Evolving Universe

In a recent book I argue that the Big Bang Theory is BS, one of the main reasons being that Hubble's Law is quite simply ridiculous. Attributing redshift of solar light reaching us from afar to the Doppler effect, it proposes that the further the star in question is from us, the more rapidly it is receding from us so that the Universe is expanding and the more distant stars are supposed to be moving at incredible, indeed ridiculous speeds.

The truth is that redshift is, in fact, caused by the interstellar medium, and perhaps gravitational redshift is also a factor in play also. So the BB theory falls in a heap (Mohr et al., 2014, 2018a).

A major contributor to BB theory was Einstein's theory of relativity and I show that this is, in fact, ridiculous and he was simply able to con single minded mathematicians and astronomers with some 'mad' ideas and sloppy maths, his followers such as Eddington (1924) presenting the Special Theory of Relativity (STR) with ridiculously erroneous mathematical steps such as reversing the sign of the velocity of light, c, at one point, and then reversing it back again on the next page to suit himself.

The STR proposes time dilation, whereas common sense dictates that there must be simultaneity of events, and Buenker's Alternative Lorentz Transformation (ALT) ensures this (Buenker, 2007). STR also gives the Lorentz-Fitzgerald length contraction, something of an illusion really, ridiculously proposing also that an object traveling at the speed of light will have infinite mass.

Appendix C: Mohr Ideas

Nothing could be further from the truth and light photons do not have zero mass as Einstein assumed, but have some small mass at rest. When traveling from stars at velocity c, however, light might be deemed to have zero mass (not infinite as STR would have it), and, rather than length contraction, a light ray might be deemed to have infinite length, or nearly so if coming from the furthest known light sources in the (infinite) Universe.

Finally, Einstein based his STR on the notion that the speed of light is constant and cannot be exceeded. In fact, there are certain circumstances in which particles can travel faster than c (Mohr et al., 2014, 2018a).

Instead of the BB, or Hoyle et al's Steady State Universe or QSSC theories, the three authors of *The Evolving Universe* proposed that the Universe is heading asymptotically towards a final, stable state as most chemical processes do, of course.

REAL IQ

Intelligence is part inherited and part developed thereafter by learning and experience, often referred to as 'nature and nurture.' It is claimed that IQ tests are "a standardized examination devised to measure human intelligence as distinct from attainments" (Carter, 2007), but many argue that they largely measure learning, not innate intelligence.

It is generally assumed that our IQ peaks at the age of 18, about when 'developmental' school education is finished in advanced countries. I contend that further education and study, however, should be able to increase IQ further so I propose a *real IQ* calculated for those over 18 as (Mohr et al., 2017):

Real IQ = IQ(18) − a(disease/injuries)

+ b(years of learning since 18)

+ c(creativity) - d[(age -18) if over 18]

Here IQ(18) is that one develops, all going OK, by age 18 as a result of hereditary factors and education and 'a', 'b', 'c' and 'd' are constants.

Appendix C: Mohr Ideas

These constants have the following roles:

(a) 'a' is a constant to calculate reduction in IQ resulting from any disease or injuries acquired later which affect the brain, including Alzheimer's disease and psychiatric conditions such as depression.[3]

(b) 'b' is a constant, perhaps circa 0.25, for the effect of learning after the age of 18.

(c) 'c' is a constant for creativity, perhaps circa 1 – 2 if creativity is measured on a scale of 1 to 10.

(d) 'd' is a constant for normal decline in intelligence with aging, perhaps about half the value of the constant 'b'.

In the terms involving the factors 'b' and 'd' the notion of 'use it or lose it' is considered, that is, learning doing intelligent things should help further increase one's intelligence, just as doing more exercise should help strengthen one's muscles.

Creativity is obviously an important factor because if one has considerable ability, but no inclination to put it to tangible use, then one cannot be seen as having much real intelligence.

As an example of this point I shall quote my greatest fan, the late John Argyris:

I have no great intelligence, I have imagination.

Whether creativity is, to any extent, in one's genes is debatable, but probably it is mostly a learnt trait, but one that relates to intelligence. In other words, without much ability to create, or intelligence, one is not likely to be very creative.

The foregoing simple equation should, indeed, encourage people to indulge in vicarious learning, surely the best kind for usually people are able to tackle subjects that genuinely interest them with more enthusiasm. In addition, being free to choose when and how one studies may improve results, of course, as this is far less painful than the all too many years spent listening to teachers regurgitate material from text books they have relatively little understanding of.

---

[3] In contrast to depression, note that positive attitudes may improve real intelligence, an example being the 'teacher expectancy effect.'

In my view, it also helps explain how people like Leonardo da Vinci and Isaac Newton, despite having only had very basic schooling, could achieve so much, namely because they did all the work themselves, whereas now most academics have research student slaves [effectively an apprenticeship historically (Mohr, 2013b)] to work on often silly topics they dream up.

Finally, an example of the great 'plasticity' of the brain was a US woman, Michelle Mack, who was found when well into her twenties to have been born with nearly all the left side of her brain missing. Nevertheless, her brain having 'rewired' itself, she had "fairly normal language abilities" and only relatively minor difficulty in coping with abstract concepts and visual-spatial processing.

THE MATERNAL GENE

MRI scans of mothers' brains show that they have a maternal instinct. Is it passed on in the female genes in some animal species, is it a learnt trait, or does this powerful instinct come, like intelligence, from both *nature* and *nurture*?

Maternal genes are required for the normal development of the embryo. These genes determine the basic body plan of the embryo before fertilization takes place. Does fertilization with an additional X chromosome somehow give rise, at least in part, to the maternal instinct? I suspect that this may be the case in many animal species to ensure the survival of the species as with all life forms physical form and growth is largely preprogrammed by DNA (Mohr, 2012b, 2018c).

Thus the brainstem, the basic 'animal' part of the brain, must involve coding for various 'essential functions' for survival, one of these being the normal 'caring' function of mothers, and genetic coding for this behaviour must be present to ensure survival of the species.

There are, however, exceptional cases such as that of Emperor Penguins in which the male cares for infants while the female hunts, perhaps a good example of the 'cell copying error' basis of evolution which sometimes has odd results like human male baldness.

Appendix C: Mohr Ideas

Ideas 'undone'

As noted in the Preface, having recently finished my memoirs which I began over 20 years ago, but not published them, instead here are just a very few of my ideas over the years that I have not had the opportunity to pursue further:

➢ Circa 1970, being a structural engineer working under the behest of architects (who praise their mistakes – engineers argue long over them – doctors bury them – lawyers charge yet more $ etc.), I felt that I should prefer my house to be built more like a motel. In that way I could have reasonable privacy: the wife would be in her own bed + room, and ditto the children, the latter able to play/watch their own rubbish on the devices that play it. I heard recently that some people with enough $, are indeed doing this sort of thing.

➢ In my book *The Doomsday Calculation* I bemoan today's 'miserable megacities', noting that a Scottish politician likened high-rise public housing to filing cabinets for people. During office hours, of course, this also applies to high-rise office buildings. Circa 50 years ago I recall the Premier of Victoria mumbling before two successive elections about "decentralization" and pledging the growth of regional cities. He never made good on his promise and, indeed, globally the growth of megacities at the expense of country towns is to be deplored, involving massive expenditures on urban freeways and massive air-conditioned buildings, accelerating the rate at which we deplete the world's non-renewable energy sources.

➢ Rather than megacities we need optimally sized cities, surrounded by sufficient farming land, that are largely self-sustainable, whereas today's global market in which products are shipped all over the planet is incredibly wasteful at a time when peak oil is long past (in terms of liquid oil deposits) and can only increase the real cost of living globally.

Appendix C: Mohr Ideas

- Daylight saving (in summer) was introduced in England as a wartime measure. In Melbourne, at least, I should prefer it in winter to make a season made worse by southerly Antarctic winds a little more bearable. It's not going to happen in my lifetime, however, unless I make PM that is.

- I have long had an interest in the electric car and still believe I could design a cheap one and by way of research I have bought an 'electric motor bike' which looked like a Vespa, and an electric tricycle.

- Noting that from circa 1920 up to 1948 "Palestine" was a British Protectorate under charter by the UN, I feel that a "two state solution" is long overdue, but recent declarations of Jerusalem as the "capital of Israel" are a step in the wrong direction.

- In three recent books (Mohr, 2012a, 2014; Mohr et al. 2018b) I propose *real democracy* and this could reduce problems such as overpopulation, resource depletion, and conflict that threaten mankind. Thus, having run for party pre-selection twice in the late 1980s, I recently researched the possibility of running as an independent candidate, noting that a Greens candidate for the Victorian upper house was elected with only 196 personal votes because the Greens 'group vote' (for 5 candidates) in the Western Metropolitan Region was circa 10% of the total vote, whilst the 4th (of 5) people elected for the region (a Liberal) got only 386 personal votes out of 443,257 votes cast in the region.

- One worthwhile objective of 'real democracy' should be to reduce the growing gap between rich and poor in excessively capitalist Western societies. Another should be to promote the message that the *consumer zombies* in such societies do not need the latest fashions, fast foods and gadgets ASAP, and that by limiting their consumption they might not only help save money, but also the planet as well (Akst, 2011; Mohr 2013b; Mohr et al., 2018e).

REFERENCES

Abelson H, Ledeen K, Lewis H, *Blown to Bits, Your Life, Liberty, and Happiness After the Digital Explosion,* Addison-Wesley, Boston (2008).

Akst D, *We Have Met the Enemy, Self-control in an age of excess,* Penguin, London (2011).

Alibek, K, *Biohazard,* Arrow Books, London (2000).

Argyris JH, Continua and discontinua, *Proceedings of the First Conference on Matrix Methods in Structural Mechanics*, Wright-Patterson AFB, Ohio, 1965.

Argyris JH, Three-dimensional anisotropic and inhomogeneous media - matrix analysis for small and large displacements, *Ingenieur Archiv* 31 (1968) 33-55.

Atrens D, Curthoys I, *The Neurosciences and Behaviour: An Introduction,* 2nd edn, Academic Press, Sydney (1982).

Atkinson RC, Shiffrin RM, Human memory: A proposed system and its control processes.

RW Spence, JT Spence (eds), *The Psychology of Learning and Motivation, Vol. 2,* Academic Press, New York (1968).

Augarde T, *The Oxford Guide to Word Games,* 2nd edn, OUP, New York (2003).

Baddeley A, *Human Memory, Theory and Practice,* Lawrence Erlbaum Associates, Hove, UK (1990).

Battersby, A, *Mathematics in Management*, Penguin, Harmondsworth UK, 1966.

Bethe, H.A, *The Road from Los Alamos.* Touchstone, New York NY (1991).

References

Black E, *IBM and the Holocaust,* Little Brown, London (2001).

Buchanan, JM, Tullock, G, *The Calculus of Consent,* Univ. of Michigan Press, Ann Arbor (1965).

Budnick FS, Mojena R, Vollmann TE, *Principles of Operations Research for Management,* Irwin, Homewood IL (1977).

Buenker RJ, *Simultaneity and Relativity: The Alternative Lorentz Transformation,* Blog Archive (June 2007).

Carter P, *Material Thinking,* Melbourne University Press, Melbourne (2004).

Carter P, *IQ and Psychometric Tests* 2nd edn, Kogan Page, London (2007).

Cissell R, Cissell H, Flaspohler DC, *Mathematics of Finance,* 8th edn, Houghton Mifflin, Boston (1990).

Cohen, *Essential Psychology,* Bloomsbury, London (1990).

Collins AM, Quillian MR, Retrieval time from semantic memory, *Journal of Verbal Learning and Verbal Behaviour,* 8 (1969) 240-247.

Copi IR, *Introduction to Logic,* 3rd edn, MacMillan, New York (1968).

Crossley JN, Ash CJ, Brickhill CJ, JC Stillwell, Williams NH, *What is Mathematical Logic?,* OUP, London (1972).

Cowie HR, Collins MB, Ryan DB, *Imperialism, Racism and Re-assessments,* Nelson, Melbourne (1994).

Darwin C, *The Expression of the Emotions in Man and Animals,* Fontona, London (1999).

Day P, *Cancer, Why We're Still Dying to Know The Truth,* Credence Publications, Tonbridge (1999).

De Bono E, *Lateral Thinking for Management,* Pelican, Harmondsworth (1982).

REFERENCES

Delgado JMR, Physical Control of the Mind: Towards a Psychocivilized Society, Colophon Books (Harper & Row), New York (1971).

Dunne JW, *An Experiment With Time*, Faber & Faber, London (1934).

Eagly AH, Chaiken S, *The Psychology of Attitudes,* Harcourt Brace Jovanovich, Orlando FA (1993).

Eddington AS, *The Mathematical Theory of Relativity,* CUP, Cambridge (1924).

Einstein A, *The Meaning of Relativity,* Methuen, London (1922).

Egerton Eastwick RW (ed.), *The Oracle Encyclopaedia,* George Newnes, London (1896).

Encarta Encyclopedia 99, Microsoft Corporation (1998).

Enrick NL, *Management Operations Research,* Hold Rinehart & Winston, New York (1965).

Federal Electric Corporation, *A Programmed Introduction to PERT,* Wiley, New York (1963).

Fiacco AV, McCormick GP, The sequential unconstrained minimization technique for nonlinear programming, *Management Science* 10 (1964) 360-372.

Foss DJ, Hakes DT, *Psycholinguistics: An Introduction to the Psychology of Language,* Prentice-Hall, Englewood Cliffs NJ (1978).

Galbraith JK (1963), *The Liberal Hour,* Pelican, Harmondsworth (1963).

Glasser W, *Reality Therapy: A New Approach to Psychiatry,* Perennial, New York (1975).

Goodall (van Lawick-Goodall) J, *In the Shadow of Man*, Houghton-Mifflin, Boston (1971).

Greene J, *Thinking and Language,* Methuen, London (1975).

References

Hall, T, *White Collar Crime in Australia,* Harper & Row, Sydney (1979).

Hewat T, *The Intelligent Investors Guide to Share Buying,* Wrightbooks, Brighton, VIC Australia (1988).

Heyn EV, *Fires of Genius, Inventors of the Past Century,* Anchor Press/Doubleday, Garden City, New York (1976).

Hillier FS, Lieberman GJ, *Introduction to Operations Research,* 3rd edn, Holden Day, Oakland CA (1980).

Hughes-Wilson Colonel J, *Military Intelligence Blunders,* Carroll & Graf, New York (1999).

Hyden H, Biochemical changes accompanying learning, in *The Neurosciences,* pp 765-771, 913-914, Quarton GC, Melnachuck T, Schmidt FO (eds), Rockefeller University Press (1967).

Jonas G, Into the brain, *New Yorker,* July 1, 1974, p 57.

Kaplan M, Kaplan E, *Bozo Sapiens, Why to Err is Human,* Bloomsbury, New York (2010).

Kaye D, *Boolean Systems,* Longman, London (1968).

Kiefer C, Constable M, *The Art of Insight, How to have more AHA! moments,* Bennet-Koehler, San Francisco (2013).

Klein LR, Pauly P, Voison P, The world economy - a global model. *Perspectives in Computing* 2 (1982).

Likert R, *New Patterns of Management,* McGraw-Hill, New York (1961).

Lindzey G, Hall CS, Thompson RF, *Psychology,* 2nd edn, Worth, New York (1978).

Lotus, *123 For Business* (1996).

Macinnis P, *100 Discoveries, The greatest breakthroughs in history,* Pier 9, Sydney (2009).

Mayeux R, Rosen WG, *Advances in Neurology Volume 38,* Raven Press, New York (1983).

References

Michell AGM, The limits of economy in frame structures, *Phil. Mag.*, series 6, 8 (1904) 589-597.

Miller, J, Engelberg S, Broad, W, *Germs: The Ultimate Weapon*, Simon & Schuster, London (2001).

Milner HR, Accurate finite element analysis of large displacements in skeletal frames, *Computers & Structures* 14 (1981) 205-210.

Mohr GA, *Design of Plate and Shell Structures using Finite Elements*, PhD thesis, University of Cambridge (1976).

Mohr GA, Power AS, Elastic boundary conditions for finite elements of infinite and semi-infinite media, *Proc. Instn Civil Engineers*, Part 2, 65 (1978) 675-684.

Mohr GA, Design of shell shape using finite elements, *Computers & Structures* 10 (1979) 745-749.

Mohr GA, A contact stiffness matrix for finite element problems involving external elastic restraint, *Computers & Structures* 12 (1980) 189-191.

Mohr GA, Numerically integrated triangular element for doubly curved thin shells, *Computers & Structures* 11 (1980b) 565-571.

Mohr GA, Milner HR, Finite element analysis of large displacements in flexural systems, *Computers & Structures* 13 (1981) 533-536.

Mohr GA, Finite element formulation by nested interpolations: application to cubic elements, *Computers & Structures* 14 (1981) 211-214.

Mohr GA, A doubly curved isoparametric triangular shell element, *Computers & Structures* 14. no. 1-2 (1981b) 9-13.

Mohr GA, A simple rectangular membrane element including the drilling freedom, *Computers & Structures* 13 (1981c) 483-487.

Mohr GA, Finite element formulation by nested interpolations: application to the drilling freedom problem, *Computers & Structures* 15, no. 2 (1982) 185-190.

REFERENCES

Mohr GA, *Finite Element Analysis of Viscous Fluid Flow,* Computers & Fluids vol. 12, no. 3 (1984) 217-233.

Mohr GA, Caffin DA, Penalty Factors, Lagrange Multipliers and Basis Transformation in the Finite Element Method, *Trans I.E.Aust,* vol. CE27, no. 2, May 1985 (pp 174-180).

Mohr GA, *The Finite Element Method for Solids, Fluids, and Optimization,* OUP Oxford (1992).

Mohr GA, Finite Element Optimization of Structures – I, II, *Computers & Structures* 53 (1994), 1217-1220, 1221-1224.

Mohr GA, Optimization of Critical Path Models using Finite Elements, *Transactions of the Institution of Engineers Australia,* CE36/2 (1994) 123-126.

Mohr GA, Numerical procedures for input-output analysis, *Applied Mathematics & Computation* 101 (1999a) 89-98.

Mohr GA, Time stepping of macroeconomic models, *Applied Mathematics & Computation* 102 (1999b) 273-278.

Mohr GA, Finite element modelling of distribution problems, *Applied Mathematics & Computation* 105 (1999c) 69-76.

Mohr GA, Optimization of primal and dual network models of distribution, *Computer Methods & Applied Mechanics in Engineering* 105 (2000) 135-144.

Mohr GA, The finite patch method: a nodal equation method based on FEM, *Advances in Engineering Software* 32 (2001) 327-335.

Mohr GA, A new facet shell element, *International Journal of Arts & Sciences,* vol. 1, no. 2 (Dec. 2001) 36-49.

Mohr GA, Chemical inhibition of corrosion in reinforced concrete, *International Journal of Arts & Sciences* vol. 1, no. 2 (Dec. 2001) 50-59.

Mohr GA, *Finite Elements and Optimization for Management Science,* International Publishers Ltd (2002).

References

Mohr GA, *Natural Finite Elements using Basis Transformation,* International Publishers Ltd (2003).

Mohr GA, Power AS, Natural cubic element formulation and infinite domain modelling for potential flow problems, *Australian & New Zealand Industrial & Applied Mathematics Journal* 44 (2003) 133-143.

Mohr GA, *Education: New Approaches,* International Publishers Limited, Melbourne (2004a).

Mohr GA, Flow ratio design of primal and dual network models of distribution, *Australian & New Zealand Industrial & Applied Mathematics Journal* 45 (2004b) 573-583.

Mohr GA, Mohr PE, Admixture inhibition of corrosion in reinforced concrete, unpublished paper (2004).

Mohr GA, Finite element modelling and optimization of traffic flow networks, *Transportmetrica* 1 (2005) 151-160.

Mohr GA, *The Doomsday Calculation, The End of the Human Race,* Xlibris, Sydney (2012a).

Mohr GA, *The War of the Sexes, Women Are Getting On Top,* Xlibris, Sydney (2012b).

Mohr GA, *The Variant Virus,* Xlibris, Sydney (2012c).

Mohr GA, *Curing Cancer & Heart Disease, Proven Ways to Combat Aging, Atherosclerosis & Cancer,* Xlibris, Sydney (2012d).

Mohr GA, *Heart Disease, Cancer & Aging, Proven Neutraceutical and Lifestyle Solutions,* Horizon Publishing Group, Sydney (2013a).

Mohr GA, *The Pretentious Persuaders, A Brief History & Science of Mass Persuasion,* 2nd edn, Horizon Publishing Group, Sydney (2013b).

Mohr GA, *The History & Psychology of Human Conflicts,* Horizon Publishing Group, Sydney (2014).

References

Mohr GA, *2045, A Remote Town Survives Global Holocaust,* Xlibris, Sydney (2014b).

Mohr GA, Sinclair R, Fear E, *The Evolving Universe, Relativity, Redshift and Life From Space,* Xlibris, Sydney (2014).

Mohr GA, Fear E, *World Religions, The History, Psychology, Issues & Truth,* Xlibris, Sydney (2015).

Mohr GA, *The 8-Week+ Program to Reverse Cardiovascular Disease,* Book Venture, Ishpeming MI (2015).

Mohr GA, *The Scientific MBA,* 5th edn, *Balboa Press,* Bloomington IN (2017).

Mohr GA, Sinclair R, Fear R, *Human Intelligence, Learning & behavior,* Inspiring Publishers, Canberra (2017).

Mohr GA, *The DIY Cardiovascular Cure: A Comprehensive Program to Reverse Atherosclerosis,* Amazon-Kindle (2018a).

Mohr GA, *Combating Cancer: Proven Neutraceutical & Lifestyle Solutions,* Amazon-Kindle (2018b).

Mohr GA, *The War of the Sexes, The Problems & the Solutions,* Amazon-Kindle (2018c).

Mohr GA, Mohr RS, Mohr PE, *The Psychology of Hope,* Balboa Press, Bloomington IN (2018).

Mohr GA, Mohr RS, Mohr PE, *New Theories of the Universe, Evolution and Relativity,* Amazon-Kindle (2018a).

Mohr GA, Mohr PE, Mohr RS, *The Population Explosion,* Amazon-Kindle (2018b).

Mohr GA, Mohr RS, Mohr PE, *Human Conflict: An Attitudinal Psychology Model,* Amazon-Kindle (2018c).

Mohr GA, Mohr PE, Mohr RS, *World Religions: From Animism to Mohronism,* Amazon-Kindle (2018d).

Mohr GA, Mohr PE, Mohr RS, *Brainwashed Zombies: Religious, Political & Consumer Persuasion,* Amazon-Kindle (2018e).

REFERENCES

Mohr WE, Bawden AE, *Network Analysis Reference Manual,* 6th edn, EPAC P/L, Melbourne (1974).

Mohr WE, *Flowline Reference Manual,* EPAC P/L, Melbourne (1977).

Mohr WE, *Project Management and Control,* 3rd edn, Dept of Architecture & Building, University of Melbourne (1981).

Morgan CT, King RA, Robinson NM, *Introduction to Psychology,* 6th edn, McGraw-Hill, Tokyo (1979).

Newbold P, Bos T, *Introductory Business Forecasting,* South-Western, Cincinnati Ohio (1990).

Norcan Data AS (US company), *Visual Mind Version 2.63,* 1999.

Ostrander S, Schroeder L, *Superlearning,* Delacorte/Confucian Press, New York (1979).

Packard V, *The Status Seekers,* Pelican, London (1961).

Packard V, *The Waste Makers*, Pelican, Harmondsworth (1963).

Packard V, *The People Shapers,* Nelson, Melbourne (1978).

Parkinson CN, *The Law,* Schwartz, Melbourne (1980).

Pavlov IP, *Conditioned Reflexes (1927),* Dover, New York (1960).

Peter LJ, Hull R, *The Peter Principle,* Souvenir Press, London (1969).

Przemieniecki JS, *Theory of Matrix Structural Analysis,* McGraw-Hill, New York (1968).

Renton NE, *Guide to Meetings and Organizations,* 2nd edn, The Law Book Co. Ltd, Melbourne (1972).

Ripps LJ, Schoben EJ, Smith EE, Semantic distance and the verification of semantic relations, *Journal of Verbal Learning and Verbal Behaviour,* 12 (1973) 203-210.

Robertson TS, *Consumer Behaviour,* Scott Foresman, Glenview IL (1970).

REFERENCES

Sampson, *The Arms Bazaar, The Companies, The Dealers, The Bribes: from Vickers to Lockheed,* Coronet, London (1977).

Sargent M, *Drinking and Alcoholism in Australia: A Power Relations Theory,* Longman Cheshire, Melbourne (1979).

Schmidt-Nielsen K, *Animal Physiology: Adaptation and Environment,* 2nd edn, Cambridge University Press, Cambridge (1979),

Schlemner RW, *Production/Operations Management: Concepts and Applications,* 4th edn, Macmillan, New York (1990).

Scott PD, *Drugs, Oil, and War, The United States in Afghanistan, Colombia, and Indochina,* Rowman & Littlefield, Lanham MA (2003).

Selmes C (ed.), *New Movements in the Study and Teaching of Biology,* Temple Smith, London (1974).

Skinner BF, *Cumulative Record,* 3rd edn, Appleton-Century-Crofts, New York (1972).

Slaybaugh J, Pareto's Law and modern management, *Management Services,* March-April 1967.

Smith KM, *Critical Path Planning: A Practical Guide,* MacDonald, London (1971).

Smith CM, Davies ET, *Anthropology for Dummies,* Wiley, New Jersey (2008).

Solomon MR, *Consumer Behaviour,* Allyn and Bacon, Boston (1992).

Sternberg S, High speed scanning in human memory, *Science* 153 (1966) 652-654.

Sykes CJ, *Dumbing Down Our Kids: Why American Children Feel Good About Themselves But Can't Read, Write or Add,* St Martin's Griffin, New York (1995).

Theil H, Boot JCG, Kloek T, *Operations Research and Quantitative Economics,* McGraw-Hill, New York (1965).

References

Traill RR, *Mind and Micro-Mechanism, A Hunt for the Missing Theory,* Ondwelle Publications, Melbourne (1999).

Ungar G, Desidero DM, Parr W, Isolation, identification and synthesis of a specific behaviour induced brain peptide, *Nature* 238 (1972) 198-202.

Ungar G, Molecular coding of memory, *Life Sciences* 14 (1974) 595-604.

Vander AJ, Sherman JH, Luciano DS, *Human Physiology, The Mechanisms of Body Function,* 6th edn, McGraw-Hill, New York (1994).

Vernon J, *Macroeconomics,* The Dryden Press, Hinsdale, Illinois (1980).

Vernon, PE, *Intelligence and Attainment Tests,* University of London Press, London (1960).

Weinberg R, *One Renegade Cell.* Phoenix, London (1999).

Weiss ML, Mann AE, *Human Biology and Behaviour: An Anthropological Perspective,* 2nd edn, Little Brown, Boston (1978).

Wild R, *Mass Production Management,* Wiley, London (1972).

References

ELEMENTARY THINKING

The book delves into a unique mix of areas, including:
- The psychology of learning, memory and thinking.
- Tools for critical thinking and assessment.
- Collective thinking of groups, corporations and the public.
- Measurement of attitudes and market research.
- Mathematical logic and computer programming.
- Planning and scheduling techniques.
- Optimization techniques, both linear and nonlinear.
- World first Finite Element Method (FEM) models of distribution, inventory and traffic flow systems and optimization of them.
- Mohr's Flow Ratio Design (FRD) optimization technique.
- Econometric modelling techniques, some of these new.

The book is the most modern, technically resourced and innovative study of thinking to date and will prove useful to a wide range of people including managers, planners, engineers, scientists, teachers, psychologists and politicians.

G. A. Mohr did his PhD at Churchill College, Cambridge. He published circa 60 papers for 20 international journals and more than 25 books, including:

A Microcomputer Introduction to the Finite Element Method
Finite Elements for Solids, Fluids, and Optimization
The Pretentious Persuaders, A Brief History & Science of Mass Persuasion
Curing Cancer & Heart Disease
The Variant Virus, Introducing Secret Agent Simon Sinclair
The Doomsday Calculation, The End Of The Human Race
Heart Disease, Cancer, & Ageing: Proven Neutraceutical & Lifestyle Solutions
2045: A Remote Town Survives Global Holocaust
The History & Psychology of Human Conflict;   The War of the Sexes
Elementary Thinking for the 21st Century
The 8-Week+ Program to Reverse Cardiovascular Disease
The Scientific MBA;   Mohr's Law of Hierarchies
The DIY Cardiovascular Cure;   Combating Cancer

Also with R.S. Mohr/Richard Sinclair & P.E. Mohr/Edwin Fear:
The Evolving Universe: Relativity, Redshift and Life from Space
World Religions: The History, Psychology, Issues & Truth
World War 3, When & How Will It End?
The Brainwashed, From Consumer Zombies to Islamic Jihad
Human Intelligence, Learning & Behaviour
New Theories of The Universe, Evolution, and Relativity
The Psychology of Hope;   The Population Explosion
Brainwashed Zombies: Religious, Political & Consumer Persuasion
Human Conflict: An Attitudinal Psychology Model

www.ingramcontent.com/pod-product-compliance
Lightning Source LLC
Chambersburg PA
CBHW052308220526
45472CB00001B/33